Seasoned with Fun

Cooking and Entertaining with Pizzazz

The Junior League of El Paso, Inc.

Seasoned with Fun

The Junior League of El Paso, Inc. is an organization of women committed to promoting voluntarism and to improving the community through the effective action and leadership of trained volunteers. Its purpose is exclusively educational and charitable. The Junior League of El Paso, Inc. reaches out to women of all races, religions and national origins who demonstrate an interest in and commitment to voluntarism.

For the past 67 years, the Junior League of El Paso, Inc. has strived to stay at the forefront of addressing community challenges. The League researches community needs and has helped to develop and support projects in the fields of arts, education, health and human welfare. Since 1933, more than 80 programs have been established and over 3 million dollars have been returned to El Paso through the League's ongoing fundraising projects.

Profits realized from the sale of **Seasoned with Fun** will be used to support the current and future projects of the Junior League of El Paso, Inc.

Cover and Division Pages designed by: Quantum Communications - Louisville, Kentucky
Benjamin Godbey, Designer

Printed in the USA by

WIMMER

The Wimmer Companies

Memphis

1-800-548-2537

For additional copies or inquiries, please contact:

The Junior League of El Paso, Inc.
520 Thunderbird
El Paso, Texas 79912
(915) 584-3511

Website: www.jlep.org
E-mail: jleague@whc.net

Table of Contents

Seasoned with Fun

Seasoned with Fun is the result of three years of hard work, dedication and countless volunteer hours; of collecting and testing thousands of recipes; of researching entertainment ideas and cooking techniques; and of building lasting friendships and fond memories through eating and laughing together. It has become a reality through the collaborative efforts of the following committee members and the loving support of their families:

Chairman .... Lori Gaman

Committee Members .... Isha Babel

Elisa Gluck

Susan Groover

Lori Harrington

Chellie Hoover

Robin James

Julie Jennings

Tatjana Lane

Lisa Saucedo

Kim Wilkinson

Sustaining Advisor .... Martha Gayle Reid

Planning a Perfect Party
and Having Fun From Day One!

Hosting parties, whether small or large, casual or glamorous, often or not, is a perfect opportunity to gather friends and family together. Introducing them to fabulous food and drink, partaking in stimulating conversation and, above all, having a great time is what entertaining is all about. You probably wish you could spend less time working and more time enjoying your guests. The good news is: you can! Any successful endeavor — especially a good party — takes planning. And that is where the fun starts! This book is filled with wonderful tips, techniques and recipes to help you launch the perfect party and "season" it with FUN! Look for these symbols throughout the recipe pages for ideas and advice on how to spice up your next event:

 Food tips and fabulous recipes

 Unique party planning and decorating ideas

 New cooking and garnishing techniques

The last section of the cookbook pays homage to El Paso's rich Hispanic heritage and contains some of the top recipes from each section translated into Spanish. In short, **Seasoned with Fun** is everything you need to put "fun and pizzazz" into cooking and entertaining!

Planning with Fun

To plan a successful party, you must begin by asking yourself five essential questions: why, who, when, where and what. There are a myriad of reasons as to **why** one should host a party and the occasion will ultimately impact the answers to the other questions. Perhaps there is a special occasion to celebrate such as an anniversary or graduation; a need to mix business with pleasure; an upcoming holiday or event such as the Super Bowl; or you just want to be social and let friends know how much you enjoy their company. There really does not need to be a special reason — having a party is a reason in and of itself!

Unless the "why" is a business event or a party in honor of someone else, there is only one reason to invite people: to gather those **who** you like and with whom you want to spend time. Make a list and then match the head count to your budget, the occasion, the other people that will be in attendance, and the capacity of the place. An elegant sit-down dinner requires an intimate atmosphere and detailed preparation; therefore, a smaller number of guests should be invited. On the other hand, a 4th of July potluck picnic provides the opportunity to invite a larger crowd. Some gatherings are appropriate for children while others are not. It is also important to consider inviting spouses or significant others when planning your guest list. The ultimate goal is to ease stress and invite as many guests as you feel comfortable in handling. When in doubt about whether or not to invite a particular person, remember that it is often easier (and less stressful) to invite someone than not! Mix it up and strive for a lively combination of personalities and interests. The guest list alone can lay the foundation for a great party!

Let the occasion of the event (and your schedule, of course) dictate **when** it will be held. Having people for breakfast, brunch, lunch, an afternoon gathering, cocktails, dinner, dessert or an open house is only right when it is right for you. In most cases, however, there are a few rules of thumb to follow. Breakfast parties should be reserved for business or meetings (unless you and your friends are real "morning" people). Brunch, starting at 11:00 a.m., is generally a more convenient and accommodating alternative. Lunch gatherings should begin at noon, while after-noon parties that do not include a meal should be held between 2:00 p.m. and 5:00 p.m. Begin a cocktail party at 6:00 p.m. and end at 8:00 p.m. For a party that includes dinner, start cocktails at 7:00 p.m. and serve dinner no later than 8:00 p.m. If children are invited, start the party at 6:00 p.m. The adults can enjoy cocktails while the children eat. Guests should be invited to arrive at an after-dinner or dessert party after 8:30 p.m. A casual open house, which is particularly nice to host during the holiday season, can be held for several hours at any time of day. Guests are free to come and go as they please and you can enjoy visiting with them by providing a nice assortment of self-serve snacks.

Inside or outdoors, at home or elsewhere...deciding on **where** to entertain also depends on what kind of party you are having, how many people are coming, what is most cost-effective, what kind of theme (if any) is involved, and what time of the year it is. Often the simplest and most comfortable place to entertain is in your own home. Be flexible and willing to clear out furniture to create open paths and ease traffic if necessary. Be inventive — use the bedroom as a bar if additional space is needed. If the weather permits, open the doors and allow the party to flow into your backyard or deck. Another thing to consider when having a party at home is your kitchen space (oven, stove, refrigerator and freezer capacities) and other paraphernalia such as serving pieces, cutlery, glassware and china. Furniture, equipment and temporary shelters can always be rented if you find you are lacking in any of these areas. In the event that your home will not work, there are plenty of other party locations to choose from: restaurants, hotels, galleries, party halls, parks, barns, your office, a boat or trolley to name just a few. Looking for a unique location is part of the fun and you can create a resource to draw on for future events in the process! Outdoor events are exciting and adventurous, but they require a bit more creativity and flexibility, particularly if the weather does not cooperate!

Exactly **what** type of event it is going to be is the last question to answer. The simplest way to decide is to do what suits you and your lifestyle best. Themed parties are not for everyone or for every occasion, but they can be a lot of fun. Just because there is a theme does not mean it has to be elaborate, expensive or time-consuming. Simply put, party themes are an added touch. Pick and embrace a theme that you think is fun and your passion is bound to lead to enthusiasm in your guests, too. Below are some ideas for themes to get you started:

Ideas for Party Themes

International/Regional Flair	With The Kids In Mind	Seasonal Get-Togethers	Other Special Events
Evening in Provence, Putting on the Ritz	Malt Shop, Diner, Ice Cream Party	New Year's Bash	Golden Anniversary
Caribbean, Hawaiian or Tropical Luau	Under the Sea Pool Party	Romantic Valentine's Dinner	Big Birthday Bash
Oriental - Wokin' the Night Away	Teddy Bear Tea Party	St. Paddy's Day Party	Grammy Awards-Watching Party
Italian Feast	Good Report Card Celebration	Easter Brunch	Blue Monday Party
Mexican - South of the Border	Back to School (or School is Out)	Mother's/Father's Day Brunch	TGIF Cocktail Party
Mediterranean Madness	Bike-a-thon	Fourth of July Blast	Video or Movie Marathon
Flyin' Down to Rio	Backwards Party	Thanksgiving Home for the Holidays	Mardi Gras
Indian Inspirations	Magical Madness	Celebrate the Harvest Dinner	Tailgating Bonanza
Cooking Cajun	Sports Day Event	Christmas Celebration	Black & White Party
Southern Fish Fry	Space Fantasy	First Snow/Shed the Cold Weather Blues	Celebration of the Decades
Texas Ho-down or Western Round-up BBQ	Graduating in Style	Labor Day or Memorial Day BBQ	Retro Party
Greek Toga Party	Gymnastics, Ballet or Cheerleading Party	Spring Garden Luncheon	Politically Correct Cocktails
Pacific Rim	Private Treasure Hunt	Halloween Costume Party	Sporting Events or Tournaments
Southwestern Salsa and Cocktails	Make-your-own Cooking Party	Hunter's Feast	Safari Zoo Party

Creating Ambience with Fun

With the basics of why, who, when, where and what decided, it is time to move forward and turn your ideas into reality. The details of your party will begin to take shape in this phase as you prepare and send out invitations; select your menu and service style; decide what music to play; and determine what lighting, flowers and table decorations you will use to create the perfect atmosphere. Envision every stage of your event and make a list of items you will need. Keep your "party-to-do" list handy at all times as you may be able to accomplish many of the tasks during the course of your daily routine. Set aside a little time each day for party preparation and slowly attack your "list" with confidence and a spirit of fun!

The **invitation** is your first opportunity to impress your guests and heighten their excitement for an event not to be missed. Be creative—make it humorous, touching, dramatic or festive, while ensuring that it reflects the occasion of your party, its theme, or the season of the year. Your invitation will be of little use if it does not include some essential information: Write out the date (including the day of the week), the starting time and the ending time (if there is one). Specify where the party is to take place and provide detailed directions depicting the easiest route, particularly if it is hard to find or guests have never been to your home. One of the most important things to include on your invitation is the dress code. Even the most savvy party-goers want to know what to wear! And finally, save time and keep it simple by asking your guests to respond only if they cannot attend. This lets you keep a head count without being overwhelmed by phone calls. The timing for sending out your invitation is equally important. Provide at least four weeks' notice for a formal event or holiday party. During less busy times of the year, two or three weeks' notice is sufficient. Sometimes, a simple telephone call, e-mail, or fax can take the place of a written invitation, especially if you are staging an impromptu gathering.

When you sit down to plan your **menu**, try to think of the kind of food you like to eat, who you are feeding, what season it is, if you are in the mood to cook and how much time you want to spend doing it, and what is available to you by way of take-out or convenience foods. Additional thought should be given to your budget as well. Your menu does not have to be "gourmet" to be good; the secret is to do what you like best. There are several things to consider, however, when selecting your food items. First, serve a varied mix of ingredients including fish and meats; dairy products; pasta, rice or grains; and some fruits and vegetables. Second, try not to repeat ingredients in the same menu, such as serving chicken twice (in the appetizer and then in the main course). Third, have a contrast of textures—soft and crisp as well as smooth and coarse. Fourth, include a spectrum of colors in the menu featuring pale with bold and bright. And finally, provide a balance of flavors (but not all in one menu) from sweet versus sour; savory or bitter; salty or sharp; and smoky and flowery. Do what works for you, and you will discover that it will work for your guests as well.

Presenting your "spread" is a matter of individual **style** and, in some respects, dependent upon the amount of space at your disposal. Without a doubt, a buffet is the easiest way to serve a crowd. Guests can help themselves and then wander off to a comfortable spot to eat. The best buffets are those that look abundant. The old cliche "more is better than less" definitely applies to this service style. Nobody wants to take the last bite, so be sure to have plenty of food on hand to refill bowls and platters as needed. Make the buffet visually enticing by placing the food on risers covered with fabric, and decorating with greens, potted plants or candles. Plan the setup to keep traffic flowing and start with the plates at one end and finish with the napkins and utensils at the other end. The buffet should feature foods that people can spoon out with one hand while they hold their plates, or be roomy enough for them to set their plates down while they serve themselves. It is also nice to write the name of each dish on a gift tag and place it alongside. A sit-down meal can be simple if served family-style, with everything on the table. Just ensure that platters are not too heavy or too hot to pass around. If the table cannot accommodate all of the food, simply create a sideboard by using a card table covered with a cloth and let the serving dishes rest there until it is time to pass them. If your heart is set on a formal sit-down dinner, try to hire someone to help you with the service if at all possible. Regardless, your menu and timing will need to be planned very carefully. To keep things flowing smoothly and to minimize the time you have to spend in the kitchen, follow these guidelines for a sit-down dinner: 1) Prepare everything for serving before your guests take their places at the table. 2) Start with a cold appetizer that can be plated long before your guests arrive and kept at room temperature or in the refrigerator until serving time. 3) Get all of the necessary plates and bowls ready. 4) Apply all garnishes and trimmings in advance. 5) To avoid having to cook between courses, keep soups simmering on the stove; side dishes, grilled foods and other entrées warming in the oven; and salads ready and waiting to be dressed at the appropriate time.

There are a number of things you can do to create the right tone for your party, **music** being one of them. Music has the power to invigorate, relax or inspire and it can be cleverly used to enhance a theme. It can fade into the background or be the star attraction of the gathering. The simplest way to add music to your party is to turn on the radio or invest in a few CD's. Try not to alienate anyone by playing only one style of music. There are many good party tapes on the market that cover a broad range of tastes. Or, you could ask each guest to bring their favorite CD for added variety. No matter what type of music you play, it does not have to be loud or deafening to be good. Volume control is essential—set it high enough so that everyone can hear the music, but low enough so that they can still hear each other! Be considerate of your neighbors as well. If you intend to play loud music for dancing, you may want to warn them in advance. But even then, do not blast it! If your budget and space allows, there is nothing like a little live entertainment. When employing professional musicians, bands or disc jockeys, be sure to spend some time with them before the party to tell them your likes and dislikes and be clear about the mood you are trying to achieve. Be mindful that they will want to take breaks and you may need to think about having an alternative source of music while they rest.

Lighting also makes a big impact on the mood of a party. You can change the feel of the room by simply turning off the overhead lights and putting low-watt bulbs (60 watts or lower) in the lamps. Add a mix of candles in different shapes and sizes and you will have a room that no one wants to leave! (Make sure the candles are positioned in safe places and away from anything that could catch fire.) Gas lanterns, luminaries, kerosene lamps and votive candles—grouped together or singly—are great for outside lighting. You can also create dramatic lighting effects by stringing tiny white lights through tree branches (inside and outdoors).

When **decorating** rooms and tables, the hardest part is not the actual decorating, but deciding how to go about it. Getting those "creative juices" flowing is a very simple process. Ask yourself what you want the party's surroundings to communicate. Are you decorating to carry out a particular theme or to honor a special occasion? Do you want to tie in with a holiday mood or season? Is glamour, fun or whimsy a look you are trying to portray? Or, do you simply want to present a relaxing and comfortable atmosphere? Once you have decided upon the impression that you wish to make, your actual decorations can be simple or elaborate, subtle or bold, homemade or store bought. There are many clever items available in party-supply stores, but you can be just as creative by using ordinary items at home in intriguing new ways. Transform colorful bottles into vases; arrange a bunch of flowers in a teapot; use an old wagon as an ice chest; arrange antiques or edible goodies for centerpieces...the possibilities are endless. Decide where you want to concentrate your efforts and money and have fun with it. Remember, decorating is not really necessary, but small touches here and there sure do add to the festivities.

Serving with Fun

Setting the table is another area where you can let your imagination run wild. **Tablecloths, placemats and napkins** are a great way to enhance your table setting as they add texture and vibrancy to the scene and warmth and color to your dinnerware. Anything goes when dressing your table — it could be an elegant linen tablecloth, a colorful woolen blanket, soft-colored placemats, a bright solid sheet with a bold printed runner, fabric remnants from the thrift shop, butcher paper or even newspaper depending on the mood you are trying to create. Placing accents such as flowers, floating candles, colored balls from the craft store, or fruits and vegetables as centerpieces complement the setting that much more. Creative napkin folding and imaginative napkin rings add style to your table. Add a graceful touch to your meal with one of these special napkin folds:

Napkin Folds

BASIC POSY - 1. Lay napkin open and flat. Bring lower right corner up to and beyond top edge, forming two small, equal triangles on either side. 2. Holding napkin in center of bottom edge, loosely pull napkin through a napkin ring, gathering in loose folds. 3. Gently shake napkin to make folds fall attractively.

BUFFET FOLD - 1. Lay the napkin open and flat. Fold the napkin in half to form a rectangle with folded edge at the bottom. Fold top edge of the first layer down 2 inches towards the middle; then fold down again 2 inches towards the bottom edge. 2. Turn napkin over. Bring right edge to center. Repeat, folding this section over on itself two more times in same direction. 3. Tuck flatware into pocket.

CARDINAL'S HAT - (Use a somewhat "stiff" cloth for best results.) 1. Lay napkin wrong side up with one point at top; bring bottom point to top. 2. Bring both side corners up to meet at the top point. 3. Turn over; keep open points at top. Fold lower corner ⅔ of way up, then bring same corner back down so it is even with bottom. 4. Bring side corners together, tucking one into the other. 5. Turn tucked-in side to back, gently pull side pieces down, then stand napkin on base.

CUMMERBUND FOLD - 1. Lay napkin open and flat. Fold napkin into quarters with closed corner pointing down towards you. Tightly roll top layer down to center. 2. Rotate napkin to the right so that roll runs on a diagonal from top left to bottom right. 3. Holding roll in the same position, fold left and right edges under until they meet and overlap slightly. The remaining rectangle should feature a band that runs diagonally from left to right.

DIPLOMA ROLL - 1. Lay napkin open and flat. Fold napkin in half to form a rectangle with folded edge at the top. Fold top right and bottom right corners in to meet and form a triangle. 2. Roll napkin all the way up from left to right. 3. Secure napkin with a napkin ring or ribbon.

ENVELOPE - 1. Lay napkin open and flat, positioning napkin one point at top. If not reversible, make sure wrong side is facing up. 2. Bring bottom point to top, then fold lower corners to middle. 3. Fold sides in to middle again. 4. Fold lower portion of napkin up to invisible line that would be the base of the triangle. 5. To finish, fold top triangle down to make flap. Position atop plate.

FLICKERING FLAMES - (You will need 2 lightweight fringed cloth or paper napkins.) 1. Place the 2 napkins on top of each other with all edges aligned. Fold up the edges nearest to you to meet the top edges. 2. Fold the napkins in half again by bringing the right edges over to the left edges. 3. Turn the napkins around, placing the open corners away from you and fold the bottom corner about a third of the way up the napkins. 4. Make accordion pleats across the napkins starting from the left point. 5. Firmly holding the bottom, gently open out the layers to form the flames and place in a glass to finish.

PARASOL - (Use a plain or patterned napkin with contrasting ribbon.) 1. Lay napkin open and flat. Make accordion pleats with the whole napkin, beginning at the edge nearest to you. 2. Place one hand firmly over the center of the completed pleats and bring the left edges over to the right edges, and so folding the napkin in half. 3. Tie a bow halfway up the pleats and then fan out the top to make a parasol.

PINWHEEL - 1. Lay the napkin open and flat. Fold the four corners into the center. 2. Fold the top edge and the bottom edge into the center. 3. Bring the left and right sides into the center. 4. Find each of the four loose corners at the center and gently bring them out to the side to form four points. 5. Fold the bottom left point to the left side and the top right point to the right.

PURE AND SIMPLE - (Far more elegant with a lace-edged napkin.) 1. Lay napkin open and flat. Start with the corners of the napkin top and bottom in the form of a diamond. Fold the corner nearest to you up to meet the top point. With a finger at the center bottom, fold the bottom left point up to the top point. 2. Fold the bottom right point up to meet the top point. 3. Turn the napkin over, keeping the open corners furthest from you. Fold the bottom point a third of the way up the napkin. 4. Carefully tuck both sides under the napkin.

SAILBOAT - 1. Lay napkin open and flat. Fold the open napkin into quarters. Keep the open corners nearest to you and fold them to the top point to make a triangle. 2. With a finger placed at the top point, fold down the right and left sides by bringing each point towards you. 3. Turn the napkin over and fold up the bottom point. 4. Turn the napkin over again and fold it in half backwards along the center line. Hold the bottom firmly and open out the top 4 layers to make the sails of the boat.

SIMPLE OBLONG - Lay napkin open and flat. Fold napkin in square. 2. Fold square in half again to make an oblong or rectangular shape. 3. Tie napkin with twine, raffia or ribbon. Insert a fresh jalapeño, dried chile pepper, or flowers under the tie for added decoration.

STRAW ROLL - 1. Lay napkin open and flat with one corner pointing down towards you. 2. Starting at the bottom corner, roll napkin into a smooth tube. 3. Fold tube in half. Tie with long ribbons or tuck folded middle into a goblet or glass.

TUXEDO - (A white napkin is best.) 1. Lay napkin open and flat. Bring bottom point to top to form a triangle; fold lower edge up about 1 inch. 2. Turn over so folded edge is at top facing down; grasp side corners and fold down to bottom corner. 3. Fold two side corners under. 4. To finish, fold bottom corner under. Lay folded napkin atop plate; tie cutlery with a piece of black ribbon and position cutlery in between the two "lapels" of the tuxedo jacket.

Seasoned with Fun

A "proper" **table setting** will probably be the last thing on your guests' minds, and therefore, should not make you feel uneasy. Still, it is reassuring to get it right! Simply put, the charger or plate and flatware should be placed one inch from the edge of the table; the knives (closest to the plate with blades facing in) and spoons go on the right with the glassware above; the forks rest on the left (beginning at the outside edge according to their logical sequence of use) with the bread and butter plate above; the dessert fork and spoon are at the top of the plate (parallel to the table edge); the salad plate sits directly left of the forks; and the coffee cup sits directly right of the spoons. Glance at the illustration below for easy reference:

Proper Table Setting

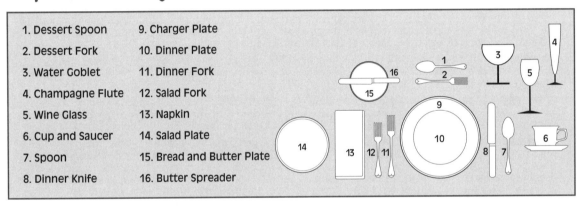

1. Dessert Spoon	9. Charger Plate
2. Dessert Fork	10. Dinner Plate
3. Water Goblet	11. Dinner Fork
4. Champagne Flute	12. Salad Fork
5. Wine Glass	13. Napkin
6. Cup and Saucer	14. Salad Plate
7. Spoon	15. Bread and Butter Plate
8. Dinner Knife	16. Butter Spreader

If you have beautiful **plates, glassware, and silver,** use them. But if not, do not worry. Things do not have to be fancy to be nice. In fact, mixing and matching is often better. Remember...diversity is the spice of life — do not be afraid to use a variety of shapes, sizes and colors. Use only what you need for each meal (usually it is just a dinner plate, dessert plate, one glass, napkin and flatware) and eliminate the rest. Setting the dining table is an adventure that you should have fun doing!

Cooking with Fun

Calculating the quantities and variety of food for a party is never easy. It is largely dependent on the type of party, who is coming, what time of day it is, the season, and how it will be served. In determining quantities, it is better to have too much than too little (you can always eat any left-overs the following day). In deciding on the range of dishes to offer, it often holds true that the fewer the selections, the bigger the impact that it will make on the table and the plate. An easy equation is to plan on 8 to 12 pieces of "finger" food items (per person, per hour) if the food is a substitute for a meal. Figure on one-half pound of meat, one-half to one cup of carbohydrates and vegetables, and one cup of salad per person for "fork" food items. With those magic figures in mind, the following chart will serve useful when determining the type and quantity of food to serve at any event:

Calculating Food Quantities for Parties

Number of People	Finger Food Only Parties		Finger and Fork Food Parties		Fork Food Only Parties	
	Spring/Summer	Fall/Winter	Spring/Summer	Fall/Winter	Spring/Summer	Fall/Winter
10-20 People	6 cold savories (8-12 pieces each)	4 cold savories 2 hot savories (8-12 pieces each)	2 cold savories (3 pieces each) 1 cold fork dish 1 salad 1 bread 1 cold dessert	2 cold savories (3 pieces each) 1 hot fork dish 1 salad 1 bread 1 cold dessert	1 cold fork dish 1 salad 1 bread 1 cold dessert	1 hot fork dish 1 salad 1 bread 1 cold dessert
30-40 People	8 cold savories (8-12 pieces each)	5 cold savories 3 hot savories (8-12 pieces each)	3 cold savories (3 pieces each) 2 cold fork dishes 2 salads 1 bread 1 cold dessert	2 cold savories 1 hot savory (3 pieces each) 1 cold fork dish 1 hot fork dish 1 cold salad 1 hot vegetable dish 1 bread 1 cold dessert	2 cold fork dishes 1 salad 1 bread 1 cold dessert	1 cold fork dish 1 hot fork dish 1 salad 1 bread 1 cold dessert
50-60 People	7 cold savories 1 cold sweet (8-12 pieces each)	4 cold savories 3 hot savories 1 cold sweet (8-12 pieces each)	3 cold savories (3 pieces each) 2 cold fork dishes 1 hot fork dish 2 salads 1 bread 2 cold desserts	2 cold savories 1 hot savory (3 pieces each) 1 cold fork dish 1 hot fork dish 1 salad 1 hot vegetable dish 1 bread 2 cold desserts	3 cold fork dishes 2 salads 1 bread 2 cold desserts	1 cold fork dish 2 hot fork dishes 1 salad 1 hot vegetable dish 1 bread 1 cold dessert 1 hot dessert

Having the right **kitchen gear** will make your job of preparing and cooking food much easier and far more enjoyable. You should never buy more than you can use or store conveniently, but the following list of kitchen tools will prove helpful, particularly for entertaining and cooking at home:

Helpful Kitchen Tools

1 set dry measures (¼ cup, ⅓ cup, ½ cup, 1 cup)
3 liquid measures (1 cup, 2 cup, 4 cup)
1 set measuring spoons
1 set stainless steel or glass mixing bowls
2 rubber spatulas
2 whisks (1 small, 1 medium)
3 mixing spoons, 1 slotted spoon
1 rolling pin
1 pastry blender
1 hand-held electric mixer
1 cutting board
1 paring knife, 1 utility knife, 1 chef's knife, 1 serrated slicing knife
1 knife sharpener or sharpening steel
1 pair kitchen shears
1 vegetable peeler
1 grater
1 colander
3 strainers in graduated sizes
1 sifter
1 timer

1 large metal spatula, 1 small spatula
1 ladle
1 set of tongs
1 long-handled meat fork
1 basting brush
1 instant-read thermometer
1 basting bulb
1 small citrus juicer
1 ruler
1 bottle opener
1 can opener
1 set of metal or wooden skewers
1 set of scales
1 electric blender and/or food processor
3 saucepans with lids (1, 2, and 3-quart)
1 double boiler
1 (4 to 5-quart) Dutch oven
1 (8 to 10-quart) stockpot
1 (6 to 8-inch) skillet
1 (10-inch) skillet with lid
1 (10-inch) nonstick skillet

1 vegetable steamer
1 broiler pan with rack
2 baking sheets
1 jelly-roll pan
1 (13 x 9 x 2-inch) baking dish
1 (11 x 7 x 1½-inch) baking dish
2 (9-inch) square or round baking pans
1 Bundt pan
2 loaf pans
1 muffin pan
1 (8-inch) square baking dish
1 (9-inch) pie plate
3 casserole dishes (1, 2, and 3-quart)
6 (6-ounce) custard cups
1 (2-quart) soufflé dish
2 wire cooling racks
1 springform pan
1 miniature muffin pan
1 (10-inch) tube pan
1 tart pan
1 pizza pan

1 large dough bowl
1 pepper mill
1 garlic press
1 oven thermometer
1 mallet
1 pie server
1 wok
1 set cookie cutters
1 pastry bag with tips
Cheesecloth
1 electric skillet
1 electric knife
1 electric, heavy-duty stand mixer
1 funnel
1 ice cream scoop
1 masher

Seasoned with Fun

Help! You have the menu and you have the tools, but what do you do if you find the pantry is lacking an essential ingredient (that you thought you had) and you are in the middle of your preparation? Or, how do you measure ounces when all you have are measuring spoons and cups? Perhaps the expiration date is a little overdue! **Equivalencies, substitutions and shelf life** challenge us all and can make us feel inadequate in the kitchen. Next time you find yourself feeling "helpless" in the kitchen at an inopportune moment, flip through these helpful cooking charts—you are bound to find a solution one way or another!

Equivalent Measures

TEASPOONS

10 drops = 1 dash
⅛ teaspoon = a few grains
1 teaspoon = 6 dashes
3 teaspoons = 1 tablespoon
8 teaspoons = 1 ounce

TABLESPOONS

1 tablespoon = ½ fluid ounce
1 tablespoon = 15 milliliters
1 tablespoon = 15 grams
2 tablespoons = 1 fluid ounce
2 tablespoons = ⅛ cup
4 tablespoons = ¼ cup
4 tablespoons = 2 fluid ounces
5 tablespoons + 1 teaspoon = ⅓ cup
8 tablespoons = ½ cup
10 tablespoons + 2 teaspoons = ⅔ cup
12 tablespoons = ¾ cup
16 tablespoons = 1 cup
16 tablespoons = 8 ounces

CUPS

⅛ cup = 1 ounce
⅛ cup = 2 tablespoons
⅜ cup = 6 tablespoons
⅝ cup = 2½ tablespoons
⅞ cup = 1 cup less 2 tablespoons
⅓ cup = 5 tablespoons + 1 teaspoon
¼ cup = 2 ounces
½ cup = 4 ounces
½ cup = 8 tablespoons

1 cup = ½ pint
1 cup = 8 ounces
1 cup = 227 grams
1 cup = 240 milliliters
2 cups = 1 pound
2 cups = 16 ounces
4 cups = 1 quart

DRY VOLUMES

2 cups = 1 pint
4 cups = 1 quart
2 pints = 1 quart
4 quarts = 1 gallon
8 quarts = 1 peck
2 gallons = 1 peck
4 pecks = 1 bushel
16 ounces = 1 pound
32 ounces = 1 quart

NUTS

4 ounces shelled almonds = 1 cup
1 pound shelled Brazil nuts = 3¼ cups
1 pound shelled cashews = 3¼ cups
1 pound chestnuts in shell = 2½ cups
1 cup whole meat hazelnuts = 1¼ cups chopped
4 ounces macadamia nuts = 1 cup whole meat
1½ pounds peanuts in shell = 1 pound shelled
1 pound shelled pecans = 4 cups whole meat
1½ ounces pine nuts = ¼ cup

3 pounds pistachios in shell = 1 pound shelled
4 ounces shelled black walnuts = 1 cup
1 pound walnuts in shell = 2 cups

CAN SIZES

6 ounces = ¾ cup
8 ounces = 1 cup
10½ ounces = 1¼ cups
16 ounces = 2 cups
20 ounces = 2½ cups
29 ounces = 3½ cups
46 ounces = 5¾ cups

INGREDIENTS

1 medium bunch celery = 4½ cups
2 medium ears corn = 1 cup kernels
4 ounces egg noodles = 3 cups cooked
1 large bell pepper = 1 cup chopped
3 medium potatoes = 2 cups cooked
1 cup long grain rice = 3-4 cups cooked
1 cup quick cooking rice = 2 cups cooked
1 medium tomato = ½ cup cooked
1 medium lemon = 2-3 tablespoons juice
5-8 medium lemons = 1 cup juice
1 lemon = 1 tablespoon grated rind

1 medium orange = 2-3 tablespoons juice
3-4 medium oranges = 1 cup juice
1 orange = 2 tablespoons grated rind

LIQUID MEASURES

1 ounce = 28 grams
1½ ounces = 1 jigger
1 quart = 2 pounds
1 liter = 1 quart + 2 ounces
1 fifth = 25 ounces
1 quart = 32 ounces
1 quart = 907 grams
1 quart = 64 tablespoons
1 pound = 454 grams

ONE POUND

2 cups butter or shortening
4 cups all-purpose flour
4½ cups cake flour
2 cups granulated sugar
3½ cups powdered sugar
2⅔ cups brown sugar
2 cups milk
3 cups rice
6 cups cooked beans
2 cups sliced carrots
6¼ cups lettuce
4 cups grated cheese
2⅔ cups cubed cheese
2 cups cottage cheese
3 cups cornstarch
4 cups ground cocoa
5 cups ground coffee
4-6 big potatoes
5-6 apples

Handy Substitutions

BAKING PRODUCTS

Arrowroot (1 teaspoon)
= 1 tablespoon all-purpose flour
= 1½ teaspoons cornstarch

Baking powder (1 teaspoon)
= ½ teaspoon cream of tartar and ¼ teaspoon baking soda

Chocolate

Semisweet (1 ounce)
= 1 ounce unsweetened chocolate and 1 tablespoon sugar

Unsweetened (1 ounce)
= 3 tablespoons cocoa and 1 tablespoon fat

Chips, semisweet (1 ounce)
= 1 ounce square semisweet chocolate

Chips, semisweet (6 ounces, melted)
= 2 ounces unsweetened chocolate, 2 tablespoons shortening and ½ cup sugar

Cocoa (¼ cup)
= 1 ounce unsweetened chocolate (decrease fat in recipe by ½ tablespoon)

Coconut

Flaked (1 tablespoon)
= 1½ tablespoons grated fresh coconut

Cream (1 cup)
= 1 cup whipping cream

Milk (1 cup)
= 1 cup whole or reduced-fat milk

Corn Syrup (1 cup, light)
= 1 cup sugar and ¼ cup water
= 1 cup honey

Cornstarch (1 tablespoon)
= 2 tablespoons all-purpose flour or granular tapioca

Flour

All-purpose (1 tablespoon)
= 1½ teaspoons cornstarch, potato starch or rice starch
= 1 tablespoon rice flour or corn flour
= 1½ tablespoons whole wheat flour
= ½ tablespoon whole wheat flour and ½ tablespoon all-purpose flour

All-purpose (1 cup, sifted)
= 1 cup and 2 tablespoons sifted cake flour
= 1 cup less 2 tablespoons all-purpose flour (unsifted)
= 1½ cups breadcrumbs
= 1 cup rolled oats
= ⅓ cup cornmeal or soybean flour and ⅔ cup all-purpose flour
= ¾ cup whole wheat flour or bran flour and ¼ cup all-purpose flour
= 1 cup rye or rice flour
= ¼ cup soybean flour and ¾ cup all-purpose flour

Cake (1 cup, sifted)
= 1 cup less 2 tablespoons all-purpose flour

Self-rising (1 cup)
= 1 cup all-purpose flour, 1 teaspoon baking powder and ½ teaspoon salt

Marshmallows

Cream (7-ounce jar)
= 16-ounce package marshmallows, melted and 3½ tablespoons light corn syrup

Miniature (1 cup)
= 10 large

Pecans (1 cup, chopped)
= 1 cup regular oats, toasted

Shortening

Melted (1 cup)
= 1 cup cooking oil

Solid (1 cup)
= 1 cup less 2 tablespoons lard
= 1⅛ cups butter or margarine (decrease salt in recipe by ½ teaspoon)

Sugar

Brown (1 cup, firmly packed)
= 1 cup granulated white sugar

Maple (½ cup)
= 1 cup maple syrup

Powdered (1 cup)
= 1 cup sugar and 1 tablespoon cornstarch (processed in food processor)

Granulated white (1 teaspoon)
= ⅛ teaspoon non-caloric sweetener solution

Granulated white (1 cup)
= 1 cup corn syrup (decrease liquid in recipe by ¼ cup)
= 1 cup firmly packed brown sugar
= 1 cup honey (decrease liquid in recipe by ¼ cup)

Tapioca (1 tablespoon, granular)
= 1½ teaspoons cornstarch
= 1 tablespoon all-purpose flour

Yeast (¼-ounce package, active dry)
= 1 tablespoon active dry yeast

Handy Substitutions continued

DAIRY PRODUCTS

Butter (1 cup)	= ⅞ to 1 cup shortening or lard and ½ teaspoon salt
Cream	
Heavy (1 cup)	= ¾ cup milk and ⅓ cup butter or margarine (for cooking and baking; will not whip)
Light (1 cup)	= ¾ cup milk and 3 tablespoons butter or margarine (for cooking and baking)
Half-and-half (1 cup)	= 1 cup evaporated milk, undiluted
	= ⅞ cup milk and ½ tablespoon butter or margarine (for cooking and baking)
	= 1 cup evaporated milk, undiluted
Whipped	= 1 (13-ounce) can evaporated milk (chilled 12 hours). Add 1 teaspoon lemon juice. Whip until stiff.
Egg	
1 large	= 2 egg yolks (for custard and cream fillings)
	= 2 egg yolks and 1 tablespoon water (for cookies)
2 large	= 3 small eggs
1 egg white (2 tablespoons)	= 2 tablespoons egg substitute
	= 2 teaspoons sifted, dry egg white powder and 2 tablespoons warm water
1 egg yolk (1½ tablespoons)	= 2 tablespoons sifted dry egg yolk powder and 2 teaspoons water
	= 1½ tablespoons thawed frozen egg yolk
Milk	
Buttermilk (1 cup)	= 1 tablespoon vinegar or lemon juice and 1 cup whole milk (let stand 10 minutes)
	= 1 cup plain yogurt
	= 1 cup whole milk and 1¾ teaspoons cream of tartar
Fat free (1 cup)	= 4-5 tablespoons nonfat dry milk powder and 1 cup water
	= ½ cup evaporated skim milk and ½ cup water
Whole (1 cup)	= 4-5 tablespoons nonfat dry milk powder and 1 cup water
	= ½ cup evaporated milk and ½ cup water
	= 1 cup fruit juice or potato water (used in baking)
Sweetened condensed	
1 (14-ounce) can	= Heat the following ingredients until sugar and butter dissolve: ⅓ cup and 2 tablespoons evaporated milk, 1 cup sugar, 3 tablespoons butter or margarine
1 cup	= Heat the following ingredients until sugar and butter dissolve: ⅓ cup evaporated milk, ¾ cup sugar, 2 tablespoons butter or margarine
	= Add 1 cup and 2 tablespoons nonfat dry milk powder to ½ cup warm water. Mix well. Add ¾ cup sugar and stir until smooth.
Sour Cream (1 cup)	= 1 cup plain yogurt and 3 tablespoons melted butter
	= 1 cup plain yogurt and 1 tablespoon cornstarch
	= 1 tablespoon lemon juice and 1 cup evaporated milk
Yogurt (1 cup, plain)	= 1 cup buttermilk

FRUIT AND VEGETABLE PRODUCTS

Lemon	
1 medium	= 2-3 tablespoons juice and 2 teaspoons grated rind
Juice (1 teaspoon)	= ½ teaspoon vinegar
Peel (1 teaspoon, dried)	= 2 teaspoons freshly grated lemon rind
	= ½ teaspoon lemon extract
Orange	
1 medium	= ½ cup juice and 2 tablespoons grated rind
Peel (1 teaspoon, dried)	= 1½ teaspoons orange extract
Mushrooms (1 pound, fresh)	= 1 (8-ounce) can sliced mushrooms, drained
	= 3 ounces dried mushrooms, rehydrated
Onion (1 medium, chopped)	= 1 tablespoon dried minced onion
	= 1 teaspoon onion powder

Handy Substitutions continued

Pepper

Red or Green (3 tablespoons, chopped)	= 1 tablespoon dried red or green pepper flakes
Sweet red (3 tablespoons, chopped)	= 2 tablespoons chopped pimiento
Shallots (3 tablespoons, chopped)	= 2 tablespoons chopped onion and 1 tablespoon chopped garlic

Tomatoes

Fresh (2 cups, chopped)	= 1 (16-ounce) can drained
Juice (1 cup)	= ½ cup tomato sauce and ½ cup water
Tomato Sauce (2 cups)	= ¾ cup tomato paste and 1 cup water

MISCELLANEOUS

Broth, Beef or Chicken	
Canned broth (1 cup)	= 1 bouillon cube dissolved in 1 cup boiling water
	= 1 teaspoon powdered broth base dissolved in 1 cup boiling water
Powdered broth base (1 teaspoon)	= 1 bouillon cube
Powdered broth base (1 teaspoon dissolved in 1 cup water)	= 1 cup canned or homemade broth
Chili sauce (1 cup)	= 1 cup tomato sauce, ¼ cup brown sugar, 2 tablespoons vinegar, ¼ teaspoon cinnamon, dash of ground cloves and dash of ground allspice
Gelatin (3-ounce package, flavored)	= 1 tablespoon unflavored gelatin and 2 cups fruit juice
Honey (1 cup)	= 1¼ cups sugar and ¼ cup water
Ketchup (1 cup)	= 1 cup tomato sauce, ½ cup sugar and 2 tablespoons vinegar (for cooking)
Macaroni (2 cups, uncooked/4 cups, cooked)	= 8 ounces spaghetti, uncooked
	= 4 cups fine egg noodles, uncooked
Mayonnaise (1 cup for salads and dressings)	= ½ cup plain yogurt and ½ cup mayonnaise
	= 1 cup sour cream
	= 1 cup cottage cheese pureed in a blender
Rice (1 cup regular, uncooked)	= 1 cup uncooked converted rice
	= 1 cup uncooked brown rice or wild rice
Vinegar (½ cup balsamic)	= ½ cup red wine vinegar (some flavor difference)

SEASONING PRODUCTS

Allspice (1 teaspoon, ground)	= ½ teaspoon ground cinnamon and ½ teaspoon ground cloves
Apple pie spice (1 teaspoon)	= ½ teaspoon ground cinnamon, ¼ teaspoon ground nutmeg and ⅛ teaspoon ground cardamom
Bay leaf (1 whole)	= ¼ teaspoon crushed bay leaf
Beau Monde Seasoning (1 teaspoon)	= 1 teaspoon seasoning salt
	= ½ teaspoon salt
Chives (1 tablespoon, chopped)	= 1 tablespoon chopped green onion tops
Dill weed (3 heads, fresh or dried)	= 1 tablespoon dill seed
Garlic	
Clove (1 small)	= ⅛ teaspoon garlic powder or minced dried garlic
Garlic salt (1 teaspoon)	= ⅛ teaspoon garlic powder and ⅞ teaspoon salt
Ginger	
Crystallized (1 tablespoon)	= ⅛ teaspoon ground ginger
Fresh (1 tablespoon, grated)	= ⅛ teaspoon ground ginger
Ground (⅛ teaspoon)	= 1 tablespoon crystallized ginger rinsed in water to remove sugar and finely cut
	= 1 tablespoon grated fresh ginger
Herbs (1 tablespoon fresh, chopped)	= 1 teaspoon dried herbs or ¼ teaspoon ground herbs

Handy Substitutions continued

Horseradish (1 tablespoon fresh, grated)	= 2 tablespoons prepared horseradish
Mustard (1 teaspoon, dried)	= 1 tablespoon prepared mustard
Onion powder (1 tablespoon)	= 1 medium onion, chopped = 1 tablespoon dried minced onion
Parsley (1 teaspoon, dried)	= 1 tablespoon fresh parsley, chopped
Pimiento (2 tablespoons, chopped)	= Rehydrate 1 tablespoon dried sweet red pepper = 2-3 tablespoons chopped fresh sweet red pepper
Pumpkin pie spice (1 teaspoon)	= ½ teaspoon ground cinnamon, ¼ teaspoon ground ginger, ⅛ teaspoon ground allspice and ⅛ teaspoon ground nutmeg
Peppermint (1 tablespoon, dried)	= 3 tablespoons chopped fresh mint
Vanilla bean (1 inch)	= 1 teaspoon vanilla extract
Worcestershire sauce (1 teaspoon)	= 1 teaspoon bottled steak sauce

ALCOHOL PRODUCTS

Amaretto (2 tablespoons)	= ¼-½ teaspoon almond extract (add water, white grape juice, or apple juice to get the specified amount of liquid when the liquid amount is crucial)
Bourbon or Sherry (2 tablespoons)	= 1-2 teaspoons vanilla extract (add water, white grape juice, or apple juice to get the specified amount of liquid when the liquid amount is crucial)
Brandy, Fruit-flavored liqueur, Port wine, Rum, or Sweet sherry (¼ cup or more)	= Equal amount of unsweetened orange or apple juice and 1 teaspoon vanilla extract or corresponding flavor
Grand Marnier (2 tablespoons)	= 2 tablespoons unsweetened orange juice concentrate or 2 tablespoons orange juice and ½ teaspoon orange extract
Kahlúa (2 tablespoons)	= ½-1 teaspoon chocolate extract and ½-1 teaspoon instant coffee dissolved in 2 tablespoons water
Marsala (¼ cup)	= ¼ cup white grape juice, or ¼ cup dry white wine and 1 teaspoon brandy
Wine	
Red (¼ cup or more)	= Equal measure of red grape juice or cranberry juice
White (¼ cup or more)	= Equal measure of white grape juice or apple juice

BAKING PAN SUBSTITUTIONS

Rectangular	
11 x 7 x 1½-inch (8 cups)	= 8 x 8 x 2-inch square
13 x 9 x 2-inch (12-15 cups)	= two 9-inch round or three 8-inch round
Square	
8 x 8 x 2-inch (8 cups)	= 11 x 7 x 1½-inch rectangular
9 x 9 x 2-inch (10 cups)	= 9 x 5 x 3-inch loaf pan or two 8-inch round
Round	
8 x 1½-inch (5 cups)	= 10 x 6 x 2-inch rectangular
8 x 2-inch (6 cups)	= 8½ x 4½ x 2½-inch loaf pan
9 x 1½-inch (6 cups)	= 8 x 2-inch round
Tube	
10 x 4-inch (16 cups)	= 10-inch ring mold or cake mold
Loaf	
8½ x 4½ x 2½-inch (6 cups)	= two or three 6 x 3 x 2-inch loaf pans
9 x 5 x 3-inch (8 cups)	= three or four 6 x 3 x 2-inch loaf pans
Pie plate	
9 x 1½-inch (5 cups)	= No substitution unless tart pans are used
10 x 1½-inch (6 cups)	= No substitution unless tart pans are used
Jelly-roll pan	
15 x 10 x 1-inch (10 cups)	= Do not substitute baking sheet for jelly-roll pan

RECOMMENDED STORAGE GUIDE

IN THE PANTRY	
Baking powder and soda	1 year
Flour, all-purpose	10-15 months
Milk	
Evaporated	1 year
Sweetened condensed	1 year
Mixes, cake	1 year
Mixes, pancake	6 months
Peanut butter	6 months
Salt and pepper	18 months
Shortening	8 months
Spices (discard if aroma fades)	
Ground	6 months
Whole	1 year
Sugar	18 months

IN THE REFRIGERATOR	
Butter and margarine	1 month
Buttermilk	1-2 weeks
Eggs (fresh in shell)	3-5 weeks
Half-and-half	7-10 days
Meat	
Casseroles, cooked	3-4 days
Steaks, chops,	
roasts (uncooked)	3-5 days
Milk, whole and skimmed	1 week
Poultry, uncooked	1-2 days
Sour cream	3-4 weeks
Whipping cream	10 days

IN THE FREEZER	
Breads	
Quick	2-3 months
Yeast	3-6 months
Butter	6 months
Cakes	
Cheesecakes and	
Pound cakes	2-3 months
Unfrosted cakes	2-5 months
Frosted cakes	Not recommended
Creamy-type	
frosted cakes	3 months
Candy and fudge	6 months
Casseroles	1-2 months
Cheese	4 months
Cookies	
Baked, unfrosted	8-12 months
Dough	1 month
Eggs (not in shell)	
Whites	1 year
Yolks	8 months
Ice Cream	1-3 months
Meat	
Cooked	2-3 months
Ground, uncooked	3-4 months
Roasts, uncooked	9 months
Steaks or chops,	
uncooked	4-6 months
Nuts	8 months
Pies	
Pastry shell	2-3 months
Fruit	1-2 months
Pumpkin	2-4 months
Custard, cream	
or meringue	Not recommended
Poultry	
Cooked	3-4 months
Parts, uncooked	9 months
Whole, uncooked	1 year
Soups and Stews	2-3 months

Drinking with Fun

When planning a party, the cocktails deserve just as much forethought as the food. After all, the bar is often the busiest place at your event! These days, there are no stringent rules about what you should and should not serve—for some events, it may just be your favorite wine and a few ice cold beers and sodas; other occasions call for a wider range of mixed drinks, sparkling wine or fruity cocktails. Let the type of party, your overall taste and comfort level, and the habits of your guests be your guide when deciding what beverages to offer.

To be on the safe side, your **bar** should be stocked with the basics: gin, whiskey and vodka, as well as wines and beers. For a fully stocked liquor cabinet, add tequila, brandy, rum, bourbon, vermouth, sherry, Dubonnet, and Campari to the selections. A full bar is not just about alcohol. You should also have plenty of bottled water, fruit juices (including orange, cranberry and tomato), tonic water, club soda, ginger ale and colas on hand for designated drivers and those who wish to socialize without imbibing. Garnishes should include lemons and limes, orange wedges, maraschino cherries, superfine sugar, salt, bitters, olives, cocktail onions, Worcestershire and Tabasco. Another crucial element is ensuring you have enough ice. Figure each guest will consume at least one-half pound of ice. If you do not have enough refrigerator space to chill all of your drinks, plan on one pound of ice per person. Ultimately, when deciding on what to buy for your bar, remember that a well-"selected" bar is better than a well-"stocked" bar; that is, one that is ready with the things you and your friends drink on a regular basis. Undoubtedly, your guests will present you with a bottle of wine or liquor as they walk through the door. If the gift enhances your drink selections, feel free to serve it. Do not feel obligated, however, if it just does not fit the occasion, menu, or you already have opened bottles...your guests will understand.

The equation for figuring **how much** to buy may seem like sheer guess work, but it actually is not. It is always better to err on the generous side than to get caught short, so plan on your guests drinking two drinks (with or without alcohol) per hour. If only wine or champagne are being served, count on one-half bottle per person and buy two bottles of white to every bottle of red. Keep in mind that there are about five glasses of wine and six champagne flutes to a standard 750 milliliter bottle. For more detailed calculations, refer to the notes below:

CALCULATING BEVERAGE QUANTITIES

Champagne or Sparkling Wine: There are six champagne flutes to a 750 milliliter bottle. For a 2-hour cocktail party, if the only other drinks that you serve are mineral water and soft drinks, allow 2½ glasses each. As an apéritif before dinner, allow 1½ glasses per person. At weddings, when you want to toast the bride and groom, a single glass per person is sufficient. A single glass is also enough to serve with dessert. When you are diluting champagne or sparkling wine with a fruit puree or juice, allow about 8 glasses per bottle.

Wines: There are about five medium wine glasses to a 750 milliliter bottle. For a 2-hour cocktail party, if you are not serving anything else, apart from mineral water and soft drinks, allow one bottle for every two people. At cocktail parties, white wine is generally more popular than red, so have two-thirds white to one-third red. For fork lunches or suppers, allow two glasses of white wine and 1½ glasses of red each. If you are providing only red or white, three glasses will generally be enough.

Spirits and Mixers: A 750 milliliter bottle will make about 17 single measures, served in old-fashioned tumblers. If you are only serving spirits or cocktails, mineral water and juice at a 2-hour cocktail party, you probably need to allow three per person.

Liqueurs: A 750 milliliter bottle of liqueur will give you about 15 liqueur or brandy glasses for an after-dinner drink. You should only need one per person.

Mineral Water: Each 1-liter bottle yields about five glasses. For a 2-hour cocktail party, provide one bottle for every four guests. Remember that some will prefer still water to sparkling, so you will need to allow an appropriate amount. For a fork lunch or supper, a bottle for every three guests is sufficient.

Soft Drinks: At a 2-hour cocktail party, when you are serving champagne or wine along with mineral water, you need to have some soft drinks as well. One six ounce glass per person should suffice. However, for parties at which you are only going to serve soft drinks and no alcohol, allow a total of three glasses each.

The process of **pairing food and wine** is highly subjective and the bottom line is you should serve whatever combination pleases you! There are, however, some historical guidelines and culinary trends to rely on if you are more of a "stickler" for the rules: white wine goes well with pale-colored foods and red wine complements dark-colored foods; champagne is often served with oysters, caviar and dessert, but no time is ever inappropriate for the "classiest" of all beverages. Refer to the suggestions listed below for pairing different food types with wine:

PAIRING FOOD AND WINE

FOOD TYPE	WINE SUGGESTION
BEEF	
Beef Stew	Burgundy, Châteauneuf-du-Pape, Beaujolais, Pinot Noir
Chili	Bandol, Zinfandel
Corned Beef	Zinfandel, Merlot
Filet of Beef	Pomerol, Vino Nobile de Montepulciano
Flank Steak	Cabernet Sauvignon, Shiraz, Beaujolais Nouveau
Hamburger	Beaujolais-Villages
Meat Loaf	Zinfandel
Rib and Loin Steaks	Beaujolais-Villages
Roast Beef	Cabernet Sauvignon, Barolo, Pommard
CHEESE, BLUES	
Stilton	Ruby Port
Roquefort	Beaujolais
Gorgonzola	Vino Nobile, Cabernet Sauvignon
Sweet Gorgonzola	Sauternes
Maytag Blue	Zinfandel
CHEESE, SOFT RIPENING	
Brie	Alsace Riesling, Bordeaux
Camembert	Merlot
Vacherin Mont d'Or	Cabernet Sauvignon, Pomerol
CHEESE, DOUBLE AND TRIPLE CRÉME	
L'Explorateur	Chardonnay
Brillat-Savarin	Beaujolais
St.-Andre	Tavel Rosé, Pink Champagne
CHEESE, SEMIHARD	
Appenzeller	Beaujolais
Cantal	Chardonnay
Cheddars	Beaujolais Nouveau, Cabernet Sauvignon, Tawny Port
CHEESE, SEMISOFT	
Morbier	Vouvray
Port-Salut	Mâcon-Villages
Reblochon	Beaujolais-Villages
Tomme de Savoie	Côtes du Rhône
Fontina	Chianti Classico
Munster	Alsace Riesling
Raclette	Alsace Riesling
Gouda	Red Rhône, Red Riesling
CHEESE, HARD	
Parmigiano-Reggiano	Vino Nobile, Barolo, Chianti Classico
Aged Cow's Milk	California Petite Sirah
Dry Jack Cheese	Napa Gamay, Beaujolais
CHEESE, CHÉVRES	
Montrachet	Zinfandel
Bucheron	Chardonnay

Pairing Food and Wine continued

FOOD TYPE	WINE SUGGESTION
CHEESE, CHÉVRES (continued)	
Banon	Sauvignon Blanc
Aged Goat	Sancerre
Crottin	Cabernet Sauvignon
Blue Capri	Beaujolais
Caprinio	Vin Santo
FISH	
Bass	Chardonnay, Orvieto
Bluefish	Chardonnay
Catfish	White Zinfandel
Cod	Bandol, Zinfandel
Flounder	Sauvignon Blanc
Gravlax, smoked	Aquavit, Gewürztraminer, Pouilly-Fuissé
Grouper	Muscadet
Herring, smoked	Chenin Blanc, Aquavit
John Dory	Fumé Blanc, Chablis
Monkfish	Montrachet
Perch	Chablis, Chenin Blanc
Pompano	Chardonnay
Salmon	Meursault
Salmon, smoked	Tokay d'Alsace, Sparkling Blanc, Pouilly-Fuissé
Sardines	Sancerre, White Rioja
Shad Roe	Puligny-Montrachet, Chardonnay
Skate	Puligny-Montrachet
Snapper	Pouilly-Fuissé
Sole	Sauvignon Blanc, Mâcon
Swordfish	Chardonnay, Beaujolais-Villages
Trout	Sancerre, Chenin Blanc
Trout, smoked	Chardonnay, Chenin Blanc
Whitefish, smoked	Pinot Blanc
GAME	
Goose	Pinot Noir, Châteauneuf-du-Pape
Grouse	Pommard, Riesling
Hare	Barbaresco, Shiraz
Partridge	Pinot Noir, Merlot
Pheasant	Brunello de Montalcino
Quail	Riesling, Gamay
Rabbit	Bordeaux, Gattinara
Venison	Barolo, Cabernet Sauvignon
Wild Duck	Gewürztraminer
GRILLED FOODS	
Chicken	Beaujolais, Chardonnay, Sauvignon Blanc
Fish	Fumé Blanc, Chardonnay
Hamburgers	Beaujolais-Villages
Lamb or Pork Ribs	Zinfandel
Mixed Grill	Chianti, Merlot
Paella	Rioja Red, Bandol Red, Zinfandel, Beaujolais, Sangría
Steak	Zinfandel, Merlot
Vegetables	Bandol Rosé, Sancerre, Beaujolais-Villages
LAMB	
Leg Roasts and Racks	Rubesco de Torgiano, Bordeaux, Cabernet Sauvignon
Moussaka and Curries	Zinfandel, Syrah, Valpolicella
Ragoûts and Stews	Côte de Beaune
Lamb Stuffed with Vegetables	Merlot

Pairing Food and Wine continued

FOOD TYPE	WINE SUGGESTION
PASTA SAUCES	
Cheese	Bardolino, Barbaresco, Gattinara
Creamy Herb	Chardonnay, Chenin Blanc
Game	Chianti Rufina, Barolo, Pinot Noir
Meat	Rubesco di Torgiano, Valpolicella
Seafood	Orvieto, Cortese di Gavi, Chardonnay
Robust Tomato	Chianti, Zinfandel
Vegetable	Beaujolais, Zinfandel
POULTRY	
Capon	Chardonnay
Roast Chicken	Châteauneuf-du-Pape, Merlot
Robust Chicken	Cabernet Sauvignon
Creamy Chicken	Chardonnay
Fried Chicken	Beaujolais
Spiced Chicken	Zinfandel
Light Chicken	Chablis, Sancerre
Chicken Salads	Riesling (dry), Chenin Blanc
Roast Duck	Vouvray
Duck Stews	Pinot Noir
Rock Cornish Hens	Vouvray, Merlot
Roast Turkey	Zinfandel, Beaujolais
Turkey, other ways	Beaujolais-Villages, Beaujolais Nouveau
Chicken Liver Pâtés	Beaujolais-Villages, Sancerre, Vouvray
Foie Gras	Sauternes, Gewürztraminer, Tokay d'Alsace
SHELLFISH	
Clams, Crab, Lobster	Beaujolais-Villages, Sancerre, Sauvignon Blanc, Muscadet, Chardonnay, Tavel Rosé
Mussels	Chablis, Fumé Blanc
Oysters	Champagne, Chardonnay
Scallops	Sauvignon Blanc, Pouilly Fumé
Shrimp	Pinot Blanc, Orvieto
Squid (Calamari)	Soave, Riesling
SOUP	
Creamy Vegetable	Sauvignon Blanc, Chardonnay, Riesling
Fruit	Johannesberg Riesling, Sauternes, Barsac
Light Vegetable	Beaujolais, Chablis
Meat, Vegetable and Noodle	Beaujolais, Cabernet Sauvignon, Merlot, Chardonnay
Robust Vegetable	Zinfandel, Côtes du Rhône, Chianti
VEAL	
Chops	Gattinara, Cortese di Gavi, Fumé Blanc
Roasts	Beaujolais Fleurie, Barolo
Robust Stews	Valpolicella, Chianti Classico, Chardonnay
Scaloppine	Beaujolais, Cabernet Sauvignon
Calf's Liver	Riesling, Gewürztraminer

For a smooth-running cocktail party, make sure your bar is stocked with plenty of **glassware** — at least twice as many glasses as people or one glass per person per hour — as they tend to get abandoned easily. To keep things simple (especially when hosting a large gathering), it is best to rely on one all-purpose glass. A 10 or 12-ounce size will usually serve all beverages; and, using plastic is perfectly okay! If, however, you want to match all of the glasses to the drink, use the following: flutes for champagne; a generous wine glass for wines, juice and water; straight-sided highballs for tall drinks served with ice; tumblers for spirits and juices; v-shaped glasses for cocktails; and balloon glasses for brandy. Again, the glassware does not all need to match. An eclectic collection of crystal, colored-glasses, plain, or thrift-store finds serve a drink as well as the next!

Seasoned with Fun

Having **essential bar accessories** will make pouring drinks a breeze. Use the checklist below as your guide and your bar will be prepared for serving any drink, any time.

Bar Accessories

MAJOR ESSENTIALS	MINOR ESSENTIALS	LUXURY ESSENTIALS
Cocktail shaker	Lemon peeler	Champagne/Wine cooler
Cocktail mixing glass	Muddler (for crushing sugar cubes and fruit)	Decanter
Ice bucket	Pepper grinder	Punch bowl with ladle
Ice tongs	Cork pourers	Cocktail tray
Pitcher	Cocktail toothpicks	
1½-ounce jigger	Bottle stoppers	
Long-handled spoon	Coasters	
Cocktail strainer	Juicer	
Cutting board	Mallet	
Paring knife		
Bottle opener (with pointed end)		
Corkscrew		
Dish towel		
Swizzle sticks		
Blender		
Cocktail napkins		

Party Menus

◎ Committee Luncheon ◎

Medley of salads to include:
Tossed Garden Greens with Soy-Ginger Dressing
Honey-Mustard Turkey Salad
Tortellini Salad with Pine Nuts
Very Berry Muffins
White Chocolate Orange Cookies

◎ Mexican Fiesta ◎

Almost-a-Meal Queso
Southwestern Black Bean Salad
Shrimp Enchiladas in Tomatillo Sauce
Southwestern Risotto
Flan Cake

◎ Garden Brunch Buffet ◎

Marinated Asparagus and Hearts of Palm
Fruit with a Bite
Canadian Bacon Scramble
Spinach Herb Cheesecake
Sweet Roll Cake

◎ Tailgate Picnic ◎

Roasted Red Pepper Roll-Ups
Mediterranean Torte
Green Bean, Walnut and Feta Salad
Pesto Potato Salad
Crispy Oatmeal-Toffee Lizzies

◎ Hunter's Feast ◎

Velvet Corn Chowder
Cranberry, Feta and Pecan Salad
Pierre's Grilled Quail
Skillet Spinach "Balsamico"
Nutty Orange Rice
Simple Dinner Rolls
Pumpkin Cheesecake with Caramel Swirl

◎ Finger Food Cocktail Party ◎

Sun-Dried Tomato Hummus
Asparagus and Sugar Snap Peas
with Honey-Mustard Dip
Italian Cheese Terrine
Stuffed Shiitake Parmigiana
Chile, Feta Cheese and Walnut Bundles
Pillows of the Greek Gods
Spicy Crab Bites
Chicken Puffs

Party Menus

◎ Patio Barbecue ◎

Mediterranean Confetti

Basil Grilled Chicken

Creamy Corn Bake

Chipotle Corn Bread

Lemon Blackberry Crisp

◎ Dinner-to-Go ◎

Spinach Salad with Raspberry Vinaigrette

Chicken Lasagna Florentine

Dilly Garlic Bread

Sinful Bundt Cake

◎ Any Occasion Shower ◎

White Gazpacho

Smoked Salmon-Caper-and-Dill Pasta

Pesto Bread with Cheese and Pine Nuts

Key Lime Tart in Coconut Crust

◎ Elegant Dinner ◎

Scallops with Roasted Garlic and Saffron Sauce

Endive, Bacon and Pecan Salad

Marinated Beef Tenderloin

Dilly Asparagus, Green Beans and Scallions

Gratin Potatoes with Boursin

Blast from the Past Dinner Rolls

Warm Fudge-Filled Cheesecake

◎ Dessert Buffet for a Crowd ◎

Array of elegant desserts to include:

Chocolate Wrapped Banana Cheesecake with Caramelized Bananas

Chocolate Truffle Cake

Caramel Cake

Lemon Meringue Cake

Mango Colada Pie

Chocolate Trifle

Fresh Fruit with Kahlúa Dip

◎ Family Dinner ◎

Mixed Greens with Chipotle Dressing

Chicken Cerveza

Green Beans Provençal

Crunchy Potato Casserole

Mexican Fiesta Spoon Biscuits

American Apple Pie

Just for Starters

Just for Starters

Black-Eyed Pea Pâté

A wonderful vegetarian version of an old favorite.

Preparation Time: 15 minutes

2   (3-ounce) packages cream cheese, softened

2   (16-ounce) cans black-eyed peas, drained

1   medium onion, quartered

1-2 cloves garlic, minced

½   cup picante sauce

3   tablespoons Worcestershire sauce

1   teaspoon hot sauce

2   envelopes unflavored gelatin

2   tablespoons cold water

¼   cup fresh parsley, minced

    Red, yellow and green bell pepper strips (optional)

    Assorted crackers (optional)

◎ In food processor, mix cream cheese, black-eyed peas, onion, garlic, picante sauce, Worcestershire sauce and hot sauce. Process 1 minute or until smooth.

◎ Sprinkle gelatin over cold water in a small saucepan and let stand 1 minute. Cook over low heat, stirring until gelatin dissolves. Add gelatin mixture to black-eyed pea mixture and process 30 seconds.

◎ Spoon into a greased 9-inch round cake pan. Cover and chill until firm.

◎ Unmold; sprinkle with parsley. Serve with bell pepper strips or assorted crackers.

Yield: 4½ cups

Host a Tasting Party

Ask each person to bring a bottle of favorite wine or an interesting beer, and an appetizer. You supply an unusual brand of beer or wine and some basic foods, including veggies, chips and dip, a variety of cheeses and breads and crackers. In the summer, if you want something more substantial, throw some gourmet sausages on the grill. In the cooler months, have a steaming pot of soup or chile simmering on the stove.

Ocean Pearls

Caviar is a rare and precious treat. When you decide to indulge, try serving it by the teaspoonfuls in these variations:

• Top thinly sliced bread with cream cheese, a layer of smoked salmon and salmon caviar

• Stuff baby new potatoes with sour cream and top with a dollop of caviar

• Stir salmon or whitefish caviar into softened butter for grilled fish

• Spoon on lightly scrambled eggs

• Stuff raw mushrooms with sour cream and caviar

• Gently toss angel hair pasta with crème fraîche and caviar

• Top potato pancakes with a dollop of sour cream and a spoonful of caviar

Caviar Dip

This is the perfect recipe for a bridal shower or brunch buffet.
Pop the champagne cork and you have a match made in heaven!

Preparation Time: 10 minutes

2	(3-ounce) packages cream cheese, whipped
3	ounces sour cream
1	tablespoon lemon juice
1	teaspoon onion, grated
1½	tablespoons fresh dill, finely chopped
1	pinch pepper, freshly ground
¼	cup fresh black caviar or natural red salmon caviar

◎ Bring cream cheese to room temperature and mix with sour cream.

◎ Gently fold in lemon juice, onion, dill and pepper, until well blended. Carefully fold in caviar.

◎ Refrigerate in a sealed container, until needed.

Yield: about 1 cup

Gazpacho Dip

This colorful starter will complement any Mexican dish. Everyone will love the refreshing taste, so take it along to the next outdoor concert!

Preparation Time: 15 minutes

3   tablespoons olive oil
½   tablespoon apple cider vinegar
1   teaspoon salt
1   teaspoon garlic salt
½   teaspoon black pepper
1   (4-ounce) can chopped black olives, with liquid

1   (4-ounce) can chopped green chiles, with liquid
4   tomatoes, diced
5-6   green onions, with tops, thinly sliced
4   avocados, chopped
    Tortilla Chips

◎ Mix olive oil, apple cider vinegar, salt, garlic salt and pepper.
◎ Add black olives with liquid, green chiles with liquid, tomatoes, green onions and avocados; toss.
◎ Serve with tortilla chips.

Try dip as a topping for barbecued steaks or pork loins.

Yield: 8 servings

This recipe can be found in
Spanish in the **Otra Vez...En Español** section.

Pack a Picnic on Ice

Galvanized tubs make a unique picnic basket that can chill and carry your food at the same time. They can even be decorated by painting them with spray paint or an oil-based enamel in a fun design; be sure to clean the tub with white vinegar before painting. Fill the tub with ice, then put fruit, cheese, salads, drinks and even flowers inside. Plastic plates, utensils and washcloths can be tucked into plastic zip-top bags and added as well.

Roasting Chiles or Peppers

To remove the tough transparent skin on chiles or peppers, follow these instructions:

• With a knife, pierce each chile or pepper near the stem to prevent bursting.

• Place on a baking sheet, and broil 4 to 5 inches from the heat source in a gas oven, 6 inches away from heat in an electric oven or 5 inches from the heat in a gas grill.

• Broil, turning with tongs. Be sure to just blister rather than burn.

• Place them in a plastic zip-top bag and seal to steam. Leave them in the bag 10 to 15 minutes for skin to loosen.

• Once they have cooled or steamed, peel by starting at the stem end and pull the skin down.

Red Bell Pepper Dip

Serve this fast and easy appetizer with blue corn chips.
It will make your taste buds dance!

Preparation Time: 20 minutes
Cook Time: 10 minutes

2 red bell peppers, seeded, roasted, peeled and pressed between paper towels to remove excess water
2 cloves garlic
1 (4-ounce) container sun-dried tomatoes packed in oil, drained and patted dry
2 teaspoons cumin
1-2 pickled jalapeños, coarsely chopped
¼ cup fresh cilantro leaves, chopped
1 bunch green onions, white parts only, coarsely chopped
2 (3-ounce) packages cream cheese, softened
½ teaspoon salt
   Blue corn chips (optional)

◎ Process red bell peppers, garlic, sun-dried tomatoes, cumin, jalapeños, cilantro, green onions, cream cheese and salt in food processor until blended.

◎ Serve with blue corn chips, if desired.

Yield: about 2½ cups

Sun-Dried Tomato Hummus

Mouthwatering medley of Mediterranean flavors visits the Desert Southwest.

Preparation Time: 15 minutes
Chill Time: 1 hour

1	(15-ounce) can garbanzo beans, drained and rinsed
1	cup sun-dried tomatoes, packed in oil
2	cloves garlic, minced or pressed
½	cup mayonnaise
¼	cup tahini (paste made from sesame seeds)

¼ cup Parmesan cheese, grated
3 tablespoons lemon juice
¼ teaspoon dried basil
⅛ teaspoon ground red pepper
½ teaspoon salt
1 teaspoon olive oil
Cilantro and parsley sprigs (optional)
Pita bread triangles

◎ Place garbanzo beans, sun-dried tomatoes, garlic, mayonnaise, tahini, Parmesan cheese, lemon juice, basil, ground red pepper and salt in a food processor and blend until smooth.

◎ Place in a bowl and refrigerate at least 1 hour.

◎ Drizzle with olive oil before serving and garnish with cilantro and parsley sprigs, if desired.

◎ Serve with pita bread triangles.

Yield: 2 cups

Tahini Who?

The rich sesame seed paste known as tahini is an essential element of hummus and is used in a number of other Mediterranean dishes as well. It is increasingly available, particularly in health food stores, usually stocked with the peanut butter. The tahini made from toasted seeds is more flavorful. The paste is oily and it separates. Spoon the contents of the jar into a bowl and work it with a spoon until blended before measuring out the quantity for the recipe. Return the remaining tahini to the jar and refrigerate. It will keep for several months.

Toasting Nuts

To toast nuts, position a rack in the middle of the oven and preheat to 375 degrees. Spread the nuts in a single layer in a metal pan and toast, stirring once or twice, until crisp and fragrant (8 to 10 minutes). Do not overcook or the nuts will be bitter. Transfer immediately to a bowl and cool to room temperature before using. Store the toasted nuts in an airtight container at room temperature for up to 3 days.

Spicy Pesto

This delicious blend of flavors will tempt your guests to double dip!

Preparation Time: 20 minutes
Cook Time: 15 minutes

6 tablespoons pine nuts, toasted	½ teaspoon salt
6 green chiles, roasted, peeled and seeded	1-2 limes, juiced
1 clove garlic, minced	1 large red bell pepper, roasted, peeled, seeded and diced sm. dice
4-6 tablespoons olive oil	French bread slices or pita triangles
1 bunch cilantro leaves, chopped	

◎ Process pine nuts, green chiles, garlic, olive oil and cilantro in food processor, until it forms a coarse paste.

◎ Add salt and lime juice to taste; stir in red bell pepper.

◎ Serve with toasted French bread slices or heated pita bread triangles.

Yield: 2 cups

Vegetable Chopped "Liver"

Serve with party rye bread or wheat crackers and they'll all be
"liver" lovers by the end of the evening!

Preparation Time: 10 minutes
Cook Time: 15 minutes

2	medium onions, chopped	6	hard-boiled eggs
2	tablespoons olive oil		Salt, pepper and garlic
1	cup pecans, chopped		powder, to taste
1	(15¼-ounce) can green beans, drained		

GARNISH with ~~a~~ chopped ~~PARSLEY~~ Chives

◎ Sauté onions in olive oil until medium to dark brown.

◎ In food processor, process pecans. Add green beans and eggs. Mix in onions.

◎ Season to taste with salt, pepper and garlic powder and blend until smooth, adding more olive oil to moisten, if necessary.

Yield: 15 to 20 servings

Baked Wontons

Baked wonton chips are a unique alternative to crackers and tortilla chips for dips and they are low in calories! Cut wonton skins in half diagonally. Arrange in a single layer on ungreased baking sheets. Spray lightly with water. Bake at 375 degrees for 8 minutes or until light brown. Serve warm or cold.

They can also be seasoned, sprayed with water and baked. Try sprinkling evenly with 2 teaspoons grated Parmesan cheese; 2 teaspoons salt-free lemon and herb spice blend; 1½ teaspoons garlic powder; or ¼ teaspoon cinnamon and 1½ teaspoons sugar.

Just for Starters

Onion Rings

Because there are so many varieties of onions, it is important to know the character and strength of each:

• Chives: These slender grass-like stalks are most often used like herbs. Chives are too delicate to stand up to heat. Simply snip and sprinkle over food before serving.

• Scallion or green onion: A baby onion complete with a thin or roundish white bulb, a scallion is good sliced and added raw to dishes or cooked just enough to wilt it. The white bulb is a little stronger than the green tops.

• Shallot: This onion is probably best characterized as a cross between garlic and onion. Its mild flavor is extraordinary in sauces and vinaigrettes.

• Pearl onion: A true pearl onion is small, not much more than an inch in diameter with a papery white skin. Pearl onions are often used in cream sauces, but they are also good sautéed or dropped in a hearty stew.

• Yellow onion: This onion makes up more than 75% of the world's supply! When a recipe calls for an onion, this is the kind to use. Since they are strong and pungent, they are almost always cooked.

• Red onion: Also called a purple onion, this onion has a delicious sweetness that is perfect for salads and sandwiches. As a rule, red onions are not cooked because the color fades and bleeds into the other ingredients. However, they are great sliced thick and grilled.

• Sweet Bermuda and Spanish onions: These onions are large and strong in flavor, but not as pungent as yellow onions. They are sweet enough to be eaten raw (sliced on burgers or in salads) and they make wonderful onion rings or stuffed baked onions.

• Walla Walla, Maui and Vidalia sweet onions: These onions (named after the places where they are grown) are all incredibly sweet and delicious. They have a high water content, which makes them extremely perishable. Keep an eye out for them in their season: Maui's are found from April to June; Vidalias are available in May and June; Walla Walla's come out in July and August.

Vidalia Onion Dip

Speedy preparation time frees you up
while your oven makes this tame onion dip come to life.

Preparation Time: 10 minutes
Cook Time: 35 to 40 minutes

2 cups Vidalia onions, finely chopped	1 cup Swiss cheese, grated
1 cup mayonnaise	Assorted crackers

◎ Mix Vidalia onions, mayonnaise and Swiss cheese well.

◎ Spoon mixture into a greased 10-inch quiche dish.

◎ Bake at 350 degrees for 35 to 40 minutes until surface is brown and bubbly.

◎ Serve as hot dip with crackers.

Yield: 8 to 10 servings

Made at least 6 times good every time

good makes alot (handwritten)

Almost-A-Meal Queso

This hearty crowd pleaser is equally popular on Mars and Venus.
Be forewarned, you'll be asked to bring it to every party!

Preparation Time: 20 minutes
Cook Time: 45 minutes

1 pound ground beef *
1 teaspoon black pepper
½ teaspoon salt
1 large onion, chopped
2 cloves garlic, minced
1 (8-ounce) link Kielbasa or smoked sausage, cubed
2 pounds processed cheese, cubed

1-Can Rotel (handwritten)
1 (14-ounce) can chopped tomatoes, drain ½ liquid
1 (4-ounce) can chopped green chiles, drained
1 tablespoon Worcestershire sauce
1 tablespoon chile powder
5-6 chipotles en adobo, chopped
Tortilla Chips   *Sauce Only* (handwritten)

◎ Cook ground beef, pepper, salt, onion, garlic and Kielbasa in skillet. Drain fat.
◎ Transfer to crock pot and add processed cheese, tomatoes, green chiles, Worcestershire sauce, chile powder and chipotles.
◎ Cook on high heat, stirring constantly, until cheese is melted.
◎ Serve with tortilla chips.

This recipe doubles as an excellent topping for baked potatoes, and leftovers can be refrigerated up to 5 days or frozen.

Yield: 10 servings

* CAN Also Add Italian Sausage Along w/beef (handwritten)

This recipe can be found in
Spanish in the **Otra Vez...En Español** section.

buy bulk if available OR links — casing Removed (handwritten)

Know Your Chiles

This list comprises a variety of chiles from the hottest to the mildest:

• **Habanero:** Considered to be 1,000 times hotter than the jalapeño, these tiny chiles are squat and fat with a neon orange color.

• **Serrano:** Serrano is the chile of choice for Mexican cooks and they are often mixed into everything from guacamole to beans. They are colored red or green and look like a fat little pinkie finger with a slight point at the end. To cool their fire, remove the ribs and seeds.

• **Santaka and Thai:** The size of a small fingernail, these peppers are often sold on the branch or as a whole plant with hundreds of peppers that dry and keep for years. The heat will not soften, even after cooking!

• **Cayenne:** Slim and twisted peppers with a long point. They are red, green and yellow-green in color and range from 3 to 6 inches in length. The smaller and more pointed, the hotter!

• **Jalapeño:** Plump little barrels with thick green skins, jalapeños are about the size of your thumb. Their spiciness is manageable and they are the most available of all the fresh chiles.

• **Fresno:** These peppers are shaped like jalapeños and are as hot, but they have a lighter green or bright red skin.

• **Hungarian wax (banana pepper):** These peppers can be very mild or medium-hot. They have long, tapering cones with a creamy yellow skin. They are wonderful pickled!

• **Ancho (poblano):** Anchos have very shiny skin, colored green or red, and are cone shaped with a long tip. They have a medium heat, but wonderful flavor. They are best eaten roasted and peeled.

• **Mexi-bell:** These chiles look exactly like a bell pepper, but they have some heat. They are great for stuffing!

• **Red cherry:** With a look like cherry tomatoes with thick deep red skin, these chiles are medium hot and are especially good pickled.

• **Anaheim:** A favorite chile for stuffing, they are elongated and cone shaped with a slight twist. They can be red or green and are mild to medium hot.

• **Pepperoncini (Tuscan peppers):** Best pickled and added to an Italian antipasto, these peppers are shaped like long cones and colored almost neon red. They have mild heat.

Garlic Chives

If you have a head of garlic that is sprouting, do not throw it away! Separate the cloves and plant them close together in a pot or in your garden. The young shoots that appear are garlic chives. They are mild with a faint garlic taste — perfect for eggs, salads and sandwiches.

Baked Goat Cheese, Roasted Garlic and Caramelized Onions

A culinary flavor sensation that is sure to collect rave reviews from the not-so-easily impressed gourmet food lovers.

Preparation Time: 15 minutes
Cook Time: 45 to 50 minutes

6	cloves elephant garlic	10	ounces goat cheese, crumbled
1	tablespoon vegetable oil	1	tablespoon balsamic vinegar
2	tablespoons butter		Salt and pepper, to taste
1	medium red onion, thinly sliced	½	cup fresh basil, sliced into strips
1	tablespoon brown sugar		Baguette slices (optional)

◎ Arrange garlic cloves in glass dish and sprinkle with vegetable oil. Cover and bake at 350 degrees for 30 to 40 minutes. Cool garlic.

◎ Melt butter in skillet and sauté red onion until brown. Add brown sugar and stir until melted. Remove from heat and cool.

◎ Place onions on bottom of 8 x 5-inch casserole dish. Sprinkle goat cheese over onions and arrange garlic on top of cheese.

◎ Bake at 350 degrees until cheese melts, taking care not to let bubble. Add balsamic vinegar and stir until blended. Season to taste with salt and pepper. Transfer to medium bowl and sprinkle with basil.

◎ Serve with warm baguette slices, if desired.

Yield: 2 cups

Green Chile and Artichoke Dip

This recipe embodies easy, yet elegant, entertaining.
Prepare the dip ahead of time, refrigerate and bake just before your guests arrive.

Preparation Time: 10 minutes
Cook Time: 20 minutes

1	(14-ounce) can artichoke hearts, drained and chopped	1	cup mayonnaise
1	cup Parmesan cheese, grated	1	(4-ounce) can chopped green chiles, drained *use fresh*
			Tortilla Chips

◎ In a mixing bowl, combine artichoke hearts, Parmesan cheese, mayonnaise and green chiles.

◎ Turn the mixture into an 8-inch round baking dish.

◎ Bake at 350 degrees for 20 minutes or until the dip is heated through.

◎ Serve warm with tortilla chips.

Yield: 12 to 15 servings

06/03 - SA, TX made Many times
10/03 ✓✓
08/09 SF, NM
08/13 Greenville, SC
08/14 SF ✓
05/15 ✓
02/17 ✓
12/19 AC, TX

Breaking the Ice

Ice breakers are a great way to introduce guests that may not be familiar with one another, and to bring out conversation and laughter. At your next party, ask guests to wear something that has a story to go with it; for example, a fake tiara, a toy gun, or an old letterman's sweater. During the evening, guests will trade props (and tales) and get to know each other. Later, each guest can share with the crowd what he or she ended up wearing and the story behind the prop.

Keep the Traffic Moving

To ensure that you have enough space for traffic flow and interaction, calculate the area of empty floor space in each room and divide by the number of guests. Allow about 16 square feet per person.

Hot Crawfish and Crab Dip

This seafood delight is amazingly adaptable. Serve it with toast rounds in a chafing dish or fill it into puff pastry shells. The possibilities are endless!

Preparation Time: 15 minutes
Cook Time: 15 minutes

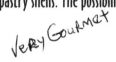

Very Gourmet

1 pound fresh mushrooms, cleaned and sliced	½ pound sharp cheddar cheese, grated
1 cup butter	1 pound lump crabmeat, chopped
2 bunches green onions with tops, chopped	4 tablespoons Vermouth
1 bunch parsley, chopped	1 teaspoon ground red pepper
1 pound crawfish tails, chopped	1 teaspoon salt
4 tablespoons flour	1 teaspoon black pepper
4 cups evaporated milk	Hot Sauce (optional)
½ pound Swiss cheese, grated	

◎ Sauté mushrooms in butter. Add green onions and parsley. Cook until onions are transparent.

◎ Add crawfish and cook until tender. Add flour and blend well. Add evaporated milk, Swiss cheese and cheddar cheese.

◎ Heat over hot water, stirring until cheese melts. Fold in crabmeat. Add Vermouth, red pepper, salt and pepper. Stir in hot sauce, if desired.

Great filling for mushrooms: Wash and remove stems from mushrooms. Brush mushroom caps with olive oil and fill with mixture. Bake at 350 degrees for 12 to 15 minutes.

Yield: 6 to 10 servings

Hot Spinach Dip

Prepare a double batch of this dip, divide into small portions and freeze.
Simply thaw and heat for spur-of-the-moment entertaining.

Preparation Time: 10 minutes
Cook Time: 15 minutes

2	(10-ounce) packages chopped frozen spinach
½	cup margarine, melted
2	tablespoons onion, grated
3	tablespoons flour
½	cup evaporated milk
1½	cups jalapeño cheese, grated
½	teaspoon pepper
¾	teaspoon celery salt
½	teaspoon garlic powder
1	tablespoon Worcestershire sauce
	Assorted vegetables or crackers

◎ Cook spinach according to package directions; squeeze to drain, reserving ½ cup liquid. Set aside.

◎ Combine margarine, onion and flour in saucepan. Stir well and cook one minute. Gradually add reserved spinach liquid and evaporated milk. Cook until thickened, stirring constantly.

◎ Add jalapeño cheese, pepper, celery salt, garlic powder and Worcestershire sauce to onion mixture, stirring until cheese is melted. Add spinach and mix well.

◎ Serve with fresh vegetables or crackers.

Yield: 1¾ cups

Thrift Shopping

You never know what you might find when you pop into a thrift shop or stop at a garage sale. Many times you might find china, silver and glassware treasures, eclectic serving pieces and other party paraphernalia at prices that are just too good to pass up.

Avocado Cheese Ball

Scrumptious Southwest flavors rolled up in one popular party appetizer.

Preparation Time: 15 minutes
Chill Time: 30 minutes

2 (8-ounce) packages cream cheese, softened	1 teaspoon garlic powder
1 cup sharp cheddar cheese, grated	1 (4-ounce) can chopped green chiles, drained
1 medium avocado, mashed	Parsley, chile powder and chopped pecans
1 small onion, minced	Assorted crackers
½ cup pecans, finely chopped	

◎ Mash cream cheese and mix well with cheddar cheese.

◎ With wooden spoon, stir in avocado, onion, pecans, garlic powder and green chiles.

◎ Form into a ball.

◎ Combine parsley, chile powder and chopped pecans.

◎ Roll cheese ball in mixture and serve with crackers.

Your favorite nut can be substituted for pecans, if desired.

Yield: 8 servings

This recipe can be found in Spanish in the **Otra Vez...En Español** section.

Herb Cheese en Croûte

Flavorful herb cheese spread is encased in savory puff pastry.

Preparation Time: 15 minutes
Chill Time: 30 minutes
Cook Time: 20 minutes

1 teaspoon Dijon mustard	¼ teaspoon fennel seeds
1 (12-ounce) package Havarti cheese	½ (17¼-ounce) package frozen puff pastry, thawed
1 teaspoon dried parsley	1 egg, beaten
½ teaspoon dried chives	Assorted crackers, apple slices or pear slices (optional)
¼ teaspoon dried dill weed	
¼ teaspoon dried basil	

◎ Spread Dijon mustard over top of Havarti cheese; sprinkle with parsley, chives, dill weed, basil and fennel.

◎ Place cheese, mustard side down, in center of puff pastry. Wrap package style, trimming excess pastry. Gently press along seam to seal. Place seam side down on lightly greased baking sheet. Brush with egg and chill for 30 minutes.

◎ Bake at 350 degrees for 20 minutes; brush with egg and bake an additional 10 minutes or until golden brown. Serve with assorted crackers or apple and pear slices.

Yield: 8 to 10 servings

Jot It Down!

Recording the details of a party is a great way to keep track of what worked, what didn't, what you served, who was there, if the quantities were right, how much you spent, special items that were particularly enjoyed or used by your guests...the next time you entertain, you can make decisions based on your own recorded experience and not a hazy memory.

Chilling Wine or Bottled Beverages...Fast

The fastest way to chill wine (or any other bottled beverage) is to put it into a deep bucket with half cold water and half ice. This method draws heat from the bottle much more quickly than ice alone does. You can chill a room-temperature bottle of white wine in about 20 minutes, which is equivalent to an hour or more in the refrigerator and is even faster than putting it in the freezer. If the ice bucket is too short to chill the top of the bottle, invert the wine in the bucket for a few minutes before opening.

Italian Cheese Terrine

A testimony to the captivating flavors of Italy.
Prepare this impressive appetizer midweek for weekend entertaining.

Preparation Time: 40 minutes
Chill Time: 8 hours to 3 days
Cook Time: 10 minutes

1 **(8-ounce) package cream cheese, softened**	9 **(1-ounce) slices Muenster or mozzarella cheese; divided**
2 **tablespoons butter, softened**	**Basil Tomato Sauce**
½ **cup Parmesan cheese, grated**	**Fresh basil sprigs (optional)**
2 **tablespoons commercial pesto**	**Assorted crackers or baguette slices**

◎ Beat cream cheese and butter with electric mixer until creamy. Add Parmesan cheese and pesto; beat until smooth. Set mixture aside.

◎ Line a 3-cup bowl or mold with plastic wrap, allowing edges to hang over 6 to 7 inches. Diagonally cut 5 slices Muenster cheese in half; arrange cheese triangles in bowl, slightly overlapping to line bowl.

◎ Spread half the cream cheese mixture over cheese; top with half of Basil Tomato Sauce. Cut 2 slices of Muenster cheese in half crosswise; arrange cheese rectangles over tomato mixture. Repeat with remaining cream cheese mixture, Basil Tomato Sauce and 2 slices Muenster cheese, cut into rectangles.

◎ Fold plastic wrap over layers, sealing securely; place a heavy object on top to compact layers.

◎ Chill at least 8 hours or up to 3 days.

◎ Invert terrine onto serving plate and peel off plastic wrap. Garnish with basil sprigs, if desired.

◎ Serve with crackers or baguette slices.

If there is leftover cream cheese pesto, you are in luck. It is an unbelievable bagel spread!

Yield: 3 cups

Italian Cheese Terrine continued

BASIL TOMATO SAUCE

1	(14½-ounce) can whole tomatoes, with liquid	2	bay leaves	
¾	cup onion, chopped	½	teaspoon sugar	
1	tablespoon fresh garlic, minced	¼	teaspoon dried basil	
2	tablespoons olive oil	1	(7-ounce) jar sun-dried tomatoes packed in oil, drained and chopped	

◎ Drain whole tomatoes, reserving ¼ cup liquid. Chop tomatoes; set aside.

◎ In large skillet, cook onion and garlic in olive oil over medium heat, stirring constantly, until tender. Stir in chopped tomato, reserved liquid, bay leaves, sugar and basil; bring to boil.

◎ Reduce heat and simmer, stirring often, 3 to 5 minutes or until thickened; remove from heat.

◎ Remove and discard bay leaves; stir in sun-dried tomatoes.

◎ Cover and chill at least 2 hours.

The Basil Tomato Sauce is an excellent dipping sauce for Italian bread sticks.

Yield: 1¼ cups

The Perfect Temperature

Different wines do taste better at different temperatures. The heavier the wine, the less chilling time it requires to taste its best. The suggested temperature and time for chilling wine in an ice bucket (with bottle starting at room temperature) is as follows:

• Light whites, sparkling wines and rosés: 45 degrees or 20 minutes in an ice bucket

• Big whites (Chardonnay) and sweet whites: 50 degrees or 15 minutes in an ice bucket

• Light reds (Beaujolais, Gamay): 55 degrees or 10 to 12 minutes in an ice bucket

• Pinot Noir, red Burgundy: 60 degrees or 5 to 8 minutes in an ice bucket

• Big reds (Cabernet, Sauvignon, red Bordeaux, Syrah): 65 degrees or 2 to 5 minutes in an ice bucket

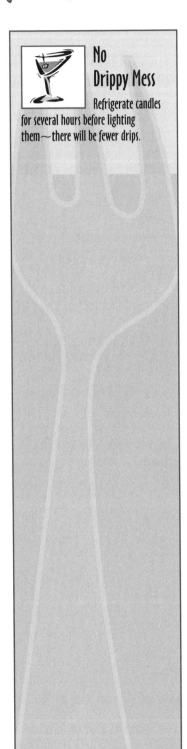

No Drippy Mess

Refrigerate candles for several hours before lighting them—there will be fewer drips.

Kahlúa-Pecan Brie

Festive both in taste and presentation;
it's an excellent choice for your next sophisticated gathering.

Preparation Time: 10 minutes
Cook Time: 3 to 5 minutes

1 **(15-ounce) miniature Brie**	1½ **tablespoons brown sugar**
½ **cup pecans, toasted and finely chopped**	**Apple, pear or baguette slices**
2 **tablespoons Kahlúa or other coffee-flavored liqueur**	

◎ Remove rind from top of Brie, cutting to within ¼ inch of outside edges. Place on an oven-safe dish.

◎ Combine pecans, Kahlúa and brown sugar and spread over top of cheese.

◎ Bake at 350 degrees for 3 to 5 minutes or just until soft.

◎ Serve immediately with apple or pear slices or baguette slices.

Yield: 12 to 15 servings

Asparagus and Sugar Snap Peas with Honey-Mustard Dip

Refreshing dip for a hot summer day.
Serve it with a glass of chilled Chardonnay or a pitcher of lemonade.

Preparation Time: 20 minutes
Cook Time: 5 minutes

1¼ pounds asparagus, trimmed	⅓ cup honey
1¼ pounds sugar snap peas, trimmed	¼ cup white wine vinegar
6 tablespoons Dijon mustard	¼ cup fresh dill, chopped
⅓ cup fresh lemon juice	½ cup olive oil
	Salt and pepper, to taste

◎ Bring large pot of water to boil. Add asparagus and blanch 2 minutes. Add sugar snap peas and blanch until vegetables are tender-crisp, about 1 minute longer.

◎ Drain. Transfer to large bowl of ice-water and cool. Drain vegetables and pat dry.

◎ Mix Dijon mustard, lemon juice, honey, white wine vinegar and dill in medium bowl. Gradually whisk in olive oil.

◎ Season to taste with salt and pepper. Place dip in bowl and set on platter. Surround with vegetables.

Yield: 12 servings

Chill It Down!

Create unusual ice chests for drinks by using household objects in interesting ways. Haul out apple barrels, metal washtubs, wicker laundry baskets, or a wheelbarrow. Your bathtub can also serve as a handy cooler. Line them with plastic if you think they might leak and fill with ice. Load them with bottles of wine, beer and cans of your favorite drinks.

Use the Power of Scent

When it comes to ambience, scents are powerful tools. Add scent by dabbing aromatic oil on light bulbs; fill a pot with water and add citrus, cinnamon sticks and cloves and let simmer on the stove; throw some fresh herbs in the fireplace; dust the inside or top of a carved jack-o-lantern with fall spices and the heat from the candle will make it smell like a freshly baked pie; or toss fresh rosemary into the barbecue pit.

Pear-Pecan Appetizers

Blue cheese adds the finishing touch to this delicious medley of tastes.

Preparation Time: 15 minutes
Chill Time: 30 minutes
Cook Time: 10 minutes

1 cup pecans, finely chopped	2 tablespoons lemon juice
2 ripe pears, thinly sliced	½ cup butter, softened
1 quart water	2 tablespoons blue cheese, crumbled

◎ Bake pecans in shallow pan at 350 degrees, stirring occasionally until toasted, about 5 to 10 minutes. Set aside.

◎ Combine pear slices, water and lemon juice in a large bowl.

◎ With a mixer, beat butter and blue cheese at medium speed until mixture is smooth.

◎ Drain pear slices on paper towels. Spread butter mixture on bottom half of pear slices; coat with pecans.

◎ Place on serving plate. Cover and chill 30 minutes.

If blue cheese is too strong for your taste buds, substitute Boursin cheese and omit all but 1 tablespoon of butter from the recipe.

Yield: 2½ dozen

Pesto-Stuffed Tomatoes and Celery

Great party pass-around appetizer with an Italian twist.

Preparation Time: 30 minutes

2 cups fresh basil leaves
¼ cup pine nuts
1 tablespoon olive oil
2 cloves garlic
1 small container cherry tomatoes

Celery sticks, washed and ends cut off
Parmesan cheese, grated
Pepper
Fresh basil sprigs (optional)

- Combine basil, pine nuts, olive oil and garlic in food processor and process until smooth.
- With thin, pointed knife, cut an opening into top of cherry tomatoes. Remove pulp.
- Fill tomatoes and celery sticks with pesto. Sprinkle with Parmesan cheese and dash of pepper.
- Arrange on platter and decorate with fresh basil sprigs, if desired.

Yield: ½ cup dip

Tomato Tidbits

Never refrigerate tomatoes...not ever! Eat ripe tomatoes within a day or two. If you have more ripe tomatoes than you know what to do with, chop them up with a couple of cloves of garlic and cook, covered, in the microwave on high for 3 minutes, stirring once. Freeze for a handy quick tomato sauce or for use in stews or soups. Most tomatoes at the grocery store are underripe. To ripen tomatoes, put them in a closed paper bag, not on a sunny windowsill. Tomatoes emit ethylene gas, which ripens them. To speed ripening, add an apple to the bag.

Roasted Pepper Trade Secret

Keep roasted and peeled peppers covered with a bit of olive oil in the refrigerator for at least a week to serve with eggs or on ham sandwiches or grilled toast.

Roasted Red Pepper Roll-Ups

A hostess' dream come true. Easy preparation, unique blend of flavors and beautiful presentation all rolled up in one tasty hors d'oeuvre.

Preparation Time: 12 minutes
Chill Time: 30 minutes

1   (3-ounce) log goat cheese, softened
4   (8-inch) flour tortillas
1   (6-ounce) container frozen guacamole, thawed

1   (7-ounce) jar roasted sweet red bell peppers, drained, patted dry and chopped
¼   teaspoon pepper, freshly ground
    Fresh cilantro sprigs (optional)

◎ Spread goat cheese evenly on tortillas. Spread guacamole on top of goat cheese. Sprinkle with red bell peppers and ground pepper.

◎ Roll up tortillas, pressing edges to seal.

◎ Wrap rolls in plastic wrap and refrigerate at least 30 minutes for easier slicing.

◎ Cut each roll into 6 slices, using a serrated knife.

◎ Garnish with cilantro sprigs, if desired.

Yield: 24 slices

Asian Vegetable Strudel

Serve this exquisite appetizer with
Soy-Ginger Dressing and you complete a work of art.

Preparation Time: 1 hour 15 minutes
Cook Time: 15 to 18 minutes

3 tablespoons reduced sodium soy sauce	1 cup carrots, shredded
1 teaspoon cornstarch	½ cup green onion, thinly sliced
1 teaspoon sugar	4 cups Chinese cabbage (Napa cabbage), finely shredded
½ teaspoon sesame oil	6 sheets frozen phyllo dough, thawed
¼ teaspoon pepper	¼ cup butter, melted
1 teaspoon fresh ginger, grated	⅓ cup peanuts, finely chopped
1 tablespoon butter	Soy-Ginger Dressing (optional)
1 cup fresh shiitake mushrooms, chopped	

◎ Stir together soy sauce, cornstarch, sugar, sesame oil and pepper in a large bowl. Set aside.

◎ In large skillet, cook ginger in butter for 15 seconds, stirring repeatedly. Add shiitake mushrooms, carrots and green onion. Cook and stir for 2 minutes. Stir soy sauce mixture and add to skillet. Cook and stir until thickened and bubbly. Stir in Chinese cabbage and remove from heat. Set aside to cool slightly.

◎ Work with one sheet of phyllo at a time, keeping remaining sheets covered with plastic wrap or a damp towel, until needed. Lightly brush one sheet of phyllo with melted butter. Place another sheet on top of the first sheet; brush with butter and sprinkle with 2 tablespoons chopped peanuts. Add other sheets of phyllo to stack, brushing each sheet with butter and sprinkling peanuts on every other sheet of phyllo. Cut phyllo stack in half crosswise.

◎ Spread half of vegetable filling (about 1 cup) lengthwise on each stack, just slightly off center. Filling should be within 3 inches of long sides and 1½ inches of short sides. Fold short side of phyllo toward center to cover filling. Fold one long side of phyllo over filling; then roll up.

◎ Place phyllo rolls, seam side down, on large baking sheet. Brush with butter. Diagonally score the top of phyllo rolls, making cuts 1 inch apart and ¼ inch deep. Do not completely cut through phyllo!

◎ Bake at 400 degrees for 15 to 18 minutes, or until golden.

◎ To transport, cover strudels loosely with foil. Upon arrival, slice strudels at cuts. Serve strudels on appetizer plates with forks and Soy-Ginger Dressing, if desired.

Soy-Ginger Dressing can be found on page 94.

Yield: 18 servings

Glass Edging

Cocktails look very attractive with a salt or sugar edging on the glass. To make it colorful, mix 2 to 3 drops of food coloring into 4 tablespoons of salt or sugar. Moisten the rim of a glass with lime juice or water and gently dip it into a plate of the sugar or table salt to produce a colored edging.

Mango Margaritas for Six

1 (26-ounce) can mangoes, plus juice

8 ounces gold tequila

1 (6-ounce) can frozen limeade

4 ounces Triple Sec or Cointreau

2 ounces Grand Marnier

Crushed Ice

Combine mangoes and juice (reserving 3 tablespoons), tequila, limeade, Triple Sec and Grand Marnier in a blender. Mix well. Pour half the liquid in a pitcher and set aside. Dip margarita glass edge in reserved liquid and then in sugar. Add crushed ice to liquid in blender. Blend until margaritas are slushy. Pour margarita mixture into glasses.

Chile, Feta Cheese and Walnut Bundles

Albuquerque meets Athens in these tasty bundles. Everyone agrees - no diplomacy needed in this delicious union of flavors!

Preparation Time: 1 hour
Chill Time: 1 hour
Cook Time: 20 minutes

1 large egg, lightly beaten	¼ cup walnuts, chopped
8 ounces feta cheese, at room temperature, crumbled	1 teaspoon dried, crushed oregano
1 New Mexican or Anaheim green chile, seeded and minced	1 pound phyllo pastry sheets, thawed
2 green onions, with tops, minced	½ cup unsalted butter, melted

- In a small bowl blend egg and feta cheese until smooth. Stir in green chile, green onions, walnuts and oregano.
- Place one phyllo sheet on smooth work surface (keep remaining phyllo covered with damp cloth). Lightly brush phyllo sheet with butter. Cover with a second sheet; lightly brush with butter. Top with a third sheet and again lightly brush with butter. Using a knife, cut phyllo stack lengthwise into four strips, 3½ inches wide. Cut strips crosswise into 3½-inch squares.
- Place 1 teaspoon cheese filling in center of each square. Gather the edges together over the center, twisting them slightly to form a frill.
- Transfer to 2 large greased baking sheets, placing bundles 1 inch apart. Brush tops with melted butter. Repeat process using remaining phyllo sheets and cheese mixture.
- Refrigerate at least 1 hour before baking.
- Bake at 350 degrees until crisp and golden brown, about 20 minutes.
- Cool 5 minutes before arranging on serving platter.
- Bundles can be made up to 1 day ahead, covered with plastic wrap and refrigerated.

Yield: 15 bundles

Olive Balls

They'll definitely have a ball and so will you with this easy, make-ahead recipe!

Preparation Time: 20 minutes
Cook Time: 7 to 10 minutes

1½ **cups biscuit baking mix**
½ **cup sharp cheddar cheese, grated**   Add 1-TBL PARM cheese
½ **cup sour cream**
2 **(2.5-ounce) jars pimiento-stuffed green olives, drained**

- Combine biscuit baking mix, cheddar cheese and sour cream. Mix well.
- Knead about 10 times on lightly floured surface.
- Pinch off 1 tablespoon dough, flatten and wrap around olive. Repeat process for remaining olives.
- Place olives on ungreased cookie sheet and bake at 425 to 450 degrees for 7 to 10 minutes.

Yield: 20 olive balls

Don't tell Anyone how you make this— they will think you Are A Real "chef!"

Munching on Olives

Olives are a natural finger food and the perfect thing to serve in a casual backyard setting. Place marinated olives in a large bowl or glass jar, then dish them out into small cones of parchment paper to serve them, just as they are sold in the French markets. Guests can stroll and nibble on olives while they visit and watch the sun set. If you prefer a dressier presentation, divide the olives with a small amount of their dressing among individual ramekins and set one at each diner's place.

Pillows of the Greek Gods

Serve this unusual variation of the traditional turnover with Tzatziki Dipping Sauce and experience the flavors of the Greek islands.

Preparation Time: 40 minutes
Chill Time: 8 hours
Cook Time: 20 minutes

1	(8-ounce) package cream cheese	3	kalamata olives, drained, pitted and finely chopped
½	cup butter	½	teaspoon salt
1½	cups flour	½	teaspoon black pepper
½	pound lean ground beef	¼	teaspoon dried oregano
1-2	cloves garlic, minced	¼-½	cup feta cheese, crumbled
½	medium onion, finely chopped	1	egg, beaten
2-3	sun-dried tomatoes, packed in oil, patted dry and finely chopped		Tzatziki Dipping Sauce (optional)

◎ Combine cream cheese, butter and flour by hand until dough forms a ball. Wrap dough ball in plastic wrap and refrigerate overnight or chill in freezer for 30 minutes.

◎ In medium skillet over medium heat, brown ground beef and drain excess fat. Add garlic, onion, sun-dried tomatoes, kalamata olives, salt, pepper and oregano. Simmer until onions are soft. Remove from heat, let mixture cool down and mix in crumbled feta. Be careful not to let feta melt.

◎ On floured board, thinly roll out ¼ of dough. Cut out circles with 2¾ or 3-inch cutter. Roll dough scraps into ball and refrigerate. (Reuse dough scraps only once; they will get tough.)

◎ On ½ of each circle, place 1 teaspoon of ground beef mixture. Brush edges with egg. Fold pastry over filling and press edges together with a fork. Prick top. Brush turnovers with egg. Repeat procedure with rest of dough.

◎ Bake on ungreased cookie sheet at 450 degrees for 12 to 15 minutes.

◎ Arrange turnovers on platter and serve with Tzatziki Dipping Sauce, if desired.

Yield: about 35 turnovers

Pillows of the Greek Gods continued

TZATZIKI DIPPING SAUCE

1   (16-ounce) container plain
    yogurt (regular or low-fat)

2   cloves garlic, minced

2   tablespoons cucumber,
    peeled, seeded and very
    finely chopped

⅛   teaspoon white pepper

½   teaspoon salt

¼   teaspoon dried oregano

◎   Combine yogurt, garlic, cucumber, white pepper, salt and oregano
    in a bowl. Cover tightly with plastic wrap and refrigerate 1 to 2 hours
    or overnight for flavors to develop. (It is normal for liquid to collect
    at top of bowl after refrigeration; simply stir into sauce.)

Yield: 2 cups

Hot Mulled Cranberry Drink

A great drink to serve in the cooler months or for the holidays. It will warm your insides up...down to the last drop!

6 cups cranberry juice

3 cups apple juice

3 cups orange juice

¾ cup maple syrup

1½ teaspoons ground cinnamon

¾ teaspoon ground cloves

¾ teaspoon ground nutmeg

12 (6-inch) cinnamon sticks (optional)

Combine all ingredients except cinnamon sticks in Dutch oven; bring mixture to a boil. Serve mixture hot with cinnamon sticks, if desired.

Yield: 3 quarts

Cilantro

Cilantro, Chinese parsley and fresh coriander leaves are different names for the same herb. Cilantro, which looks like a lighter green and more delicate parsley, is often found in many Asian, Mediterranean and Latin American dishes. Coriander is the seed of the herb cilantro. It is pungent and essential for curries, couscous and gingerbread, but cannot be substituted for fresh cilantro.

Roasted Squash and Red Pepper Quesadillas with Chipotle Lime Sour Cream

Some like it hot - some do not. Feel free to add some of your favorite chiles to kick up the heat in this recipe!

Preparation Time: 30 minutes
Cook Time: 45 minutes

Good Easy

1	¾-pound seedless butternut squash, peeled and cut into ¾-inch pieces	8	(5-inch) flour tortillas
1	medium onion, unpeeled, cut into eighths	1	large red bell pepper, chopped
1	large clove garlic, unpeeled	1	cup Monterey Jack cheese, coarsely grated
1	tablespoon vegetable oil	¼	cup unsalted butter, melted
	Salt and pepper, to taste		Chipotle Lime Sour Cream Dip

- In shallow baking pan, arrange squash, onion and garlic in one layer; drizzle with vegetable oil and toss to coat.
- Roast mixture on middle rack of 400 degree oven for 15 minutes or until garlic is tender. Remove garlic and set aside.
- Continue to roast squash and onion until tender, about 15 minutes. Discard peels from onion and garlic.
- In food processor, puree squash, onion and garlic with salt and pepper, to taste, until smooth.
- Spread ¼ squash puree on each of 4 tortillas and sprinkle each with ¼ red bell pepper and ¼ Monterey Jack cheese. Top each quesadilla with a plain tortilla, pressing gently. Brush each side of tortilla with ½ tablespoon butter.
- Heat griddle or 7-inch nonstick skillet over moderate heat until hot and cook quesadillas, one at a time, 3 minutes on each side or until golden.
- Transfer to cutting board and cut each quesadilla into 6 or 8 wedges.
- Serve warm with Chipotle Lime Sour Cream Dip.

Yield: 24 to 32 wedges

Roasted Squash and Red Pepper Quesadillas continued

CHIPOTLE LIME SOUR CREAM DIP

1-4 chipotle chiles en adobo,   2   teaspoons lime juice
minced and seeded   1   cup sour cream

◎ In a small bowl, stir chipotle chiles and lime juice into sour cream
until well combined.

Yield: 1 cup

this is A good dip for other uses

This recipe can be found in
Spanish in the **Otra Vez...En Español** section.

Party with an Island Beat

Rumba, zouk, Afro-Cuban, merengue, reggae, steel band music, soca, salsa...you may have so much fun at a Caribbean party that you have no need for food or drink!

Grapefruit Sangría

Combine 4 cups grapefruit juice, 3 cups Rhône wine and 1½ cups ginger ale in a large pitcher. Put in any combination of freshly sliced fruit. Stir gently and serve over ice.

Good!

Smoked Gouda and Caramelized Onion Quesadillas

Everyone will enjoy this unexpected variation of the border favorite.

Preparation Time: 20 minutes
Cook Time: 45 minutes

4	tablespoons butter, melted; divided
1	onion, thinly sliced
1	tablespoon brown sugar
¼	teaspoon white wine vinegar

1½ cups smoked Gouda cheese, grated
4 (8-inch) flour tortillas
2 ounces prosciutto, chopped
Pepper, to taste

Add GRN Chili

◎ Melt 2 tablespoons butter in medium-sized skillet over medium heat. Add onion, brown sugar and white wine vinegar. Sauté until onion is golden brown, stirring frequently, about 25 minutes. Remove from heat and cool to room temperature.

◎ Preheat oven to 350 degrees.

◎ Sprinkle Gouda cheese over each tortilla, dividing equally. Sprinkle prosciutto and sautéed onion over cheese. Season with pepper. Fold each tortilla in half. Brush tortillas with melted butter.

◎ Brush large skillet with melted butter. Place over medium-high heat. Working in batches, grill quesadillas just until brown spots appear, brushing skillet with butter between batches, about 2 minutes per side.

◎ Transfer quesadillas to large baking sheet. Bake until tortillas are golden and cheese is melted, about 5 minutes.

◎ Transfer quesadillas to work surface. Cut each into 6 wedges. Arrange on platter and serve hot.

Yield: 24 wedges

Stuffed Shiitake Parmigiana

Treat your guests to a gourmet restaurant experience!

Preparation Time: 20 minutes
Cook Time: 30 minutes

12	large shiitake mushrooms, washed and stems removed
2	tablespoons butter or margarine
1	medium onion, diced
½	(4-ounce) package sliced pepperoni, chopped
¼	cup green bell pepper, diced
1	clove garlic, minced
⅓	cup chicken broth

12	round buttery crackers, crushed
3	tablespoons Parmesan cheese, grated
1	tablespoon fresh parsley, chopped
½	teaspoon seasoned salt
¼	teaspoon dried oregano
1	dash pepper

- ◎ Place mushroom caps in a 15 x 10-inch jelly-roll pan; set aside.
- ◎ Melt butter in large skillet over medium-high heat. Add onion, pepperoni, green bell pepper and garlic. Sauté until tender.
- ◎ Add chicken broth, crackers, Parmesan cheese, parsley, seasoned salt, oregano and pepper.
- ◎ Spoon into mushroom caps. Add water to pan to depth of ⅛ inch.
- ◎ Bake at 325 degrees for 25 minutes and serve.

Yield: 4 to 6 servings

Shiitake Mushrooms

Shiitakes are large, tawny mushrooms with parasol-shaped caps and cream-colored insides. They are rich, meaty and smoky-flavored.

Variations on the Pepper

• Cayenne is a dried, crushed spice. It is orange-red in color and very hot. In recipes, it is often referred to simply as ground red pepper.

• Crushed red pepper is flaked, dried red peppers and is sometimes called "pizza pepper." The same pepper is also available in whole dried pods, called dried red peppers.

• Paprika is ground and dried sweet red peppers. Paprika is available sweet, moderately hot, and hot!

Chicken Puffs

Serve these great buffet appetizers at a
large gathering or bring them to the next party!

Add Chopped GRN Chile

Preparation Time: 15 to 20 minutes
Cook Time: 20 minutes

1½ cups cooked chicken, finely chopped	1 tablespoon dried parsley flakes
⅓ cup almonds, toasted and chopped	1 teaspoon seasoned salt
1 cup chicken broth	1 teaspoon celery seed
½ cup vegetable oil	⅛ teaspoon cayenne pepper
2 teaspoons Worcestershire sauce	1 cup flour
	4 eggs

◎ Combine chicken and almonds; set aside.

◎ In large saucepan combine chicken broth, vegetable oil, Worcestershire sauce, parsley flakes, seasoned salt, celery seed and cayenne pepper; bring to a boil. Add flour and stir until a smooth ball forms.

◎ Remove from heat, let stand 5 minutes. Add eggs, one at a time, beating mixture well after each egg until texture is smooth. Stir in chicken and almonds.

◎ Drop dough by heaping teaspoonfuls onto greased baking sheet, spacing puffs about 2 inches apart. Repeat process with remaining dough on several baking sheets.

◎ Bake at 450 degrees for 12 to 14 minutes or until golden brown.

◎ Serve warm.

Yield: about 6 dozen puffs

Crawfish Cakes with Cilantro-Lime Cream

Serve this refreshing combination as an appetizer or entrée.

Preparation Time: 15 minutes
Cook Time: 20 minutes

1 **pound crawfish tails, cooked and peeled**	1 **tablespoon Worcestershire sauce**
3 **cups soft breadcrumbs; divided**	1 **teaspoon Cajun seasoning**
½ **cup mayonnaise**	¼ **teaspoon ground red pepper**
½ **cup green onions, chopped**	1 **large egg, lightly beaten**
2 **cloves garlic, pressed**	3 **tablespoons vegetable oil**
1 **tablespoon lemon juice**	**Fresh cilantro sprigs, lemon and lime slices (optional)**
	Cilantro-Lime Cream

◎ Stir together crawfish, 2 cups breadcrumbs, mayonnaise, green onions, garlic, lemon juice, Worcestershire sauce, Cajun seasoning, red pepper and egg. Shape into 12 patties and coat with remaining 1 cup breadcrumbs.

◎ In large skillet, cook patties, in batches, in hot vegetable oil until lightly browned, about 3 to 4 minutes.

◎ Drain on paper towel and arrange on platter. Surround cakes with cilantro sprigs and round lemon and lime slices, if desired. Serve with Cilantro-Lime Cream.

Lump crabmeat or 1 pound frozen cooked crawfish tails, thawed and drained, may be substituted.

Yield: 10 to 12 appetizer servings

CILANTRO-LIME CREAM

½ **cup sour cream**	1 **tablespoon lime juice**
2 **tablespoons fresh cilantro, chopped**	¼ **teaspoon salt**

◎ Stir together sour cream, cilantro, lime juice and salt.

Yield: ½ cup

Crawfish

Crawfish, or crayfish on the West Coast, are sweet freshwater shellfish that look like tiny lobsters. There are two types available in America ~ one from Louisiana and one from the West Coast ~ but there is very little difference between the two. If you are not from one of those areas, cooked crawfish tails can generally be found in the frozen section of most grocery stores.

Radish Roses

Slice stem end and root tip from radish. Hold radish with root tip up and slice 4 or 5 petals around the radish by slicing from top to, but not through, bottom. Leave a little red between each petal. Drop radish in ice water and refrigerate at least 1 hour for rose to open.

Hoisin Crab Pot Stickers

Invite the taste of the Orient to the banks of the Rio Grande!

Preparation Time: 20 minutes
Cook Time: 15 minutes

½   **pound fresh lump crabmeat**
5   **fresh mushrooms, finely chopped**
⅔   **cup green onions, sliced**
1   **teaspoon fresh ginger, grated**
3   **tablespoons hoisin sauce**
1   **tablespoon dark sesame oil**

1   **(12-ounce) package wonton wrappers**
2   **tablespoons vegetable oil; divided**
1   **cup chicken broth; divided**
  Soy sauce (optional)

◎ Drain and flake crabmeat, removing any bits of shell. Combine crabmeat, mushrooms, green onions, ginger, hoisin sauce and sesame oil. Place 1 teaspoon crabmeat mixture in center of each wonton wrapper; moisten edges of wrapper with water. Fold wrappers in half, forming triangles; pinch edges to seal. Stand pot stickers on folded edge; press down to flatten slightly.

◎ Pour 1 tablespoon vegetable oil into large nonstick skillet; place over medium-high heat until hot. Fry half of pot stickers in hot oil, about 3 minutes or until golden brown on both sides.

◎ Add ½ cup chicken broth; reduce heat to medium. Cover and cook 8 minutes until tender. Repeat procedure with remaining pot stickers.

◎ Serve with soy sauce, if desired.

Canned or frozen crabmeat can be substituted for fresh crabmeat.

Yield: 4 dozen pot stickers

Spicy Crab Bites

Guests are sure to have more than one bite of these piquant treats!

Preparation Time: 10 minutes
Cook Time: 15 minutes

1	pound fresh crabmeat, drained and flaked
1	egg, beaten
1½	cups fine dry breadcrumbs; divided
1	cup red bell pepper, finely chopped
⅓	cup parsley, finely chopped
3	tablespoons mayonnaise or salad dressing
1	tablespoon green onion, finely chopped

1	teaspoon coarse ground black pepper
½	teaspoon salt
1½	teaspoons Old Bay Seasoning
1	teaspoon Worcestershire sauce
¼	teaspoon dry mustard
1⅛	teaspoons red pepper
2	tablespoons vegetable oil
2	tablespoons butter
	Red and green grapes, parsley and citrus slices (optional)

◎ Combine crabmeat, egg, 1 cup breadcrumbs, red bell pepper, parsley, mayonnaise, green onion, pepper, salt, Old Bay Seasoning, Worcestershire sauce, dry mustard and red pepper in a bowl and mix well. Shape into patties, using 1 tablespoon mixture for each; dredge in remaining ½ cup breadcrumbs.

◎ Combine oil and butter in large skillet over medium-high heat. Cook crabmeat patties in hot vegetable oil mixture until golden brown on both sides. Drain well on paper towels.

◎ Arrange on tray, and garnish with grapes, parsley and citrus slices, if desired.

◎ May be prepared and fried 30 minutes ahead and reheated at 350 degrees for 5 to 10 minutes.

Yield: about 3 dozen cakes

Don't Be Too Shy to Fry

If the oil is hot enough, a brittle shell forms around the food, preventing oil absorption, sealing in natural juices and yielding food that is neither greasy nor soggy. This technique can be tricky. Too high a temperature browns the surface before the inside is done; too low a temperature takes longer for the food to cook, resulting in fat absorption and an overcooked exterior. The ideal temperature for frying ranges from 325 to 400 degrees. To keep an accurate oil temperature, use a thermometer and avoid fluctuations by adding small amounts of food at a time. All pieces should float freely.

Citrus Cups

Cut a very thin slice from each end of the fruit so that the cups will sit level. Insert the blade of a small sharp knife at a downward angle into the middle of the fruit; remove the blade. Insert the knife again at an upward angle to make a zigzag pattern. Continue cutting in this fashion all the way around fruit. Separate the halves by twisting slightly and carefully pulling them apart. Scoop out pulp if using the cups as a container for dip, sherbert or other foods.

Coconut Fried Shrimp

Get ready to limbo, 'cause the "coco" may drive 'em loco. Your guests will be delighted as they take a trip to the islands with every crunchy bite!

Preparation Time: 25 minutes
Cook Time: 20 minutes

1 pound medium-sized fresh shrimp, unpeeled	¾ cup flour
¾ cup biscuit baking mix	2½ cups flaked coconut
1 tablespoon sugar	Vegetable oil
¾ cup beer	Orange-Lime Dipping Sauce

◎ Peel shrimp leaving the tails intact; devein, if desired, and set shrimp aside.

◎ Combine biscuit baking mix, sugar and beer, stirring until smooth; set mixture aside.

◎ Coat shrimp with flour; dip into beer mixture, allowing excess to drain. Gently roll coated shrimp in flaked coconut.

◎ Pour vegetable oil to a depth of 3 inches in large saucepan; heat to 350 degrees. Cook shrimp, a few at a time, 1 to 2 minutes or until golden; drain on paper towels, and serve immediately with Orange-Lime Dipping Sauce.

Yield: about 3 dozen

ORANGE-LIME DIPPING SAUCE

1 (10-ounce) jar orange marmalade	3 tablespoons spicy brown mustard
	1 tablespoon fresh lime juice

◎ Combine orange marmalade, spicy brown mustard and lime juice in a small saucepan; cook over medium heat, stirring constantly, until marmalade melts. Remove from heat; cool.

Dip may be stored in refrigerator up to 1 week.

Yield: 1¼ cups

Seared Scallops with Tomato Mango Salsa

Garnish this light south-of-the-border scallop variation with kiwi slices and cilantro sprigs for a beautiful presentation.

Preparation Time: 15 minutes
Chill Time: 30 minutes
Cook Time: about 3 minutes

1 medium tomato, finely chopped	1 tablespoon capers
¾ cup ripe mango, finely chopped	1 tablespoon olive oil
3 tablespoons purple onion, finely chopped	12 sea scallops
2 tablespoons fresh basil, finely chopped	¼ teaspoon salt
2 tablespoons red wine vinegar	¼ teaspoon pepper
	¼ avocado, sliced
	Kiwi slices and cilantro sprigs (optional)

◎ Combine tomato, mango, purple onion, basil, red wine vinegar and capers; cover and refrigerate at least 30 minutes.

◎ Heat olive oil in skillet over medium-high heat until hot. Add scallops and cook 3 minutes or until done, turning once. Be aware that scallops cook very quickly and become tough and chewy, when overcooked! Remove scallops from skillet; sprinkle with salt and pepper.

◎ Arrange scallops, salsa and avocado slices evenly on plates. Garnish with kiwi slices and cilantro sprigs, if desired.

Scallops may be threaded on skewers and grilled. Cook, covered with grill lid, over hot coals (400 to 500 degrees) for 3 to 5 minutes on each side or until done.

Yield: 6 appetizer servings

This recipe can be found in
Spanish in the **Otra Vez...En Español** section.

Succulent Scallops

• Scallops can range in color from off-white to pale pink. Those that appear too white have excess water added and almost no flavor. Select scallops that smell sweet and have a moist sheen.

• Small bay scallops are sweeter and have a richer flavor than larger sea scallops. One pound of sea scallops contains about 30 pieces, while a pound of bay scallops has about 100 pieces.

• Use small scallops in pasta sauces, risotto, or wherever flavor is more important than size. For grilling or broiling, sea scallops are easier to handle.

• Pat scallops dry before you sauté them so they will not "water out" in the recipe.

Great Garlic

Garlic heads or bulbs should be large, firm and tight-skinned. Old heads will be yellowed, soft and sprouting. Store garlic in a cool, dry place for up to one month. Do not refrigerate it and keep it out of the sun.

Garlic is as strong as you want it to be. It is mildest as whole, unpeeled cloves because the juices have not escaped; peeled whole garlic is a little stronger; sliced and minced cloves exude pungent juices; and mashed garlic lets it all hang out—it is the most powerful.

Scallops with Roasted Garlic and Saffron Sauce

A tangy trio of taste! Prepare this dish a day ahead and add fast-cooking scallops, once your guests are seated.

Preparation Time: 10 minutes
Cook Time: 40 to 45 minutes

good Sauce

1	head garlic	1	pinch saffron powder
3	tablespoons olive oil	1	tablespoon fresh lemon juice
2	tablespoons butter	1	teaspoon sugar
¼	cup shallots, minced	½	teaspoon Old Bay Seasoning
½	cup dry white wine	¾	pound bay scallops
1	cup whipping cream		Salt and pepper, to taste

◎ Preheat oven to 400 degrees. Cut top off garlic head, exposing cloves. Place garlic in small baking dish. Drizzle with olive oil. Bake until garlic is very soft, about 30 minutes. Squeeze garlic out of skin into small bowl. Mash with fork. Set aside.

◎ Melt butter in large skillet over medium-high heat. Add shallots and sauté until translucent, about 3 minutes. Add white wine and boil until reduced by ½, about 2 minutes. Add whipping cream and saffron. Reduce heat and simmer until reduced to sauce consistency, about 3 minutes. Stir in mashed garlic and lemon juice. Add sugar and Old Bay Seasoning.

◎ Can be prepared 1 day ahead. Cover and refrigerate. Bring to simmer just before continuing.

◎ Add scallops to sauce and simmer just until cooked through, about 3 minutes. Season to taste with salt and pepper. Divide among 4 plates and serve.

As a main dish, serve with Basmati or Jasmin rice, cooked according to package directions, to enjoy every drop of the savory sauce.

Yield: 4 servings

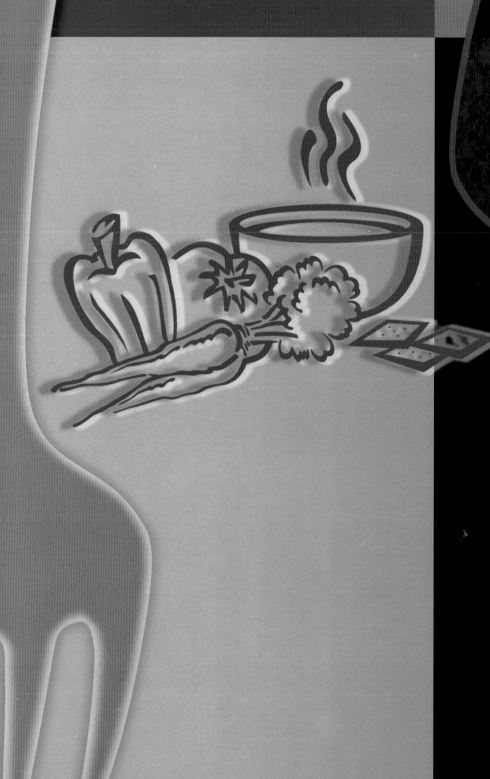

Soups, Salads & Salsas

Soups, Salads & Salsas

Wild Potato Soup

Great on a cold winter's day and the rice adds a delicious crunch.

Preparation Time: 10 minutes
Cook Time: 20 minutes

Fast / Easy

½	cup wild rice	2	(10¾-ounce) cans cream of potato soup
9	strips bacon	2	pints milk
1	small onion, chopped	2	cups cheddar cheese, grated

◎ Cook wild rice as directed on package.

◎ In skillet, fry bacon until crisp. Remove bacon and crumble. Sauté onion in the bacon drippings.

◎ In large saucepan, mix cream of potato soup and milk. Add rice, bacon and onion.

◎ Cook mixture until ingredients are heated through, stirring occasionally.

◎ Add cheddar cheese and stir until melted.

Yield: 6 servings

Bread Bowls

For an unusual way to serve hot soup, cut the top quarter off of individual round loaves of country bread and hollow them out to make a bowl. Be careful not to cut through the bottom. Brush the insides of the bread with olive oil and toast (with their lids) at 350 degrees for 10 minutes, until a bit crusty. Ladle the hot soup into the bread bowls and serve immediately.

Flavor Adjusting

When the soup is too salty, add a cut raw potato to the pot, then discard the potato once it is boiled.

If the dish is too sweet, add salt. On a main dish or vegetable, add a teaspoon of vinegar.

If the food is too sharp, a teaspoon of sugar will soften the taste.

Velvet Corn Chowder

A quick and tasty family addition all will love.

Preparation Time: 10 minutes
Cook Time: 30 minutes

Add 1-Cup Chopped GRN Chile

2	medium potatoes, peeled and cut in cubes	1	(15¼-ounce) can cream style corn
1	large onion, chopped	1	(15¼-ounce) can whole kernel corn, with liquid
3	stalks celery, chopped		
½	pound mushrooms, sliced	4	cups milk
3	tablespoons butter	10	ounces processed cheese or cheddar cheese, cubed or shredded
	Salt and pepper, to taste		

- ◎ Boil potatoes in large pot with water to cover until tender; drain and set aside.
- ◎ Sauté onion, celery and mushrooms in butter; add salt and pepper to taste.
- ◎ Add cream style corn and whole kernel corn with liquid; simmer for 20 minutes.
- ◎ Add potatoes and milk to corn mixture. Heat thoroughly, but do not boil.
- ◎ Add processed cheese slowly. Stir soup gently until cheese is melted.

Yield: 6 servings

Tortilla Soup

Border at its best!

Preparation Time: 15 minutes
Cook Time: 1 hour 5 minutes

4	tablespoons butter
⅓	cup oil
1	large onion, chopped
1	fresh jalapeño, chopped and seeded
4	cloves garlic, minced
2	carrots, diced
6	ribs celery, diced
1	pound boneless chicken breasts, diced
1	teaspoon cumin
1	teaspoon salt
1	teaspoon chile powder

1	teaspoon lemon pepper
½	cup flour
1	(14-ounce) can chopped tomatoes
4	(10½-ounce) cans chicken broth
6-7	stems cilantro
2	tablespoons lime juice
	Tortilla chips, slightly crushed
	Sour cream
	Avocados, diced
	Monterey Jack cheese, shredded

◎ Heat butter and oil in large pot.

◎ Sauté onion, jalapeño, garlic, carrots, celery and chicken; simmer 5 minutes.

◎ Add cumin, salt, chile powder, lemon pepper and flour. Stir to blend.

◎ Add tomatoes and chicken broth. Simmer 1 hour.

◎ Add cilantro and lime juice.

◎ Put in individual serving bowls in this order: tortilla chips, sour cream, avocados, Monterey Jack cheese and then soup.

Yield: 8 servings

This recipe can be found in
Spanish in the **Otra Vez...En Español** section.

Too Hot to Handle

When peeling and chopping fresh jalapeño peppers, always wear rubber gloves and keep your hands away from your face and eyes. The same compound that causes the peppers' hot flavor is also a potent skin and eye irritant.

Soup Garnishes

- Avocado slices
- Bacon bits
- Basil
- Caraway
- Carrots, grated
- Celery, diced
- Cheese, grated
- Chervil
- Chili powder
- Chives, snipped
- Cilantro
- Croutons
- Cucumber, sliced
- Curry powder
- Dill
- Eggs, hard-cooked
- Fennel
- Herb butters
- Lemon rind or slices
- Mint sprigs
- Mushrooms, sliced
- Nuts, all varieties

Tomato Basil Soup

A simple and elegant tomato soup that should be in everyone's collection.

Preparation Time: 15 minutes
Cook Time: 45 minutes

4	cups (8-10) tomatoes, peeled and chopped
4	cups tomato juice
12-14	fresh basil leaves
1	cup heavy whipping cream
½	cup unsalted butter

Salt, to taste
¼ teaspoon cracked black pepper
Fresh basil leaves, chopped (optional)

- Combine tomatoes and tomato juice in saucepan; simmer over medium-low heat 30 minutes.
- Cool slightly. Place in blender or food processor with basil leaves and puree in batches.
- Return to saucepan and add whipping cream and butter. Stir over low heat until cream and butter are incorporated.
- Season with salt and pepper.
- Garnish with basil leaves, if desired.

Substitute fresh tomatoes with 4 cups canned chopped tomatoes. Substitute tomato juice with a mixture of tomato juice and vegetable stock or chicken stock.

Delicious served with crusty bread.

Yield: 8 servings

Zucchini Soup

People will ask for this recipe every time.

Preparation Time: 15 minutes
Cook Time: 20 minutes

5	**cups water**
7	**chicken bouillon cubes**
5	**small zucchini, sliced**

8	**ounces cream cheese**
	Cayenne pepper, to taste

- ◎ Boil water, chicken bouillon cubes and zucchini for 20 minutes.
- ◎ Put in blender with cream cheese; puree in batches until smooth.
- ◎ Serve with a dash of cayenne pepper.

This soup can be served cold, at room temperature, or hot.

Yield: 6 servings

Sounds to easy to be good... Oh! Wait it is good don't tell Anyone how you made this Recipe

Soup Garnishes

- Olives, ripe or green
- Onion slices
- Orange rind or slices
- Parmesan cheese
- Parsley, minced
- Pepitas
- Peppers, diced
- Pimiento
- Popcorn
- Poppy seeds
- Radishes
- Sesame seeds
- Scallions
- Sour cream
- Sunflower seeds
- Tarragon
- Tomatoes
- Tofu
- Watercress
- Whipped cream dollops

Soup's On!

- Do not compromise on quality; lackluster ingredients will make a lackluster soup.

- Sauté vegetables in butter or oil before adding them to soup. This seals in their flavor and keeps them firm. Give onions a little extra time; slow cooking brings out their natural sweetness.

- You can make a very good soup with water, so the lack of a stock should not stop you from trying a recipe. But a rich, homemade stock will add a depth of flavor that water cannot duplicate.

- Most soups (with the exception of fresh fruit soups) improve with age and can be made a day or two in advance. And, the leftovers freeze well!

- It is simple to defat a soup if you chill it first; the fat will solidify on top and can be easily removed with a spoon.

- To guard against burns, allow hot soup to cool slightly before pureeing.

- Leftovers make terrific soups. Sauté aromatic vegetables such as onions, carrots and garlic in oil or butter. Add bite-size pieces of leftover meats and vegetables along with a little stock or milk and simmer until flavorful.

- The addition of wine frequently enhances the flavor of a soup. A not-too-dry sherry or Madeira blends well with subtle veal or chicken, while a little dry red table wine will complement the flavor of beef.

- To ensure that soups arrive at the table piping hot, serve them in tureens, lidded bowls or well-heated cups. Serve cold soups ice cold in chilled bowls or goblets.

- For a crisp, rich addition to soups, sauté small cubes or thin, decoratively shaped slices of bread in butter or olive oil with herbs or pepper flakes. Then dust them with freshly grated Parmesan cheese while still hot. Serve the croutons in a small dish on the side and let guests help themselves.

White Gazpacho

Zesty cold soup...perfect on a hot day!

Preparation Time: 15 minutes
Cook Time: 10 minutes
Chill Time: 2 hours

3 cups chicken broth	3 tablespoons white wine vinegar
3 cucumbers, peeled and minced	3 tablespoons cilantro, chopped
2 cups sour cream	3 tablespoons parsley, chopped
3 green onions, with tops, sliced	1 teaspoon salt (or more to taste)
3 tablespoons fresh dill, chopped	⅓ cup slivered almonds, (optional)
3 cloves garlic, crushed	

- Combine chicken broth, cucumbers, sour cream, green onions, dill, garlic, white wine vinegar, cilantro, parsley and salt.
- Chill at least 2 hours.
- Garnish with slivered almonds, if desired.

3 teaspoons dried dill may be substituted for fresh dill.

Yield: 8 servings

This recipe can be found in
Spanish in the **Otra Vez...En Español** section.

Steak Soup

A tasty soup that is easily transported to the homes of friends and family.

Preparation Time: 15 minutes
Cook Time: 30 minutes

2	pounds ground beef	1	(15-ounce) can corn, with liquid
1	cup onion, chopped	1	(14½-ounce) can green beans, drain liquid
5	cups water		
1	(12-ounce) jar spaghetti sauce	2	beef bouillon cubes
1	cup celery, chopped		Salt and pepper, to taste
1	cup carrots, chopped	1	cup macaroni

◎ Brown beef with onion; drain.
◎ Add water.
◎ Add spaghetti sauce, celery, carrots, corn, green beans, beef bouillon, salt and pepper. Simmer until vegetables are tender.
◎ Add macaroni and cook until pasta is done.

Vary the amount of water to achieve desired thickness. May add chopped cabbage, peas, diced potatoes or any other vegetables.

Yield: 10 servings

This recipe can be found in
Spanish in the **Otra Vez...En Español** section.

Wrinkle-free Tablecloth

To iron a large tablecloth, position the ironing board next to the dining room table. As you finish ironing a section, spread the cloth from the board directly to the table to eliminate any creases or wrinkles.

Mushroom Tips

• Don't peel mushrooms...that's where the flavor is!

• Use the stems if they are not woody or soft. If you need only the caps, save the stems for flavoring soups or sauces.

• Cook mushrooms, especially wild mushrooms, as soon as you can. They dry out and lose their flavor quickly.

• Handle mushrooms gently and store them in just one or two layers to keep them from bruising.

• To keep mushrooms white, wipe with water mixed with a little lemon juice.

• If you have a pound of mushrooms of different sizes for sautéing, keep the little ones whole and slice the larger ones so they all cook in the same time.

• Add the liquid from steeping dried mushrooms to soups or sauces. It's great!

Cream of Shiitake Soup

Perfect as an appetizer or as a meal!

Preparation Time: 15 minutes
Cook Time: 20 minutes

½	pound fresh shiitake mushrooms	2	(14¾-ounce) cans chicken broth
¼	cup butter or margarine	2	cups whipping cream
2	cups onion, chopped	¼	teaspoon pepper
3	tablespoons flour	¼	teaspoon ground nutmeg

◎ Remove stems from mushrooms; discard. Finely chop mushrooms.

◎ Melt butter in saucepan over medium-high heat. Add mushrooms and onion. Cook, stirring constantly, until tender.

◎ Add flour. Cook 1 minute, stirring constantly. Gradually add chicken broth; cook, stirring constantly, until thickened. Remove from heat.

◎ Stir in whipping cream, pepper and nutmeg.

May use rehydrated dry mushrooms for fresh shiitake mushrooms.

Yield: 6 servings

White Chile

Surprise your family with this fun variation of chile.

Preparation Time: 15 minutes
Cook Time: 4 hours

1	pound Northern white beans	1½	teaspoons oregano
6	cups chicken broth	¼	teaspoon ground cloves
2	cloves garlic, minced	¼	teaspoon cayenne pepper
2	onions, chopped; divided	4	cups cooked chicken, diced
1	teaspoon vegetable oil	3	cups Monterey Jack cheese, grated
2	(4-ounce) cans chopped green chiles		Salsa
2	teaspoons ground cumin		Sour cream

- ◎ Soak Northern white beans overnight in cold water.
- ◎ Combine beans, chicken broth, garlic and ½ of onions in large soup pot and bring to boil.
- ◎ Reduce heat and simmer until beans are soft, at least 3 hours.
- ◎ Sauté remaining onions in vegetable oil until tender. Add green chiles, cumin, oregano, cloves, and cayenne pepper.
- ◎ Add sautéed vegetables to beans and chicken.
- ◎ Simmer 1 hour.
- ◎ Garnish with Monterey Jack cheese, salsa and sour cream.

Yield: 10 servings

Tone down the heat!

Condiments are the best way to subdue the spiciness of your favorite chile. Put out a platter of raw celery and carrot sticks and individual bowls of chopped onions; garnish with sour cream and lime wedges or mixed sour cream with lime juice and cilantro; top with grated Monterey Jack or cheddar cheese; or serve with cole slaw, guacamole, soft tortillas or a big basket of corn bread. If the recipe does not call for beans, cook up some pinto, kidney or red beans and serve the chile over them. Some like to put their chile over rice.

Sipping on Soup

Soup can be served as an appetizer at a "heavy hors d'oeuvres" party by serving it in demitasse cups. It is fun, unique and a wonderful way to show off pretty china.

Cream of Red Bell Pepper Soup

This colorful, creamy soup is great to serve when entertaining.

Preparation Time: 45 minutes
Cook Time: 20 to 25 minutes

1	tablespoon olive oil	½	cup half-and-half
1	cup shallots, chopped	2	teaspoons red wine vinegar
2	cloves garlic, minced	⅛	teaspoon cayenne pepper
1	tablespoon fresh thyme, chopped		Salt and pepper, to taste
3	cups vegetable broth		Sliced fresh basil
2½	pounds red bell pepper, roasted, peeled, seeded and sliced		

◎ Heat olive oil in heavy large saucepan over medium heat. Add shallots, garlic and thyme. Sauté for 3 minutes. Add vegetable broth and all but 4 slices of roasted red bell pepper. Simmer, uncovered, until peppers are very tender, about 20 minutes.

◎ Working in batches, puree soup in blender and strain until smooth.

◎ Return pureed mixture to pot. Add half-and-half, red wine vinegar and cayenne pepper.

◎ Rewarm soup, thinning with additional broth, if desired.

◎ Season to taste with salt and pepper.

◎ Ladle soup into bowls. Garnish with reserved red bell pepper strips and basil.

Yield: 4 servings

Cranberry, Feta and Pecan Salad

This salad is colorful, unique and oh so good!

Preparation Time: 20 minutes
Chill Time: 1 hour

10	ounces mixed salad greens	2	tablespoons balsamic vinegar
1	cup sweetened dried cranberries	1	tablespoon honey
1	(4-ounce) package crumbled feta cheese	1	teaspoon Dijon mustard
¼	teaspoon black pepper
½	cup pecans, chopped	¼	cup extra virgin olive oil

◎ Combine salad greens, cranberries, feta cheese and pecans in a large salad bowl.

◎ Whisk balsamic vinegar, honey, Dijon mustard and pepper in a small bowl. Add olive oil in a thin stream, whisking constantly until well blended.

◎ Toss salad mixture with salad dressing.

Yield: 8 to 10 servings

Buying Greens

It may seem obvious, but the best gauge of freshness when choosing greens is how they look and smell: sparkling fresh, with a good color and no wilted, dry or yellowing leaves or tough or thick stems. They should not show excessive ripping or insect damage. And, they should smell very, very fresh. Look at the stem base where the greens were cut. If it is very brown, slimy or too dry, do not buy it—it was harvested too long ago. Also be sure to check the center of the head because decay sometimes begins there. Weight is another clue when choosing greens: the heavier the head or bunch, the tighter, firmer and fuller the leaves. Greens are almost all water. If they feel light, they are drying out!

Perk Up Lettuce

It is possible to revive wilted salad greens by dousing them quickly in warm water, then in ice water containing a small amount of vinegar.

Endive, Bacon and Pecan Salad

A very refreshing first course.

Preparation Time: 15 minutes
Cook Time: 10 minutes

3 cups Boston lettuce, loosely packed	6 slices bacon
3 cups curly endive, loosely packed	1½ teaspoons brown sugar
1 medium purple onion, sliced	¼ cup red wine vinegar
¾ cup pecans, coarsely chopped and toasted	¼ teaspoon salt
	¼ teaspoon pepper

◎ Combine lettuce, endive, purple onion and pecans in a large bowl; set aside.

◎ Cook bacon until crisp; remove bacon, reserving 2 tablespoons drippings in skillet. Crumble bacon and set aside.

◎ Add brown sugar, red wine vinegar, salt and pepper to skillet; cook over low heat until thoroughly heated. Pour over lettuce; toss gently.

◎ Sprinkle bacon over lettuce; serve immediately.

Yield: 6 servings

Spinach Salad
with Raspberry Vinaigrette

An incredibly easy salad that tastes like you spent all day making it.

Preparation Time: 10 minutes

2	tablespoons raspberry vinegar
2	tablespoons raspberry jam
⅓	cup vegetable oil
8	cups spinach leaves

¾	cup macadamia nuts, coarsely chopped
1	cup fresh raspberries
3	kiwis, peeled and sliced

◎ Combine raspberry vinegar and raspberry jam in blender. Add vegetable oil slowly in a thin stream, while processing.

◎ Toss spinach leaves with macadamia nuts, raspberries, kiwi slices, and dressing.

Yield: 8 to 10 servings

Leafy Spinach Stuff

When picking out fresh spinach, look for the leaves to be crisp and dark green with no sign of yellowing or wilting. Try to buy it in bundles (rather than in bags) because it will be fresher. If you do buy it in the bag, open it up when you get home, sort through it for wet or rotting leaves and store it in the crisper drawer in the refrigerator. It will not last much longer than 3 or 4 days. One to 1½ pounds of fresh spinach will yield just 1 cup cooked or 2 servings. Served raw in a salad, 1½ pounds will serve four.

Spinach is very sandy, so soak it in water and rinse thoroughly before cooking. Never cook spinach in an aluminum pan, never serve it in silver, and chop it with a stainless-steel knife to keep it from discoloring. It is delicious when quickly wilted and served with plenty of lemon wedges and ground black pepper. But don't stop there...try some of these other favorite toppings too: basil, caraway seeds, Parmesan cheese, feta cheese, ricotta cheese, goat cheese, chervil, chives, dill, garlic, mint, nutmeg, onion, oregano, parsley, rosemary, shallots, thyme and watercress.

Don't Get a Big Head

Cabbage should be stored in a plastic bag in the refrigerator. Never wash it before storing. Green and red cabbage will keep up to two weeks; however, if you use just part of it, it will only last for a few more days after being cut...a good reason to buy small heads of cabbage!

Mediterranean Confetti

The blend of colors makes a beautiful presentation.

Preparation Time: 15 minutes
Chill Time: 8 hours

1 medium purple onion, sliced	¾ cup feta cheese, crumbled
1 small cabbage, shredded	⅔ cup olive oil
2 tomatoes, cut into thin wedges	⅓ cup red wine vinegar
1 cucumber, halved and sliced	2 cloves garlic, minced
1 small yellow bell pepper, cut into thin strips	1 teaspoon ground cumin
1 (4-ounce) can sliced ripe olives, drained	½ teaspoon salt
	¼ teaspoon pepper

◎ Half each purple onion slice, and separate into half rings.

◎ Layer purple onion, cabbage, tomatoes, cucumber, yellow bell pepper, olives and feta cheese in a large bowl; set aside.

◎ Combine olive oil, red wine vinegar, garlic, cumin, salt and pepper in a jar. Cover tightly and shake vigorously; pour over salad.

◎ Cover and refrigerate 8 hours. Toss and serve with a slotted spoon.

Yield: 6 to 8 servings

Marinated Asparagus and Hearts of Palm

An elegant salad that makes a lasting impression.

Preparation Time: 10 minutes
Chill Time: 8 hours
Cook Time: 5 minutes

3 pounds fresh asparagus	½ cup cider vinegar
2 (14-ounce) cans hearts of palm, drained and cut into ½-inch slices	3 cloves garlic, crushed
	1½ teaspoons salt
1 cup vegetable oil	1 teaspoon pepper
	Cherry tomatoes (optional)

◎ Snap off tough ends of asparagus. Remove scales from stalks with a knife. Place asparagus in steaming rack over boiling water; cover and steam 4 minutes. Drain and submerge in ice water to cool. Drain well.

◎ Combine asparagus and hearts of palm in zip-top, heavy-duty plastic bag.

◎ Combine vegetable oil, cider vinegar, garlic, salt and pepper in a jar; cover with lid and shake vigorously. Pour dressing over vegetables. Seal bag, and marinate in refrigerator 8 hours; turn bag occasionally. Garnish with cherry tomato halves, if desired.

Yield: 12 servings

Asparagus Candle Holder

Tie a bundle of fresh asparagus with ribbon; then stand the asparagus upright allowing a few stalks to spread outward. Slip a candle in the center of the bundle until it feels secure.

Broccoli Salad

Even kids will eat broccoli prepared this way...delicious!

Preparation Time: 10 minutes

1	head broccoli, chopped	1	cup sunflower seeds
2	tablespoons balsamic vinegar	1	cup mayonnaise
1	medium red onion, chopped	¼	cup sugar
1	cup raisins	6	slices crisp bacon, crumbled

◎ Mix broccoli, balsamic vinegar, red onion, raisins, sunflower seeds, mayonnaise and sugar in a large bowl. Stir in bacon crumbs, reserving a small amount for garnish.

Yield: 8 servings

Buying Broccoli

Broccoli is one of nature's healthiest foods and is available all year round! Choose only tight green broccoli heads on firm stalks. Broccoli on several slender stalks, rather than on one or two large stalks, will have more tender stems for eating. Store it in the refrigerator, unwashed, in an open plastic bag or wrap it in damp paper towels and put it in the crisper drawer. A 2-pound bunch will serve four people generously.

Dilled Cucumber Salad

The perfect salad to prepare for an outdoor picnic or barbecue.

Preparation Time: 15 minutes
Chill Time: 1 hour 20 minutes

¼ teaspoon salt	1 tablespoon fresh dill, chopped
4½ cups cucumber, thinly sliced	1 clove garlic, minced
1 (8-ounce) container plain nonfat yogurt	6 lettuce leaves
2 tablespoons tarragon vinegar or cider vinegar	

◎ Sprinkle salt over cucumber slices; toss gently to evenly coat all sides. Let stand 20 minutes. Drain cucumber between layers of paper towels; set aside.

◎ Combine yogurt, tarragon vinegar, dill and garlic. Pour over cucumbers; toss gently, and chill up to 1 hour. Arrange on lettuce leaves.

Yield: 6 servings

good

Cucumbers are Cool

If you have garden-fresh cucumbers, there is no need to peel them, but they should be scrubbed under cold water. The peel and seeds of store-bought cucumbers are often bitter. Therefore, to determine whether or not you need to peel and seed the cucumber really depends on how fresh it is. Cut off a slice and taste it. If it seems bitter, peel and seed it. If it tastes fresh and tender, it is a matter of choice. To peel the cucumber, use a paring knife or vegetable peeler. To seed it, cut it lengthwise in half and scoop out the seeds with a teaspoon.

Because cucumbers have so much water, they do not store well. Three to five days is about all they will last in the refrigerator in a closed plastic bag. Two medium cucumbers weigh ¾ to 1 pound. A pound of cucumbers (peeled, seeded and sliced) will measure 2½ to 3 cups.

Buying Olive Oil

There are so many types of olive oil on the market, it is hard to know what kind to buy. While each has its own benefits, the more expensive oils generally are of higher quality. Extra-virgin olive oil is made from the very first pressing of the olives. It is usually green, sometimes greenish-black. Its intense flavor and aroma is similar to green olives. Extra-virgin olive oil is best used in salads, marinades or tossed on piping hot vegetables. Virgin olive oil is also a direct product of the olive fruit, but it is the result of the second pressing. It has a sweetish, nutty flavor. Pure olive oil is made up of oils extracted by treating the previously pressed olive pulp with solvents. Fine olive oil is oil that has been extracted from the olive pulp and mixed with water. It is perfect for cooking and frying.

Green Bean, Walnut and Feta Salad

Mediterranean in style, easy to make and big on taste!

Preparation Time: 15 minutes
Chill Time: 1 hour
Cook Time: 15 minutes

1 cup walnuts, coarsely chopped	¼ teaspoon salt
¾ cup olive oil	¼ teaspoon pepper
¼ cup white wine vinegar	1½ pounds fresh green beans
1 tablespoon fresh dill, chopped	1 small purple onion, thinly sliced
½ teaspoon garlic, minced	1 (4-ounce) package crumbled feta cheese

◎ Bake walnuts in a shallow pan at 350 degrees, stirring occasionally, 5 to 10 minutes or until toasted; set aside.

◎ Combine olive oil, white wine vinegar, dill, garlic, salt and pepper; cover and chill. *Add ½ tea CAvenders*

◎ Cut green beans into thirds, and arrange in a steamer basket over boiling water. Cover and steam 15 minutes or until green beans are crisp-tender. Immediately plunge green beans into cold water to stop cooking process; drain and pat dry.

◎ Combine walnuts, green beans, onion and feta cheese in a large bowl; toss well. Cover and chill.

◎ Pour oil mixture over bean mixture 1 hour before serving; toss just before serving.

Yield: 6 servings

Made in S.F.
10/08
07/17 - at Dan's house

Hearts of Palm Salad

Try a little something different...this salad is unique and appetizing.

Preparation Time: 15 minutes
Chill Time: 8 hours

1	cup olive oil	6	ripe olives, finely chopped
½	cup white vinegar	2	cloves garlic, pressed
½	cup celery, finely chopped	¼	teaspoon capers
¼	cup red bell pepper, finely chopped	1	(16-ounce) can hearts of palm, drained and cut into ½-inch pieces
¼	cup onion, finely chopped		
¼	cup dill pickle, finely chopped	6	cups torn Romaine lettuce

◎ Combine olive oil, white vinegar, celery, red bell pepper, onion, dill pickle, olives, garlic and capers; chill at least 8 hours.

◎ To serve, arrange hearts of palm on bed of lettuce on individual serving plates. Top with dressing.

Yield: 6 servings

MARgARet liked this SALAd

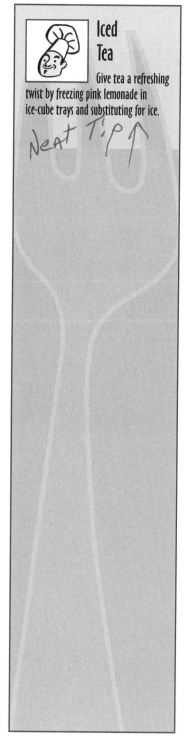

Iced Tea

Give tea a refreshing twist by freezing pink lemonade in ice-cube trays and substituting for ice.

Neat Tip ↑

Parsley Pointer

Generally, recipes call for only a small amount of parsley and it only comes in one large bunch! Don't let your parsley go bad. Put it in a zip-top plastic bag and freeze it. It will come in handy the next time a small amount of parsley is needed.

Snow Pea Salad

A great salad for summertime.

Preparation Time: 20 minutes
Chill Time: 1 hour
Cook Time: 15 minutes

¼ cup sesame seeds, lightly browned	2 teaspoons sugar
1½ teaspoons salt	1-2 cloves garlic, crushed
⅔ cup olive oil	1 pound snow peas, blanched
2 tablespoons lemon juice	1 head iceberg lettuce, shredded
2 teaspoons vinegar	½ cup parsley, chopped

◎ Lightly brown the sesame seeds for 15 minutes at 350 degrees.

◎ Mix sesame seeds, salt, olive oil, lemon juice, vinegar, sugar and garlic in a large bowl.

◎ Toss snow peas, lettuce and parsley with dressing. Chill 1 hour.

Yield: 6 to 8 servings

Southwestern Black Bean Salad

A tangy salad or salsa.

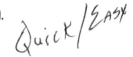

Quick/Easy

Preparation Time: 15 minutes ←
Chill Time: 3 to 4 hours

2   **medium tomatoes, chopped**

2   **ripe avocados, chopped**

1   **(15¼-ounce) can corn, drained**

1   **(16-ounce) can black beans, drained**

½   **cup red onions, chopped**

Add - 4 oz Chopped GRN. Chile

1   **cup thick and chunky salsa (mild)**

2   **tablespoons lime juice**

2   **tablespoons olive oil**

2   **tablespoons cilantro, chopped**

1   **teaspoon sugar**

1 - TBL Chopped Parsley

◎ Combine tomatoes, avocados, corn, black beans, red onions, salsa, lime juice, olive oil, cilantro and sugar in a bowl.

◎ Toss gently to coat well.

◎ Cover; chill 3 to 4 hours before serving.

Yield: 6 to 8 servings

This recipe can be found in
Spanish in the **Otra Vez...En Español** section.

07/19 - AC
09/20 - AC Charlies -BD

Mince - Dice - Chop

Mince is the smallest; about ¼-inch cubes.

Dice is in the middle cutting size; about the size of playing dice or ½-inch cubes.

Chop is chunks; a 1-inch cube or a nice little bite.

Plan on Pesto

Use pesto to zip up sandwiches, spread on pizza as a basic sauce, add a dash to a baked potato with butter or oil, lightly spread inside or under the skin of poultry before roasting, or blend with butter and serve with grilled fish. Pesto can be frozen in ice cube trays or in small containers for access at any time.

Pesto Potato Salad

A zesty recipe that prompts friends to ask, "May I have your recipe?"

Preparation Time: 15 minutes
Chill Time: 15 minutes
Cook Time: 15 minutes

2½ **pounds tiny new potatoes (about 24)**	2 **tablespoons pine nuts**
1 **clove garlic**	½ **teaspoon salt**
⅓ **cup Parmesan cheese, freshly grated**	2 **tablespoons water**
1 **cup fresh basil leaves, loosely packed**	3 **tablespoons olive oil**

- Cook potatoes in boiling water to cover 15 minutes or until tender.
- Drain and cool 15 minutes.
- Leaving skins intact, cut potatoes into ¼-inch slices.
- Position knife blade in food processor; top with cover. Drop garlic through food chute with processor running; process 3 to 5 seconds or until garlic is minced.
- Add Parmesan cheese, basil leaves, pine nuts, salt and water to processor; process until smooth.
- With processor running, pour olive oil through food chute in a slow, steady stream until combined.
- Combine basil mixture and potatoes in a large bowl and toss gently, being careful not to break slices.
- Serve potato salad warm or at room temperature.

Yield: 8 to 10 servings

Big short-cut use jarred pesto from Sam's or Costco

Layered Chicken Salad

A delicious salad under a blanket of tasty dressing.

Preparation Time: 15 minutes
Chill Time: 8 hours
Cook Time: 30 minutes

3 cups cooked chicken, chopped; divided	1 cup cucumber, thinly sliced
2 cups lettuce, torn	1 small red bell pepper, chopped
1 cup cooked long-grain rice	1 small green bell pepper, chopped
1 (10-ounce) package frozen green peas, thawed	Creamy Dressing
¼ cup fresh parsley, chopped	Red bell pepper rings (optional)
2 large tomatoes, seeded and chopped	

◎ Layer 1½ cups chicken and lettuce in a 3-quart bowl. Combine rice, peas and parsley; spoon evenly over lettuce.

◎ Layer tomatoes, cucumber, red bell pepper, green bell pepper and remaining 1½ cups chicken.

◎ Spoon dressing evenly over top of salad, spreading to edge of bowl. Garnish with red bell pepper rings, if desired; cover and chill 8 hours. Toss before serving.

Yield: 8 servings

CREAMY DRESSING

1 cup mayonnaise	2 tablespoons milk
½ cup sour cream	½ teaspoon celery seeds
½ cup raisins	½ teaspoon dill seeds
½ cup onion, finely chopped	½ teaspoon dry mustard
¼ cup sweet pickle relish	½ teaspoon garlic salt

◎ Combine mayonnaise, sour cream, raisins, onion, pickle relish, milk, celery seeds, dill seeds, dry mustard and garlic salt. Stir well.

Yield: 2¾ cups

Celery Fans

Slice celery stalks into 3 or 4-inch lengths and place on a cutting board. Using a sharp knife, cut several slits at one or both ends of each piece of celery, cutting almost to, but not through, the center. Place celery in ice water, and refrigerate until the fans curl. Follow the same directions for green onion fans, but slice off root and most of onion's top portion before beginning.

Passion Fruit Punch

1 cup pineapple juice

⅓ cup passion fruit juice

2 tablespoons lime juice

2 cups ginger ale

Combine pineapple juice, passion fruit juice and lime juice. Slowly stir in ginger ale just before serving.

Oriental Chicken Salad

Crisp and crunchy...you'll love it!

Preparation Time: 15 minutes
Chill Time: 2 hours
Cook Time: 45 minutes

Ginger Dressing
Vegetable oil

1 (3¾-ounce) package cellophane noodles

½ head lettuce, shredded (about 4 cups)

3 cups cooked chicken or turkey, cut in bite-size pieces

1 medium carrot, shredded

¼ cup green onions with tops, sliced

1 tablespoon sesame seeds, toasted

- Prepare Ginger Dressing.
- Pour 1-inch vegetable oil in deep skillet and heat to 425 degrees.
- Fry ¼ of the noodles at a time, turning once, until puffed, about 5 seconds; drain.
- Pour Ginger Dressing over lettuce, chicken, carrot and onions in 4-quart bowl. Toss with half of noodles. Spoon salad over remaining noodles; sprinkle with sesame seeds.

Make-ahead Tip: Cellophane noodles can be fried as directed and stored in an airtight container at room temperature no longer than 5 days.

5 cups chow mein noodles can be substituted for the fried cellophane noodles. Toss half of the noodles with chicken-dressing mixture; continue as directed.

Yield: 6 servings

GINGER DRESSING

⅓ cup vegetable oil

¼ cup white wine vinegar

1 tablespoon sugar

2 teaspoons soy sauce

½ teaspoon salt

½ teaspoon pepper

½ teaspoon ground ginger

- Put vegetable oil, white wine vinegar, sugar, soy sauce, salt, pepper and ginger in jar. Cover tightly and shake vigorously until ingredients are combined. Refrigerate at least 2 hours.

Yield: ½ cup

Honey-Mustard Turkey Salad

Great for Thanksgiving Turkey leftovers.

Preparation Time: 10 minutes

2 cups cooked turkey, chopped	1½ tablespoons Dijon mustard
6 slices bacon, cooked and crumbled	¾ teaspoon soy sauce
1 (4½-ounce) jar whole mushrooms, drained	¾ teaspoon lemon juice
¼ cup red bell pepper strips	1 (2-ounce) package roasted cashews
¼ cup green onions, sliced	Lettuce leaves (optional)
½ cup mayonnaise or salad dressing	Red bell pepper rings (optional)
2 tablespoons honey	Chow mein noodles

◎ Combine turkey, bacon, mushrooms, red bell pepper and green onions; set aside.

◎ Combine mayonnaise, honey, Dijon mustard, soy sauce and lemon juice; fold into turkey mixture. Cover and refrigerate.

◎ Just before serving, stir in cashews. Serve on lettuce leaves and red bell pepper rings, if desired. Sprinkle with chow mein noodles.

Yield: 4 to 6 servings

Whip It Right

If cream is difficult to whip, add one egg white, and stand the bowl in a larger bowl of cold water before whipping. This also increases the amount without flavoring the cream. If the cream goes watery, dissolve a little gelatin in 2 tablespoons of water and whip.

Colorful Greens

Salads do not always have to be green. Radicchio is a brilliant ruby-colored lettuce with a peppery-taste. Mix it with Boston, loose-leaf lettuces, spinach, Belgian endive or arugula and toss it with a vinaigrette dressing.

Tuna and Red Pepper Salad

The Asian touch and hot pepper add an exciting new twist to tuna.

Preparation Time: 15 minutes
Chill Time: 1½ hours

2	(6⅛-ounce) cans solid white tuna packed in water, drained and separated into chunks
2	large red bell peppers, cut into thin strips
1	cup fresh parsley, chopped
½	cup fresh cilantro, chopped
2	tablespoons rice vinegar
1	tablespoon vegetable oil
1	tablespoon sesame oil
¼	teaspoon dried crushed red pepper
¼	teaspoon salt
	Radicchio (optional)
	Leaf lettuce (optional)

◎ Combine tuna, red bell peppers, parsley and cilantro in a large bowl.

◎ Combine rice vinegar, vegetable oil, sesame oil, crushed red pepper and salt. Drizzle over tuna mixture and toss gently.

◎ Cover and chill up to 1½ hours.

◎ Arrange on radicchio and leaf lettuce, if desired.

1 pound fresh tuna may be substituted. Place tuna in a lightly greased shallow baking pan. Bake at 375 degrees for 10 to 12 minutes or until done. Double dressing recipe and serve on the side.

Yield: 4 servings

This recipe can be found in Spanish in the **Otra Vez...En Español** section.

Smoked Salmon-Caper-and-Dill Pasta

Perfect as a side or a main dish pasta salad.

Preparation Time: 10 minutes
Cook Time: 10 minutes

½	cup vegetable oil	12	ounces bow-tie pasta, cooked
1	(8-ounce) container sour cream	2	cucumbers, peeled, seeded and cubed
2	tablespoons lemon juice	6	cherry tomatoes, halved
⅓	cup fresh dill, chopped	5	ounces smoked salmon, cut into small pieces
2	teaspoons minced onion	¼	cup fresh chives, chopped
¼	teaspoon salt	¼	cup capers
¼	teaspoon pepper		

◎ Whisk together vegetable oil, sour cream, lemon juice, dill, onion, salt and pepper in a large bowl. Combine bow-tie pasta, cucumbers, cherry tomatoes, salmon, chives and capers.

◎ Toss pasta mixture with dressing.

◎ Cover and chill.

Yield: 4 servings

Very Easy
Very Tasty

Candied Flowers

Pastry chefs have long been using candied flower petals to decorate cakes. To make candied petals, hold the flower on its backside at the base of the stem and just brush the petals lightly (using an artist's paint brush) with egg whites that have been beaten until frothy. Gently sprinkle it with fine sugar. Allow the flower to dry face up on a plate. Rose petals and violets are two of the most popular candied flowers, but pansies, snapdragons and daisies will also work.

Homemade Infused Oils

Place herb or spice in a heavy saucepan; add 1 cup canola oil. Warm over low heat, stirring occasionally, 20 minutes; cool overnight. Pour through a fine wire-mesh strainer, discarding solids. Cover and refrigerate up to 2 weeks and then discard.

• Basil Oil: 1 cup chopped fresh basil

• Mint Oil: 1 cup chopped fresh mint

• Dill Oil: 1 cup chopped fresh dill

• Oregano Oil: 1 cup chopped fresh oregano

• Thyme Oil: 1 cup chopped fresh thyme

• Chive Oil: 1 cup chopped fresh chives (reduce oil to ³/₄ cup)

• Sage Oil: ¹/₂ cup chopped fresh sage

• Rosemary Oil: ¹/₂ cup chopped fresh rosemary

• Black Pepper Oil: ¹/₂ cup coarsely ground black pepper

• Ginger Oil: Place ¹/₃ cup chopped fresh ginger in heatproof container; heat oil and pour warm over ginger.

• Chile Pepper Oil: Crumble 2 dried red chile peppers in a heatproof container; heat oil and pour warm over chiles.

• Roasted Garlic Oil: Place 8 heads garlic on sheet of aluminum foil. Drizzle garlic with ¹/₄ cup canola oil; seal foil and bake at 400 degrees for 45 minutes; cool. Squeeze pulp from each clove into a heatproof container. Heat oil and pour over garlic.

Tortellini Salad with Pine Nuts

A dish of fun for a picnic under the sun.

Preparation Time: 30 minutes
Cook Time: 15 minutes

2	pounds fresh tortellini pasta	½	cup pine nuts, chopped
1	cup green bell peppers, seeded and chopped	¼	cup fresh basil, chopped
1	cup red bell peppers, seeded and chopped	¼	cup fresh dill, chopped
1	cup chopped green onions, with some green tops	¼	cup Parmesan cheese, grated Vinaigrette Dressing

◎ Cook the tortellini until it is al dente in a large pot of rapidly boiling water.

◎ Drain tortellini and place in a large bowl with the green bell peppers, red bell peppers, green onions, pine nuts, basil, dill and Parmesan cheese.

◎ Pour Vinaigrette Dressing over tortellini and chill.

VINAIGRETTE DRESSING

¼	cup balsamic vinegar		Freshly ground black pepper
1	clove garlic, minced	¾	cup peanut oil
¼	teaspoon salt		

◎ Combine balsamic vinegar, garlic, salt and pepper in a small bowl. Whisk in the peanut oil until well combined.

Yield: 8 to 10 servings

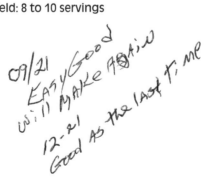

09/21
EASY Good
will MAKE AGAIN

12-21
Good As the last time

Pine Nut, Rice and Feta Salad

A flavorful salad with texture and taste.

Preparation Time: 10 minutes
Chill Time: 4 hours
Cook Time: 25 minutes

1 (7-ounce) package long-grain and wild rice mix	⅔ cup pine nuts, toasted
1 (4-ounce) package crumbled feta cheese	1 (2-ounce) jar diced pimiento, drained
½ cup green bell pepper, chopped	⅓ cup extra virgin olive oil
½ cup yellow bell pepper, chopped	2 tablespoons tarragon wine vinegar
½ cup onion, chopped	⅛ teaspoon pepper
	Lettuce leaves (optional)

- Prepare rice according to package directions; cool.
- Stir together rice, feta cheese, green bell pepper, yellow bell pepper, onion, pine nuts and pimiento in a bowl.
- Stir together olive oil, tarragon wine vinegar and pepper; add rice to mixture, tossing to coat.
- Cover and chill 4 hours or up to 24 hours.
- Serve on lettuce leaves, if desired.

Yield: 6 to 8 servings

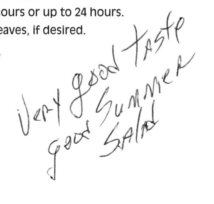

Very good taste
good Summer
Salad

Strike Oil

Experiment with these easy ideas for using infused oils:

- Savor them at their simplest as a dip for French bread.

- Drizzle any herb-infused oil over a platter of sliced tomatoes and garnish with the same herb.

- Toss cooked pasta or rice with a sprinkling of infused oil.

- Drizzle infused oil over mashed potatoes, steamed vegetables or fresh mozzarella or goat cheese.

- Marinate kalamata olives in oregano, rosemary or roasted garlic oil overnight.

- Pop popcorn in chile pepper oil for a spicy snack.

- Sprinkle dill oil over cooked zucchini, green beans or new potatoes.

- Brush any infused oil on fish, chicken, scallops or shrimp before grilling.

Punch Chiller

For an ice ring on the outside of the punch bowl, start with a large bowl. Place a container the same size as the punch bowl inside it and weigh it down. Freeze water in layers around the weighted container, adding citrus slices and mint or lemon leaves. After freezing, remove the duplicate container and unmold ice ring onto a tray. Place the punch bowl into the center of the ring.

Pebble Salad

Who knew "pebbles" had so much flavor?

Preparation Time: 5 minutes
Chill Time: 3 hours
Cook Time: 25 minutes

1	(6-ounce) package long grain and wild rice mix
1	(12-ounce) can white shoe peg corn, drained
1	small cucumber, seeded and chopped
2	medium carrots, chopped
¼	cup green onions, sliced
⅓	cup fresh parsley, chopped
¼	cup olive oil

¼	cup lemon juice
1	clove garlic, minced
½	teaspoon dill weed
¼	teaspoon dry mustard
⅛	teaspoon pepper
½	cup dry-roasted sunflower kernels
	Romaine lettuce leaves (optional)
⅓	cup slivered almonds, toasted

◎ Prepare rice according to package directions; cool.

◎ Combine rice, corn, cucumber, carrots, green onions and parsley in a large bowl; set aside.

◎ Combine olive oil, lemon juice, garlic, dill weed, dry mustard and pepper; pour over rice mixture and toss gently. Cover and chill 3 hours.

◎ Just before serving, stir in sunflower kernels.

◎ Arrange lettuce leaves in a large serving dish, if desired; spoon salad on top and sprinkle with almonds.

Yield: 8 to 10 servings

Chipotle Dressing

Absolutely amazing chipotle sauce!

Preparation Time: 10 minutes

¼ onion, peeled	¼ cup Worcestershire sauce
1 cup sugar	2-3 whole chipotles plus 2 to 3 teaspoons chipotle sauce from can (adobo sauce)
⅔ cup chili sauce	
½ cup white vinegar	2 cups vegetable oil

- In a blender, mix onion, sugar, chili sauce, vinegar, Worcestershire sauce and chipotles with adobo sauce until thickened. Add the oil a little at a time until all ingredients are well mixed.
- Put into a container. Chill.

Serving suggestions:

1. Serve cold on mixed green salad with chopped avocado, green bell pepper, yellow bell pepper, red bell pepper, tomato, jícama, black olives, cilantro and cucumber. Garnish with crushed tortilla chips.

2. Baste over chicken breasts while baking.

3. Marinate vegetables or meats and grill.

Yield: 2 cups

good Roasted Shrimp dip.

11-21
12-21
Roasted Shrimp
served w/ Football game

Jícama

When just the right crisp, cool flavor and texture are called for, the versatile jícama shines. Delicate in flavor, this tuber imparts a subtle sweetness. Well-peeled and thinly sliced, it enhances salads, crudités and stir-fries.

Green Salad Garnishes

- Tomato slices marinated in balsamic vinaigrette
- Lemon slices
- Cooked baby beets, cut into rounds or julienned
- Toasted walnuts, sesame seeds, sunflower seeds, pecans, almonds or pine nuts
- Capers
- Pomegranate seeds
- Orange sections
- Seedless or seeded table grapes
- Sliced red onions
- Fennel slices
- Cucumber slices
- Julienned green, red and yellow bell peppers
- Black or white truffle slivers
- Sliced hard-cooked eggs
- Small cherry or plum tomatoes
- Croutons
- Coconut
- Raisins
- Cheese
- Bacon
- Fresh edible flowers

Soy-Ginger Dressing

Great twist for salad or fresh veggies.

Preparation Time: 10 minutes

2 whole green onions (bottoms trimmed)	2 tablespoons rice vinegar (unflavored)
2 large cloves garlic	2 tablespoons fresh ginger, chopped
2 tablespoons sesame oil	1 tablespoon honey
2 tablespoons soy sauce	¼ cup canola oil

Blend green onions, garlic, sesame oil, soy sauce, rice vinegar, ginger and honey in a food processor until well mixed. Slowly add canola oil to mixture at a slow speed.

Toss with your choice of salad greens and cut vegetables such as carrots, cucumber, radishes and tomatoes. Garnish with toasted sesame seeds.

Yield: 1 cup

Kahlúa Fruit Dip

Perfect for fun or fancy entertaining.

Preparation Time: 5 minutes

1	(8-ounce) package cream cheese, softened
1	cup frozen nondairy whipped topping

¾	cup light brown sugar, firmly packed
⅓	cup Kahlúa or coffee-flavored liqueur
1	cup sour cream

◎ Mix cream cheese and frozen nondairy whipped topping until smooth.

◎ Add brown sugar, Kahlúa and sour cream. Blend well.

◎ Refrigerate until served. Serve with fruit.

Yield: 3 cups

This recipe can be found in
Spanish in the **Otra Vez...En Español** section.

Yours for the Picking

There are ways to tell when a melon is ripe. These tips are tried and true:

• A ripe watermelon will be yellow on the bottom, heavy for its size and uniformly round or oval.

• The rind of a cantaloupe should have a golden netting over a yellow background. If the background is green, it is not ripe.

• Honeydew has a creamy, faintly green rind when it is fully ripe.

Delicious Fruit Combos

• Fresh blackberries, sliced purple figs and a wedge of lime sprinkled with orange juice

• Cantaloupe and watermelon balls with chopped crystallized ginger in syrup

• Sliced pears drizzled with maple syrup

• Clementine sections in pomegranate juice topped with pomegranate seeds

• Sliced strawberries and raspberries sprinkled with balsamic vinegar and powdered sugar

• Oranges drizzled with orange water and sprinkled with chopped crystallized ginger and pistachio nuts

• Pineapple chunks, kiwi slices and strawberries drizzled with honey and candied lemon zest

• Sliced bananas and pink grapefruit sections sprinkled with brown sugar and lightly broiled

• Pitted peach and apricot halves, drizzled with wildflower honey and grilled on a skewer

• Halved green grapes, honeydew melon balls and diced kiwi drizzled with hot fudge sauce

• Pitted summer cherries with dollops of kirsch-flavored cream

• Raspberries, blackberries and strawberries with orange juice and fresh mint

• Kiwi slices, strawberries, raspberries and cantaloupe wedges sprinkled with poppy seeds and a citrus juice

• Baked bananas in banana liqueur, sprinkled with cinnamon sugar

• Banana slices sprinkled with toasted coconut and served with a dollop of crème fraîche and chopped macadamia nuts

Fruit with a Bite

Don't let the combination of ingredients frighten you...this is delicious!

Preparation Time: 20 minutes

1	pint any combination of four or five fruits or berries that are in season (cherries, strawberries, blueberries, raspberries, green grapes, melon)

4	tablespoons fresh jalapeño, seeded
½	cup raspberry vinegar
4	tablespoons fresh cilantro, finely chopped
1	cup orange marmalade

◎ Wash and cut up fruit. Combine in a bowl.

◎ Place jalapeño in microwave-safe bowl. Cover with water and micro-wave on high for 1 minute to soften.

◎ In a blender add jalapeño, raspberry vinegar and cilantro. Blend well.

◎ Add marmalade; cover and blend.

◎ Pour over fruit and toss, or serve sauce on the side.

May substitute 4 tablespoons canned chopped jalapeño for fresh jala-peño.

Yield: 2 cups sauce

Bread & Breakfast

Bread & Breakfast

Apple Orange Raisin Bread with Lemon Glaze

This recipe is a breeze to prepare in a food processor.

Preparation Time: 30 minutes
Cook Time: 30 minutes

1	apple, peeled, cored and sliced	½	cup orange juice
½	medium orange, cut into 6 pieces	1¼	cups sugar
1	cup yellow raisins	1	teaspoon vanilla
1	cup pecans	3	cups flour
2	eggs	2	teaspoons baking powder
½	cup oil	1	teaspoon baking soda
			Lemon Glaze

◎ Place apple, orange, yellow raisins, pecans, eggs, oil, orange juice, sugar and vanilla in the bowl of a food processor and blend for 30 seconds. Scrape down the sides and continue blending until fruit and nuts are finely chopped (not pureed), about 30 seconds. In the absence of a food processor, grate the apple and orange and chop the raisins and pecans.

◎ In a large bowl, stir together the flour, baking powder and baking soda. Add fruit and nut mixture to the bowl and stir until the dry ingredients are just moistened. Do not overmix.

◎ Divide batter between 5 greased miniature loaf pans (6 x 3 x 2-inch).

◎ Place pans on a cookie sheet and bake at 350 degrees for 30 minutes or until a toothpick, inserted in the center, comes out clean. Cool in pans for 15 minutes and then remove from pans and continue cooling on a rack. When cool, drizzle with Lemon Glaze.

Walnuts can be substituted for pecans.

Yield: 5 mini-loaves

LEMON GLAZE

1	tablespoon lemon juice	¾	cup powdered sugar, sifted

◎ Stir together lemon juice and powdered sugar until blended.

Play Clay

While mom is busy in the kitchen making her own "creations," kids can have fun too with their own dough. Remove crusts from 6 pieces of day old white bread. Tear or cut the bread into small pieces and place in a mixing bowl. Add two teaspoons of water and three teaspoons of white household glue. Mix with hands until it becomes the consistency of pie dough. Begin playing with it immediately to mold sculptures and figures, or roll out the clay with a rolling pin on wax paper. Cut into interesting shapes with cookie cutters. Set on a cooling rack to air dry and harden. To make beads, roll the clay into balls, poke a toothpick or wooden skewer through the middle to make the holes. Allow to harden 24 hours. Paint and decorate as desired.

One of Marybeth's favorite — gave away as Christmas gifts

Carrot Curls and Flowers

Curls: Scrape carrot; cut off ½ inch from each end. Using a vegetable peeler, cut thin lengthwise strips from carrot. Roll strips jelly roll fashion; secure with wooden picks. Drop in ice water and refrigerate at least 1 hour for curls to set. Remove picks before serving.

Flowers: Scrape carrot. Using a sharp paring knife, cut 4 or 5 grooves, evenly spaced, down the length of carrot; then slice the carrot to produce flower.

Spiced Carrot and Orange Bread with Raisin Orange Glaze

This spiced bread is especially nice around the winter holidays and makes a wonderful holiday gift.

Preparation Time: 25 minutes
Cook Time: 45 to 50 minutes

¾	cup butter	1½	cups walnuts, chopped
1	cup sugar	2	cups flour
3	eggs	1	teaspoon baking powder
1½	cups carrots, finely grated	1	teaspoon baking soda
½	orange, grated (about 3 tablespoons)	3	teaspoons pumpkin pie spice
			Raisin Orange Glaze

◎ Beat together butter, sugar, eggs, carrots, orange and walnuts until blended.

◎ Combine flour, baking powder, baking soda and pumpkin pie spice. Add to butter mixture and stir until the dry ingredients are just moistened. Do not overmix.

◎ Divide batter between 5 greased miniature loaf pans (6 x 3 x 2-inch).

◎ Place pans on a cookie sheet and bake at 325 degrees for 45 to 50 minutes or until a toothpick, inserted in the center, comes out clean. Cool in pans for 15 minutes and then remove from pans and continue cooling on a rack. When cool, drizzle with Raisin Orange Glaze.

Pecans can be substituted for walnuts.

Yield: 5 mini-loaves

RAISIN ORANGE GLAZE

2	tablespoons orange juice	2	tablespoons yellow raisins, finely chopped
1	cup powdered sugar, sifted	1	tablespoon orange peel, grated

◎ Stir together orange juice, powdered sugar, yellow raisins and orange peel until blended.

Honey Spiced Walnut Bread with Honey Butter Topping

This sticky bread is dense, but delicious and makes you want to lick your fingers to get every last crumb.

Preparation Time: 20 minutes
Cook Time: 45 to 50 minutes

½ cup butter, softened	2 teaspoons baking powder
¾ cup sugar	¼ teaspoon ground cloves
2 eggs	1 teaspoon cinnamon
¾ cup honey mixed with 1 cup hot water	¾ cup walnuts, chopped
2¼ cups flour	⅓ cup yellow raisins, chopped
1 teaspoon baking soda	Honey Butter Topping

◎ Beat together butter, sugar, eggs and honey mixture until blended.

◎ Combine flour, baking soda, baking powder, cloves, cinnamon, walnuts and yellow raisins. Add to butter mixture and stir until the dry ingredients are just moistened. Do not overmix.

◎ Divide batter between 4 greased and lightly floured miniature loaf pans (6 x 3 x 2-inch).

◎ Place pans on a cookie sheet and bake at 325 degrees for 45 to 50 minutes or until a toothpick, inserted in the center, comes out clean. Cool in pans for 15 minutes and then remove from pans and continue cooling on a rack. When cool, spoon on and brush tops with Honey Butter Topping.

Pecans can be substituted for walnuts.

Yield: 4 mini-loaves

HONEY BUTTER TOPPING

2 tablespoons orange juice	2 tablespoons butter
¼ cup honey	⅓ cup walnuts, chopped

◎ Heat together orange juice, honey, butter and walnuts until butter is melted and mixture is nicely blended.

Sticky Fingers

Unless you're hoping to lick your fingers, before measuring honey, coat the cup or spoon with vegetable cooking spray. The honey will slide right off without having to give it a nudge with your fingers! The same technique can be used for anything sticky or syrupy.

The Perfect Cup

Start with fresh coffee beans and cold water; choose the grind for your coffee maker; and brew the proportions as follows:

• Regular-strength coffee: 2 tablespoons coffee to ¾ cup water

• Extra-strength coffee: 2 tablespoons coffee to ½ cup water

• Double-strength coffee: ¼ cup coffee to ¾ cup water

• For large crowds: ½ pound of coffee with 1¼ to 1½ gallons of water will serve 50 cups.

Lemon Poppy Seed Bread

Delicious warm or cold!

Preparation Time: 15 minutes
Cook Time: 35 minutes

1	lemon cake mix (with pudding)	4	eggs
6	tablespoons flour	½	cup poppy seeds
⅓	cup oil	1¼	cups water

◎ Pour contents of lemon cake mix into a large bowl. Stir in flour. Add oil, eggs, poppy seeds and water. Mix together.

◎ Pour batter into 5 miniature loaf pans (6 x 3 x 2-inch). Let rise at room temperature for 10 minutes.

◎ Bake at 350 degrees for 35 minutes or until golden and the center of the bread cracks.

You can also use two 9 x 5-inch loaf pans.

Yield: 5 mini-loaves

This recipe can be found in Spanish in the **Otra Vez…En Español** section.

Pineapple Pecan Quick Bread with Pineapple Vanilla Glaze

A quick and easy bread that can be stored in the refrigerator for up to 1 week.

Preparation Time: 25 minutes
Cook Time: 50 to 65 minutes

1 cup margarine	1 cup buttermilk
2 cups sugar	1-2 tablespoons lemon peel
4 eggs	½ teaspoon lemon extract
3 cups flour	1 (20-ounce) can crushed pineapple, with liquid
½ teaspoon baking powder	
½ teaspoon baking soda	½ cup pecans, chopped
½ teaspoon salt	Pineapple Vanilla Glaze

◎ Preheat oven to 350 degrees.

◎ Grease and flour bottom only of two 8 x 4-inch or 9 x 5-inch loaf pans.

◎ Beat together margarine and sugar until light and fluffy. Add eggs one at a time. Add flour, baking powder, baking soda, salt, buttermilk, lemon peel and lemon extract; beat until smooth.

◎ Drain pineapple juice, reserving the liquid for the Pineapple Vanilla Glaze. Stir in drained pineapple and pecans.

◎ Divide batter between 2 loaf pans. Bake at 350 degrees for 50 to 65 minutes until toothpick inserted in center comes out clean.

◎ Spoon Pineapple Vanilla Glaze over loaves while warm and still in the pans. Let stand for 10 minutes before removing from the pans.

Yield: 2 loaves

PINEAPPLE VANILLA GLAZE

3 tablespoons pineapple liquid	½ cup sugar
½ teaspoon vanilla	

◎ Stir together pineapple liquid, vanilla and sugar until well blended.

Cutting a Pineapple

To cut a pineapple, first, cut off the top and trim the bottom so it stands upright. Using a sharp knife, cut away the skin, then go back and trim any eyes. Slice in wedges or rings and cut away the core. Cut pineapple can be refrigerated for up to one week.

Muffin Musts

• Remember to combine dry and wet ingredients just until batter holds together (usually no more than 15 seconds). The less a muffin is beaten, the better. Overbeating results in muffins that are tough with undesirable tunnels inside.

• If all cups in the muffin pan are not filled, pour some water or place ice cubes into the empty cups to keep the pan from buckling.

• Muffins are done when the tops form domes and are dry to the touch, sides have slightly pulled away from the cups, and a wooden pick comes out clean when inserted in the center of the muffin.

• Muffins are best eaten fresh the day they are made, but freeze well too.

Very Berry Muffins

This recipe is wonderful with any type of fresh or frozen berries.

Preparation Time: 20 minutes
Cook Time: 25 minutes

1 cup butter, softened	4 cups flour, sifted
1½ cups sugar	1 cup milk
4 large eggs	4-5 cups fresh or frozen berries
2 teaspoons vanilla	Nutmeg, sugar, cinnamon and raw sugar (optional)
4 teaspoons baking powder	
½ teaspoon salt	

◎ Preheat oven to 375 degrees.

◎ Cream butter and sugar together. Add eggs, vanilla, baking powder and salt. Do not overbeat. Add flour and milk alternately. Fold in berries. (If using frozen berries, thaw and drain them first.)

◎ Spoon mixture into muffin papers. If desired, top each muffin with a sprinkling of nutmeg and sugar or cinnamon and raw sugar.

◎ Bake 25 minutes.

Use a combination of berries or one berry of your choice.

Yield: about 24 muffins

Date Pecan Muffins

A wonderful, healthy treat!

Preparation Time: 20 minutes
Cook Time: 20 to 25 minutes

1 cup regular rolled oats	1 cup whole wheat flour
1 cup buttermilk	½ teaspoon baking soda
½ cup brown sugar, firmly packed	2 teaspoons baking powder
½ cup oil	½ cup pitted dates, chopped
2 large egg whites	½ cup pecans, chopped

- In a large bowl, mix rolled oats, buttermilk, brown sugar, oil and egg whites.
- In a separate bowl, mix whole wheat flour, baking soda, baking powder, dates and pecans.
- Add flour mixture to the oats mixture. Stir until evenly moistened.
- Spoon mixture into greased muffin pan or muffin papers.
- Bake at 375 degrees for 20 to 25 minutes. Cool in pan for 5 minutes and serve warm or cold.

Yield: 12 muffins

Butter It Up!

Flavored butters add a tasty touch to muffins, scones, biscuits and waffles. To ½ cup softened butter, try adding:

- ¾ cup pure maple syrup
- 1 tablespoon brown sugar and 1 teaspoon cinnamon
- ½ teaspoon fresh orange or lemon zest
- 2 large strawberries with powdered sugar to taste
- ⅓ cup toasted and finely chopped pecans and 2 tablespoons of honey

Maggie favorite

The Pine Nut

Pine nuts are also called pignoli. This nut is small, pellet-shaped and creamy white with a sweet, rich flavor. It is popular in Mediterranean cuisine and seen in pestos, stuffing, sauces, soups, stews, rice dishes, pastries and cookies.

Pesto Bread with Cheese and Pine Nuts

A wonderful complement to a warm bowl of homemade soup. Try this bread topped with sweet butter.

Preparation Time: 20 minutes
Cook Time: 45 minutes

2 eggs	½ teaspoon baking powder
3 tablespoons sugar	1½ teaspoons sweet basil flakes
⅓ cup oil	⅓ cup Parmesan cheese, grated
¾ cup cream	¼ cup pine nuts, lightly toasted
2 cups self-rising flour	

◎ Beat together eggs, sugar, oil and cream.

◎ In a separate bowl, combine flour, baking powder, basil and Parmesan cheese. Add dry ingredients mixture to egg mixture. Stir until dry ingredients are blended. Do not overmix. Stir in pine nuts.

◎ Spread batter into a greased 8 x 4-inch loaf pan.

◎ Place pan on a cookie sheet and bake at 350 degrees for 45 minutes or until a toothpick, inserted in the middle, comes out clean.

◎ Allow to cool in the pan for 15 minutes and then remove from the pan and continue cooling on a rack.

◎ Use a serrated bread knife and cut into slices.

If you use all-purpose flour, increase baking powder to 3 teaspoons, and add a pinch of salt.

Yield: 1 loaf

Blast from the Past Dinner Rolls

*These rolls will remind you of your grandmother's
kitchen and the succulent smell of homemade bread.*

Preparation Time: 40 minutes
Chill Time: 3 hours to rise; refrigerate until ready to bake
Cook Time: 20 to 30 minutes

1 cup shortening	1 cup warm water
¾ cup plus 1 teaspoon sugar; divided	2 eggs, slightly beaten
1 cup hot water	1 cup all-bran cereal
2 packages yeast	1½ teaspoons salt
	6 cups flour

◎ Mix together shortening, ¾ cup sugar and hot water. Set aside to cool.

◎ In a separate bowl, dissolve yeast and 1 teaspoon sugar in warm water. Add cooled shortening mixture to yeast mixture; mix well. Add eggs.

◎ Combine all-bran cereal, salt and flour. Gradually add dry ingredients to wet mixture. Stir until combined.

◎ Let rise until doubled in bulk. Punch down and cover tightly with plastic wrap and refrigerate until ready to bake.

◎ Approximately 1½ hours before baking, shape punched down dough into four small balls per greased muffin cup. Let rise in muffin pan until doubled in size.

◎ Bake at 425 degrees for 20 to 30 minutes.

Yield: 48 rolls

Yeast...Alive and Kicking

Proofing the yeast insures that it is active. Pour the yeast over ½ cup of warm (100 to 115 degrees) liquid from the recipe. Add 2 teaspoons of sweetener from the recipe. After 5 to 8 minutes, the mixture will bubble and foam indicating active yeast. Add the yeast to the recipe as directed.

Shapely Butter

For molding butter, rubber, plastic or porcelain molds unmold more easily than wooden ones. The molds come in both large and pat-size designs. To make butter molds, first soften the butter. Spread butter into cavity of the mold, scraping the back surface of the butter to level it. Freeze for 30 minutes or until the butter is firm. Then invert the mold, and pop the butter out. Cover and chill until ready to use.

To make butter curls, you will need a hook-shaped instrument known as a butter curler. Work with a stick of butter at refrigerator temperature. Place the butter on a flat surface, and pull the butter curler, ridges down, lengthwise down the stick. The butter will curl up and over the curler. Place finished curls in ice water until all are made. Remove them from the water, and place on a serving dish. Cover and chill until ready to use.

Simple Dinner Rolls

Homemade rolls that are easy to make.

Preparation Time: 30 minutes
Chill Time: 1 hour to rise; can be refrigerated up to three days before baking
Cook Time: 12 minutes

2	cups water	2	teaspoons salt
⅔	cup butter or margarine	2	packages dry yeast
½	cup sugar	2	eggs
6	cups flour; divided		

◎ Combine water, butter and sugar in a saucepan; heat until butter melts, stirring occasionally. Cool to 120 to 130 degrees.

◎ In a separate large bowl, combine 2 cups flour, salt and yeast ; stir well. Gradually add liquid mixture to flour mixture, beating well at high speed of an electric mixer. Add eggs, and beat an additional 2 minutes at medium speed. Gradually stir in remaining 4 cups flour, making a soft dough. Cover and refrigerate up to 3 days; punch down dough and cover if it begins rising out of the bowl.

◎ When ready to use, punch dough down; turn out onto a floured surface, and knead lightly 4 to 5 times. Divide dough into thirds. Divide each third into 12 pieces; shape each into a ball. Place each ball in cup of lightly greased muffin pan. Repeat procedure with remaining dough.

◎ Cover and let rise in a warm place (85 degrees), free from drafts, 1 hour or until doubled in bulk.

◎ Bake at 400 degrees for 12 minutes or until golden brown.

To make cloverleaf rolls, punch dough down; divide and shape dough into 108 balls; place 3 balls in each cup of lightly greased muffin pan. Cover and let rise until doubled in bulk; bake as directed.

Yield: 24 rolls

Mexican Fiesta Spoon Biscuits

Add a little spice and flavor to ordinary biscuits.

good

Preparation Time: 20 minutes
Cook Time: 45 minutes

1	(17-ounce) can large refrigerated buttermilk biscuits
1	(10-ounce) can large refrigerated buttermilk biscuits
1	(16-ounce) jar chunky salsa

2	cups (8 ounces) Monterey Jack cheese, shredded
1	small green bell pepper, seeded and chopped
½	cup green onions, sliced
1	(2¼-ounce) can sliced ripe olives, drained

◎ Cut each biscuit into 8 pieces.

◎ Combine biscuits and salsa, tossing gently to coat. Spoon mixture into a lightly greased 13 x 9 x 2-inch baking dish. Top with Monterey Jack cheese, green bell pepper, green onions and olives.

◎ Bake at 350 degrees for 45 minutes or until edges are golden and center is set. Let stand 15 minutes. Cut into squares.

Substitute a (4.5-ounce) can chopped green chiles for the green bell pepper.

Yield: 15 servings

This recipe can be found in
Spanish in the **Otra Vez...En Español** section.

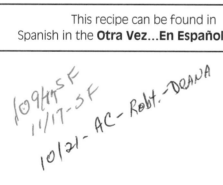

The Red Jalapeño

Chipotles are red-ripe jalapeños, smoked and then either dried or canned in a vinegary sauce known as adobo. The canned variety is more readily available and more useful. Many grocery stores stock them or they can be found in specialty food shops. Very hot and very smoky, chipotles are usually minced to distribute their flavor and fire throughout a dish. Brands vary in heat, flavor and thickness of the adobo. Transfer unused chipotles to a tightly covered storage container and refrigerate for up to one month.

Chipotle Corn Bread

A moist corn bread with "a kick."

TRY

Preparation Time: 10 minutes
Cook Time: 35 minutes

1 cup yellow cornmeal	1 cup buttermilk
1 cup flour	3 large eggs
¼ cup sugar	6 tablespoons unsalted butter, melted and cooled
2 teaspoons baking powder	
1 teaspoon baking soda	2 tablespoons canned chipotle chiles, seeded and minced
1 teaspoon salt	
1 cup Monterey Jack cheese, grated	

◎ Preheat oven to 375 degrees.

◎ Grease 9 x 5 x 2½-inch metal loaf pan.

◎ Combine cornmeal, flour, sugar, baking powder, baking soda and salt. Stir in Monterey Jack cheese.

◎ Whisk buttermilk, eggs, butter and chipotle chiles in medium bowl.

◎ Add buttermilk mixture to dry ingredients; stir until blended.

◎ Spoon batter into prepared pan. Bake for 35 minutes or until a toothpick, inserted in the center, comes out clean. Cool in pan on rack 15 minutes. Turn bread out onto rack; cool completely.

Yield: 1 loaf

This recipe can be found in
Spanish in the **Otra Vez...En Español** section.

Party Cheese Bread

This bread looks great and is even better to eat!

Preparation Time: 10 minutes
Cook Time: 20 minutes

1	loaf French bread	1	tablespoon poppy seeds
½	cup margarine, softened	8	(1-ounce) slices Swiss cheese
3	green onions, finely chopped	4	slices bacon, cooked and
1	tablespoon Dijon mustard		chopped

◎ Cut bread, but not completely through, into 16 slices.

◎ Combine margarine, green onions, Dijon mustard and poppy seeds.

◎ Cut Swiss cheese slices in half and insert between the slices of bread. "Ice" bread with butter mixture. Top with bacon.

◎ Place bread on foil covered cookie sheet and bake at 400 degrees for 20 minutes.

Yield: 16 servings

Lining a Bread Basket

• Spread a large square napkin, right side facing down, on a table or other flat surface. Fold each of the four corners to meet exactly in the center.

• Preserving the folds you have made, carefully turn the napkin over and fold each corner to meet exactly in the center once again.

• Place in the basket, holding down the ends in the center. Bring each loose corner up from underneath, making a flowery nest for your bread rolls.

Dessert Dish Designs

Jazz up a dessert presentation by decorating the dishes:

• Sprinkle sifted powdered sugar or cocoa around the brim of the plate.

• Garnish with fresh berries.

• Arrange mint leaves or long twists of fresh orange or lemon peel on the plate.

• Use a squeeze bottle to make a design with liquid chocolate or sauces.

Dilly Garlic Bread

Add a new twist to your Italian dinner.

Preparation Time: 10 minutes
Cook Time: 8 minutes

½	cup margarine or butter, softened	1	(16-ounce) loaf French bread, cut in half horizontally
2	cloves garlic, pressed	¼	cup Parmesan cheese, grated
¼	cup fresh dill weed, finely chopped		

◎ Combine margarine, garlic and dill weed. Spread mixture evenly on cut sides of bread. Sprinkle with Parmesan cheese.

◎ Place bread on foil covered cookie sheet and bake at 375 degrees for 8 minutes or until golden brown. Slice crosswise into 1-inch slices and serve.

Yield: 10 to 12 servings

Blue Corn Muffins

These muffins are colorful and flavorful, complementing any meal.

Preparation Time: 20 minutes
Cook Time: 20 to 25 minutes

½ cup red bell pepper, diced	1 cup flour
½ cup yellow bell pepper, diced	⅓ cup sugar
¼ cup onion, diced	1 tablespoon baking powder
1 tablespoon vegetable oil	1 teaspoon salt
¼ cup plus 2 tablespoons butter or margarine	2 eggs, slightly beaten
½ cup shortening	1 cup milk
¾ cup blue cornmeal	½ cup half-and-half
¾ cup yellow cornmeal	1 cup cooked ham, diced

Add GRN. Chile

◎ Sauté red bell pepper, yellow bell pepper and onion in vegetable oil until tender; set aside.

◎ Combine butter and shortening in a small saucepan; melt over low heat. Set aside to cool.

◎ In a separate large bowl, combine blue cornmeal, yellow cornmeal, flour, sugar, baking powder and salt; mix well and set aside.

◎ Combine eggs, milk, half-and-half and ham. Stir in sautéed vegetables and melted butter mixture. Add to dry ingredients, stirring just until moistened.

◎ Spoon into greased and floured muffin pans filling ¾ full.

◎ Bake at 350 degrees for 20 to 25 minutes.

White or yellow cornmeal may be substituted for the blue cornmeal.

Yield: 24 muffins

Delicious Corn Bread

Corn bread can be made with different cornmeals for varying textures. Coarse stone-ground cornmeal gives a rustic and gritty texture to the bread; fine yellow cornmeal makes a soft, tender bread. When making corn bread, add the liquid in two stages to avoid a lumpy batter because cornmeal does not absorb liquid quickly. For a dark, crisp cornbread, bake the batter in a preheated, greased cast-iron skillet. Serve fresh with sweet butter and honey or jalapeño jelly.

Canadian Bacon Scramble

Light, fluffy and delicious!

Preparation Time: 20 minutes
Cook Time: 45 minutes

¼ cup plus 5 tablespoons butter or margarine; divided	¼ cup green bell pepper, chopped
¼ cup flour	¼ cup green onions, sliced
2 cups milk	½ pound fresh mushrooms, sliced
1 teaspoon salt	18 eggs, slightly beaten
½ teaspoon pepper	1 cup soft breadcrumbs
1 (6-ounce) package Canadian bacon, chopped	

◎ Preheat oven to 350 degrees.

◎ Melt ¼ cup butter in a large saucepan over low heat; add flour, stirring until smooth. Cook one minute, stirring constantly.

◎ Gradually add milk; cook over medium heat, stirring constantly, until thickened and bubbly.

◎ Stir in salt and pepper; set white sauce aside.

◎ In a skillet, add 2 tablespoons butter and sauté Canadian bacon, green bell pepper, green onions and mushrooms until vegetables are tender, but crisp; drain.

◎ Melt 1 tablespoon butter in skillet; add eggs. Cook without stirring until mixture begins to set on bottom of skillet. Drag spatula across bottom of skillet to form large curds. Continue cooking eggs until thickened but still moist; do not stir constantly.

◎ Remove from heat. Stir in Canadian bacon mixture and white sauce.

◎ Spoon egg mixture into a greased 13 x 9 x 2-inch baking dish.

◎ Combine breadcrumbs and remaining 2 tablespoons melted butter, stirring well. Sprinkle evenly over egg mixture.

◎ Bake, uncovered, for 20 to 25 minutes or until thoroughly heated.

To make ahead, prepare casserole as directed, but do not bake. Cover and refrigerate up to 24 hours. Remove from refrigerator; let stand 30 minutes. Bake as directed.

Yield: 12 servings

(handwritten: TRY)

Chile n' Cheese Breakfast Casserole

(handwritten: GREAT TIPS ↓)

A different spin on the traditional breakfast casserole.

Preparation Time: 15 minutes
Chill Time: 8 hours
Cook Time: 50 minutes

(handwritten: Tried 12/15 Very Good)

3	English muffins, split
2	tablespoons butter or margarine, softened
1	pound bulk pork sausage
1	(4-ounce) can chopped green chiles, drained *+ A little more*
3	cups cheddar cheese, shredded
1½	cups sour cream
12	eggs, beaten

◎ Spread cut side of each English muffin with 1 teaspoon butter and place, buttered side down, in a lightly greased 13 x 9 x 2-inch baking dish.

◎ Cook sausage in a skillet until browned, stirring to crumble; drain.

◎ Layer ½ of sausage, ½ of green chiles and ½ of cheddar cheese over English muffins.

◎ Combine sour cream and eggs; pour over casserole. Repeat layers with remaining sausage, green chiles and cheddar cheese. Cover and refrigerate 8 hours.

◎ Remove from refrigerator and let stand at room temperature for 30 minutes.

◎ Preheat oven to 350 degrees.

◎ Bake, uncovered, for 35 to 40 minutes.

Yield: 8 to 10 servings

(handwritten: Made for ~~Brunch~~ 10/17 INSF A Hit!)

This recipe can be found in
Spanish in the **Otra Vez...En Español** section.

Eggs-actly

• Salt toughens eggs...add it to your dish after it is prepared, not while it is cooking. In addition, salted butter can cause fried or scrambled eggs to stick to a pan (use vegetable oil, cooking spray or unsalted butter instead).

• When cooking an egg in the microwave, pierce the yolk first or it will explode.

• Plunge hard-cooked eggs into cold water while they are hot to prevent a greenish ring from forming around the egg yolks.

• To reduce fat, calories and cholesterol, use fewer egg yolks and more egg whites.

• Avoid washing eggs before storing them as their protective coating may wear off and they will not last as long. On the average, an egg's shelf life is about 10 days in the refrigerator. If you are unsure of an egg's age, place it in a pan of cold water. If it lies on its side, it's fresh; if it tilts at an angle, it's 3 to 4 days old; if it stands upright, it's about 10 days old; if it floats, toss it!

• Add a teaspoon of salt or a tablespoon of vinegar to water before hard-cooking eggs to make them easier to peel.

• Avoid placing eggs near odoriferous foods — they'll absorb those odors right through their shells.

• To make scrambled eggs fluffier, add ¼ teaspoon cornstarch per egg; to make them rich and creamy, add 1 tablespoon sour cream per 2 eggs; to give them a delightful flavor, add 1 teaspoon sherry per egg.

Keeping Avocados Green

If you are using half an avocado, leave the pit in the unused half, cover it with plastic wrap and refrigerate. This will retard discoloration. If the avocado's cut surface turns brown, gently scrape off the discoloration. The avocado should be fine underneath.

Individual Mexicali Quiches with Avocado Topping

Makes a wonderful presentation and is very tasty, too!

TRY FOR A PARTY

Preparation Time: 30 minutes
Cook Time: 25 minutes

6   (6-inch) corn tortillas
½   pound ground spicy pork sausage
¼   cup onion, finely chopped
1   tablespoon chile powder
1   teaspoon cumin
3   large eggs, slightly beaten

1   (4½-ounce) can chopped green chiles; divided
1½ cups half-and-half
½   teaspoon salt
⅛   teaspoon pepper
1½ cups Monterey Jack cheese, shredded; divided
     Avocado Topping

- Preheat oven to 350 degrees.
- Bring 2 inches of water to boil in a large skillet; remove from heat.
- Dip each tortilla in water to soften; drain on paper towels. Place tortillas in 6 lightly greased custard cups; set aside.
- Cook sausage, onion, chile powder and cumin in skillet over medium heat until meat is browned, stirring until it crumbles; drain and set aside.
- Combine eggs, ½ of green chiles, half-and-half, salt and pepper in a large bowl. Stir in sausage mixture.
- Spoon ½ of egg mixture evenly into tortilla shells; sprinkle with ½ of Monterey Jack cheese. Pour remaining egg mixture evenly over cheese.
- Bake for 20 minutes. Sprinkle with remaining cheese and bake an additional 5 minutes.
- Remove from oven, and let stand 5 minutes. Remove from custard cups and sprinkle with remaining green chiles. Serve with Avocado Topping.

To make a Mexicali Quiche in a 9-inch deep-dish pie plate, soften 8 corn tortillas in boiling water, as directed; place in lightly greased pie plate, overlapping and extending tortillas about ½-inch over edge. Spoon ½ of egg mixture into shell; sprinkle with ½ of Monterey Jack cheese, and spoon remaining egg mixture over cheese. Bake at 350 degrees for 30 minutes. Sprinkle with remaining Monterey Jack cheese, and bake an additional 5 minutes. Remove from oven and let stand 5 minutes. Sprinkle with remaining green chiles. Serve with Avocado Topping.

Yield: 6 servings

Individual Mexicali Quiches continued

AVOCADO TOPPING

1 avocado, peeled and mashed	1 clove garlic, minced
1 tomato, peeled, seeded and chopped	2 tablespoons lime juice

◎ Combine avocado, tomato, garlic and lime juice until blended.

Storing Spices

• Store spices in airtight containers in a cool, dark place up to six months. If keeping them longer than six months, store in freezer.

• Label each jar with date of purchase so you know when it is time to replace them.

• Alphabetize spice rack to make locating spices easier.

Brunch Bites

• Clear pitchers of freshly squeezed juices in sunshine colors are enticing. Add a few sprigs of mint.

• Smoked fish platters are lightened when presented with tissue-thin melon slices. Garnish with lemon halves instead of wedges.

• Present bowls of plain and fruity yogurts alongside a selection of favorite toppings, including raisins, chopped nuts, granola and melon chunks.

• Slice a French bread lengthwise; spread with butter and toast under the broiler. Serve with thinly sliced country ham...yum!

• Hot sweet potatoes are delicious in the winter with Orange Butter, maple syrup or brown sugar.

Spinach-Herb Cheesecake

Munch on this for brunch or lunch!

Preparation Time: 25 minutes
Cook Time: 45 minutes

¼ cup pine nuts or pecan pieces, toasted	3 large eggs
¼ cup Italian-seasoned breadcrumbs	4 cups spinach, loosely packed and shredded
2 tablespoons butter or margarine, melted	2 cloves garlic, pressed
3 (8-ounce) packages cream cheese, softened	2 tablespoons flour
1 (15-ounce) container ricotta cheese	1 tablespoon fresh dill, chopped
1 (8-ounce) package feta cheese, crumbled	½ teaspoon salt
	½ teaspoon pepper
	Fresh dill sprigs and tomato slices (optional)

◎ Preheat oven to 350 degrees.

◎ Place nuts in food processor and process until ground.

◎ In medium bowl, stir together ground nuts, breadcrumbs and butter. Press into bottom of 9-inch springform pan and bake for 10 minutes. Cool on wire rack.

◎ Reduce heat to 325 degrees.

◎ Beat cream cheese at medium speed with an electric mixer until creamy; add ricotta cheese, feta cheese and eggs, beating until blended. Stir in spinach, garlic, flour, dill, salt and pepper. Pour into crust.

◎ Bake at 325 degrees for 45 minutes. Cool on wire rack for 10 minutes. Gently run a knife around the edge of cheesecake and release sides. Cool ten minutes more. Garnish with dill sprigs and tomato slices, if desired.

Serve this warm or cold at your next wine and cheese party.

Yield: 8 to 12 servings

Vegetable Frittata

Delicious, beautiful and full of healthy vegetables!

Preparation Time: 15 minutes
Chill Time: 10 minutes
Cook Time: 1 hour

1 clove garlic, minced	¼ cup milk
3 tablespoons butter or margarine, melted	6 large eggs
1½ cups fresh mushrooms, sliced	1½ cups cheddar cheese, shredded
1½ cups zucchini, chopped	3 slices white bread, cut into cubes
1 cup red bell pepper, chopped	¾ teaspoon salt
1 cup green onion, sliced	½ teaspoon pepper
1 cup frozen whole kernel corn or canned corn, drained	1 medium tomato, cut into wedges
1 (8-ounce) package cream cheese, softened	

◎ Preheat oven to 350 degrees.

◎ Cook garlic in butter in a large skillet over medium-high heat, stirring constantly, until tender.

◎ Add mushrooms, zucchini, red bell pepper and green onion, stirring constantly 8 to 10 minutes or until vegetables are tender and excess liquid evaporates.

◎ Stir in corn and remove from heat; set aside.

◎ Beat cream cheese and milk at medium speed with an electric mixer until smooth.

◎ Add eggs one at a time, beating after each addition.

◎ Fold egg mixture in vegetable mixture with cheddar cheese, bread, salt and pepper.

◎ Pour into a lightly greased 10-inch springform pan. Bake for 45 to 50 minutes or until center is set.

◎ Cool in pan for 10 minutes.

◎ Remove sides of springform pan and arrange tomato wedges on top.

Yield: 8 servings

This recipe can be found in
Spanish in the **Otra Vez...En Español** section.

Frittatas

Frittatas are to Italians what omelets are to the French. In a frittata (or tortillas in Spain), the filling is mixed with the eggs and the whole mixture is cooked slowly in a skillet until set, then quickly browned under the broiler. Frittatas are a bit drier than omelets, not so fussy in their timing, and much easier to make for a crowd. The filling ingredients are what make the frittata so good, but it is the eggs that bind everything together.

Frittatas can be served hot, right in the skillet, or left to cool at room temperature. They can be cut into pie-shaped wedges for brunch or supper or little squares for appetizers. They are also perfect for picnics!

TRY

Citrus Party Punch

2½ dozen small fresh mint leaves

2 cups sugar

1 gallon water

1½ cups lemon juice

1 (12-ounce) can frozen orange juice concentrate, thawed and undiluted

1 (46-ounce) can unsweetened pineapple juice

1 tablespoon vanilla extract

1½ teaspoons almond extract

Place 1 mint leaf in each compartment of 2 ice cube trays. Fill trays with water, making sure mint leaves do not float; freeze. Combine sugar and water in a large punch bowl, stirring until sugar dissolves. Stir in lemon juice and remaining ingredients. To serve, add minted ice cubes.

Mediterranean Torte

This towering hot sandwich is wonderful for brunch, lunch or dinner.

Preparation Time: 30 minutes
Cook Time: 45 minutes

1 (32-ounce) package frozen bread dough, thawed	2 tablespoons butter
2 (10-ounce) packages frozen chopped spinach, thawed	1 pound small fresh mushrooms, sliced
1 (14-ounce) can artichoke hearts, sliced	8 ounces salami, thinly sliced
1 (12-ounce) jar marinated red bell pepper strips	8 ounces provolone cheese, thinly sliced
1 (6-ounce) can pitted ripe olives, sliced	8 ounces cooked ham, thinly sliced
	1 large egg
	1 tablespoon water

◎ Preheat oven to 350 degrees.

◎ Cut one bread loaf in half crosswise. Roll out ½ on a lightly floured surface into a 10-inch circle. Cover and set aside.

◎ Press together remaining 1½ dough loaves, and roll out on a lightly floured surface into a 12-inch circle. Fit dough into a 9-inch springform pan, allowing edges to overhang.

◎ Drain spinach, artichoke hearts, red bell pepper strips and olives. Press spinach and red bell pepper strips between layers of paper towels and set aside.

◎ Melt butter and sauté mushrooms in a skillet for 8 minutes; drain.

◎ Layer ½ of salami, mushrooms and olives in dough-lined pan; top with ½ of provolone cheese slices. Layer with ½ of ham, spinach, red bell peppers, remaining salami, remaining ham and artichokes; top with remaining provolone cheese slices.

◎ Stir together egg and water; brush on overhanging pastry edges.

◎ Top torte with remaining pastry round. Fold overhanging edges over top pastry, crimping as necessary and press to seal. Brush top with remaining egg mixture.

◎ Bake on bottom oven rack for 30 to 35 minutes.

◎ Remove from oven and cover with aluminum foil, if necessary to prevent excessive browning.

◎ Bake 15 to 20 more minutes. Cool in pan on a wire rack. Remove sides of pan and cut into wedges.

Yield: 8 servings

Hot Apple Cranberry Bake

Scrumptious!

Preparation Time: 15 minutes
Cook Time: 1 hour

3 cups Granny Smith apples, peeled, seeded and chopped

2 cups cranberries, fresh or frozen

1½ teaspoons lemon juice

¾ cup sugar

1⅓ cups old-fashioned oats

1 cup walnuts, chopped

⅓ cup brown sugar, firmly packed

½ cup butter or margarine, melted

◎ Preheat oven to 325 degrees.

◎ Combine apples, cranberries, lemon juice, sugar, oats, walnuts, brown sugar and butter.

◎ Put in greased casserole dish.

◎ Bake for 1 hour.

Can be served as a dinner side dish or as a dessert with ice cream or whipped cream, too!

Yield: 10 to 12 servings

Can't Find Cranberries

Fresh cranberries can sometimes be difficult to find. Buy cranberries when they are in the store and freeze them in the 12-ounce bags they come in for up to one year.

Flavorful Coffee

An easy and delicious way to enhance brewed coffee (without buying flavored beans) is to put a small handful of red hots in the filter with the ground coffee. When it brews, the cinnamon flavor flows through as well, creating a wonderful, rich taste.

Apple Pancake

This pancake will melt in your mouth!

Preparation Time: 20 minutes
Cook Time: 30 minutes

4 tablespoons margarine	6 tablespoons powdered sugar or less, depending on sweetness of apples
4 medium apples, peeled, cored and sliced	3 eggs, room temperature
3 tablespoons lemon juice	¼ teaspoon salt
¼ teaspoon cinnamon	½ cup flour
	½ cup milk

- Preheat oven to 425 degrees.
- Melt margarine in 10-inch stovetop-safe dish. Remove dish from stove. Take one tablespoon of the melted margarine and set aside.
- Put apple slices into large bowl with lemon juice.
- Mix cinnamon and powdered sugar together and sprinkle over apples; toss to mix.
- Return stovetop-safe dish with melted margarine to burner, add apples and cook, stirring often, for about 3 to 4 minutes or until apples are tender but still hold their shape.
- In a separate bowl (or blended in a food processor) combine eggs, salt, flour, milk and the reserved 1 tablespoon of melted margarine; beat until smooth.
- Spread the apples evenly over the bottom of the stovetop-safe dish and pour the egg mixture on top.
- Bake for 20 minutes or until golden brown and fluffy.
- Turn over onto a warm platter so that apples are on top.
- Dust with powdered sugar, if desired, and serve warm.

Yield: 6 servings

Brunch Popover Pancake

Your taste buds will go wild with every bite!

Preparation Time: 20 minutes
Cook Time: 30 minutes

4 large eggs, lightly beaten	3 tablespoons orange marmalade
1 cup milk	1 tablespoon lemon juice
1 cup flour	1 (16-ounce) package frozen sliced peaches, thawed and drained
¼ teaspoon salt	
⅓ cup plus 3 tablespoons butter or margarine, melted; divided	1 cup frozen blueberries, thawed and drained

◎ Preheat oven to 425 degrees.

◎ Place a well greased 12-inch cast-iron skillet or baking dish in oven for 5 minutes.

◎ Combine eggs, milk, flour, salt and ⅓ cup butter in bowl and blend with a wire whisk.

◎ Remove skillet from oven. Pour in batter.

◎ Bake for 20 to 25 minutes (this will resemble a large popover and will quickly fall after removing from oven).

◎ Combine marmalade, 3 tablespoons butter and lemon juice in a saucepan; bring to a boil.

◎ Add peaches and cook over medium heat, stirring constantly, 2 to 3 minutes. Spoon on top of baked pancake; sprinkle with blueberries.

Yield: 4 servings

Look What Popped Up!

A popover is a crisp, golden balloon with a soft, moist hollow center. Eggs are the only leavening in popovers. Popovers are served hot and puffed right out of the oven. If you want to serve them a little later, just pierce the top with the tip of a knife to let the steam escape.

Gingerbread Pancakes

This recipe is a new twist to a traditional favorite.

Preparation Time: 20 minutes
Cook Time: 10 minutes

1½ cups flour	3 egg whites, lightly beaten
1½ tablespoons baking powder	1½ cups milk
1½ teaspoons cocoa	2½ tablespoons molasses
½ teaspoon ground ginger	2½ teaspoons vegetable oil
½ teaspoon ground cloves	Maple syrup or honey (optional)
½ teaspoon cinnamon	
2½ tablespoons pecans, chopped	

◎ Combine flour, baking powder, cocoa, ginger, cloves, cinnamon and pecans in a bowl. Make a well in the center of mixture.

◎ Combine egg whites, milk, molasses and vegetable oil. Add to dry mixture; stir just until moistened.

◎ Spoon about 2 tablespoons batter for each pancake onto a moderately hot, lightly greased griddle. Cook pancakes until tops are covered with bubbles and edges look cooked; turn and cook other side.

◎ Pour maple syrup or honey over the pancakes, if desired.

Assorted fruit can be served with these pancakes.

Yield: 18 (3-inch) pancakes

Banana Oatmeal Waffles with Praline Pecan Sauce

Out of this world!

Preparation Time: 10 minutes
Cook Time: 10 minutes

1¼ cups flour
¾ cup regular oats, uncooked
3 tablespoons brown sugar
1 tablespoon baking powder
½ teaspoon baking soda
¼ teaspoon cinnamon
   Pinch nutmeg

1½ cups buttermilk
2 large eggs
¼ cup butter or margarine, melted
2 medium bananas, sliced
   Praline Pecan Sauce

◎ Position knife blade in food processor. Put in flour, oats, brown sugar, baking powder, baking soda, cinnamon, nutmeg, buttermilk, eggs and butter. Process until smooth, stopping once to scrape down sides.

◎ Add bananas and pulse 3 to 4 times or until chopped.

◎ Bake in preheated, greased waffle iron until golden. Waffles will be slightly soft.

◎ Serve with warm Praline Pecan Sauce or syrup.

Yield: 12 (4-inch) waffles

← *Sounds good*

PRALINE PECAN SAUCE

1 cup brown sugar, firmly packed
½ cup light corn syrup
½ cup pecans, chopped
¼ cup water

   Dash salt
1 tablespoon butter or margarine
1 teaspoon vanilla extract

◎ Combine brown sugar, corn syrup, pecans, water and salt in a small saucepan and bring to a boil, stirring constantly until sugar dissolves. Remove from heat.

◎ Stir in butter and vanilla extract.

Serve this sauce warm over ice cream. Sauce may be stored in refrigerator up to two weeks.

Yield: 1½ cups sauce

Punch Bowl Stand

With grapevine wreaths and a tablecloth, you can create a beautiful display to serve punch. Wind ribbon and greenery through the wreath and arrange on the table. Set the punch bowl in the center. Place votive candles on the table for a glittering display of lights.

Baked Orange Pecan French Toast

Sleep in! This recipe can be made the night before.

Preparation Time: 10 minutes
Chill Time: 2 hours
Cook Time: 30 minutes

4 **eggs**	¼ **teaspoon nutmeg**
⅔ **cup orange juice**	8 **(½-inch thick) slices Italian or French bread**
⅓ **cup milk**	
¼ **cup sugar**	¼ **cup butter or margarine**
½ **teaspoon vanilla extract**	½ **cup pecans, chopped**

- In medium bowl, beat together eggs, orange juice, milk, sugar, vanilla extract and nutmeg.
- Arrange bread in single layer in baking dish; top with egg mixture. Refrigerate at least two hours or overnight.
- Preheat oven to 350 degrees.
- Melt butter in 10 x 15 x 2-inch pan, arrange soaked bread on top. Bake for 20 minutes.
- Sprinkle with pecans and bake an additional 10 minutes.
- Serve with warm Orange Syrup.

Yield: 8 servings

ORANGE SYRUP

½ **cup sugar**	1 **cup orange juice**
½ **cup butter**	

- Combine sugar, butter and orange juice. In small saucepan, cook over low heat. Do not boil.
- Cool for 10 minutes.

Praline French Toast

A breakfast or brunch treat that can be prepared in advance!

Preparation Time: 15 minutes
Chill Time: 8 hours
Cook Time: 50 minutes

1 cup light brown sugar, firmly packed	6 large eggs
½ cup butter or margarine	1½ cups milk
2 tablespoons light corn syrup	1 teaspoon vanilla extract
2 (6¼-ounce) packages frozen butter crescent rolls, thawed	¼ teaspoon salt

◎ Stir together brown sugar, butter and corn syrup in a small sauce-pan. Cook over low heat, stirring often, until butter melts and mixture is smooth.

◎ Pour into a lightly greased 13 x 9-inch baking dish.

◎ Place crescent rolls in a single layer over syrup.

◎ Whisk together eggs, milk, vanilla extract and salt; pour over rolls.

◎ Cover and chill for 8 hours.

◎ Remove from refrigerator and let stand at room temperature for 30 minutes.

◎ Bake at 350 degrees for 45 minutes and serve immediately.

Yield: 6 servings

Party Ice Ring

The day before serving your punch, prepare a pretty ring by boiling about 7 cups of water for 1 minute; let cool at room temperature. (This eliminates cloudiness in the ice ring.) Pour 3 cups of the water into a 6-cup ring mold; freeze. Set remaining water aside.

Slice lemons, limes or oranges and cut the slices in half. Arrange citrus slices and mint leaves on top of ice in the ring. Slowly fill the mold to top with remaining water. Freeze. (Other combinations or fruit or edible flowers can also be used.)

To unmold, let the mold sit at room temperature 5 minutes or until loosened. Carefully float ice ring in punch.

Stick Dipping

Impress your guests at your next party by offering homemade chocolate dipped cinnamon swizzle sticks to flavor and sweeten their coffee. To make, combine 4 ounces semisweet chocolate (or sweet dark chocolate) with 1½ tablespoons whipping cream in a 1-cup glass measuring cup. Microwave at medium power for 1 minute, stirring midway through, or until chocolate melts. Stir in ⅛ teaspoon almond extract. Dip each cinnamon stick in melted chocolate. Allow excess to drip off and place on waxed paper-lined baking sheet. Allow to harden in the freezer for 15 minutes or until set. Spoons can be substituted for the cinnamon sticks by dipping the bowl of the spoon and ¼ inch up handle in chocolate.

Sweet Roll Cake

This will definitely become a Saturday morning favorite!

Preparation Time: 10 minutes
Chill Time: 8 hours
Cook Time: 30 minutes

½ cup pecans, chopped	½ cup butter, melted
1 (25-ounce) package frozen dinner roll dough, thawed	½ cup brown sugar, firmly packed
1 (3.4 ounce) package butterscotch pudding mix	¾ teaspoon cinnamon

- Sprinkle pecans in bottom of greased Bundt pan.
- Arrange dough in pan and sprinkle with dry pudding mix.
- Stir together butter, brown sugar and cinnamon; pour over dough.
- Cover and chill for 8 hours.
- Preheat oven to 350 degrees.
- Remove from refrigerator and bake for 30 minutes or until golden brown.
- Invert onto a serving plate and serve immediately.

Yield: 10 to 12 servings

This recipe can be found in
Spanish in the **Otra Vez...En Español** section.

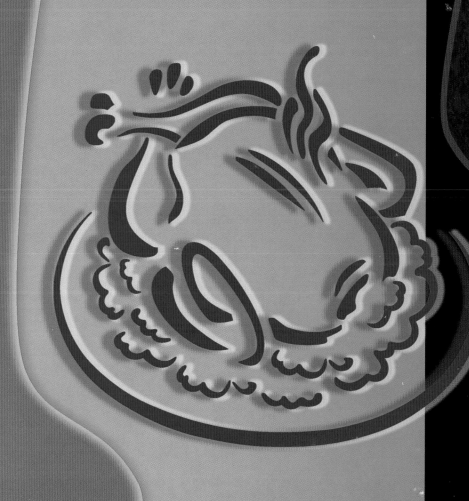

The Main Event

The Main Event

Shake, Rattle and Roll Chicken

Oven-fried chicken at its best and a dish the kids will love to help you shake and bake!

Preparation Time: 20 minutes
Cook Time: 20 minutes

1 cup flour	1 teaspoon seasoned salt
2 teaspoons garlic powder	6 chicken breast halves, skinned and boned
1 teaspoon ground black pepper	2 eggs
1 teaspoon basil	¼ cup buttermilk
1 teaspoon oregano	2 teaspoons Dijon mustard
½ teaspoon salt	5 cups crushed cornflakes cereal
1½ teaspoons Cajun seasoning	

◎ Preheat oven to 450 degrees.

◎ Place flour, garlic powder, pepper, basil ,oregano, salt, Cajun seasoning and seasoned salt in a brown paper bag; mix together.

◎ Put chicken pieces into bag, one piece at a time, to coat.

◎ Mix eggs with buttermilk and Dijon mustard in a bowl. Dip chicken in egg mixture.

◎ Press chicken into cornflakes cereal and place on a greased cookie sheet, not touching each other.

◎ Bake for 20 minutes and serve immediately.

12 chicken thighs, skinned and boned, may be substituted for chicken breasts.

Yield: 6 servings

Table Etiquette

• As soon as you are seated, place your napkin in your lap.

• Wait to begin eating until the hostess takes the first bite. Also, follow the hostess' lead when in doubt about which utensil to use. (The hostess can suggest that the company begin without her if she is going to be delayed.)

• Once you pick up a piece of flatware, never place it back on the table; rest it on your plate. Leave the knife at the upper plate edge with the blade toward the plate. Leave the fork centered on the plate.

• Never butter a whole piece of bread at one time; instead, break off a bite-sized piece, butter, and eat it. Biscuits are an exception.

• Remove olive pits or any seeds from your mouth with the same utensil you used to eat the food.

• For formal service, present a served dinner plate at the left of the recipient; remove plates from the right.

• For family-style service, pass food around the table to the right.

• When passing salt and pepper, place the shakers or mills on the table rather than handing them directly to the person requesting them. Always pass both salt and pepper, even if only one is requested.

• Place your knife and fork together at the "3:15" position on your plate to signal that you have finished.

• At the end of the meal as you leave the table, place your napkin on the table, not in your chair or on your plate.

Carve Poultry with Confidence

1. Remove leg and thigh. Place bird, breast side up, on a large platter. Pull the leg away from the body and slice through skin between the leg and body. Cut down to the joint where the thigh connects to the back; push on the leg to open joint and cut through.

2. To sever the joint between drumstick and thigh, feel for a small indentation and cut through it, bending the drumstick back gently while cutting.

3. To cut off wings, roll bird on its side and pull the wing away from body. Cut into the hollow between wing and body. Pulling wing away from body, cut around wing joint. Bend wing back, exposing the joint and cut through.

4. To slice breast meat, make a deep horizontal cut into breast above where wing was attached. Beginning at the outer edge of one side of breast, cut thin, even slices from the top down to the base.

5. Repeat steps for other side of bird.

Wine Chicken

This dish will quickly become a family favorite.

Preparation Time: 20 minutes
Cook Time: 1 hour

½ cup butter	Pepper, to taste
1 whole chicken, cut in pieces	½ cup white wine
1 onion, sliced	½ cup tomato juice
Seasoned salt, to taste	½ cup water
Garlic powder, to taste	

- Melt butter in large skillet. Brown chicken pieces on both sides until a nice golden color. Remove chicken and place in a roasting pan.
- Put onion slices in remaining butter and sauté until soft.
- Sprinkle chicken pieces with seasoned salt, garlic powder and pepper, to taste. Pour white wine, tomato juice and water on top of chicken. Top with sautéed onion.
- Bake uncovered at 350 degrees for 1 hour.

Spoon the gravy over egg noodles as a side dish.

Yield: 4 servings

Stuffed Chicken Breasts with Mushroom Sauce

Enjoy with a glass of wine.

Keeping the Crumbs
Coating will adhere to chicken better if it has been chilled for an hour before cooking.

Preparation Time: 30 minutes
Cook Time: 40 minutes

8 chicken breast halves, boned and skinned	2 teaspoons water
4 (1-ounce) slices cooked ham, cut in half	1 cup seasoned dry breadcrumbs
4 (1-ounce) slices Swiss cheese, cut in half	½ cup butter
1 egg, beaten	1 teaspoon Italian seasoning
	Mushroom Sauce

- Place each chicken breast half on a sheet of waxed paper; flatten to ¼-inch thickness using a meat mallet or rolling pin.
- Place one piece of ham and one piece of Swiss cheese in center of each chicken piece. Roll up lengthwise, and secure chicken, ham and cheese with wooden picks.
- Combine egg and water; dip each chicken breast in egg, and coat well with breadcrumbs.
- Melt butter in a large skillet; stir in Italian seasoning.
- Add chicken and cook over low heat 30 to 40 minutes, browning all sides.
- Serve with Mushroom Sauce.

Yield: 8 servings

A good basic Mushroom Sauce use w/ other dishes

MUSHROOM SAUCE

½ pound fresh mushrooms, sliced	3 tablespoons white wine
¼ cup onion, chopped	½ cup milk
3 tablespoons butter, melted	1 (10¾-ounce) can cream of mushroom soup, undiluted

- Sauté mushrooms and onion in butter in a medium saucepan until tender.
- Stir in white wine, milk and cream of mushroom soup; heat thoroughly.

Grilling Chicken

Chicken has a tendency to burn on the grill, so cook over medium-hot coals for best results. If it begins to burn, place a disposable aluminum pan directly under the chicken to catch drippings and push coals to both sides of pan.

Basil Grilled Chicken

Great for a summer backyard barbecue.

Preparation Time: 20 minutes
Cook Time: 20 minutes

¾ teaspoon coarsely ground pepper	1 tablespoon Parmesan cheese, grated
4 chicken breast halves, skinned and boned	¼ teaspoon garlic powder
⅓ cup plus ½ cup butter; divided	⅛ teaspoon salt
¼ cup plus 2 tablespoons fresh basil, chopped; divided	⅛ teaspoon pepper
	Fresh basil sprigs (optional)

◎ Press pepper into meaty sides of chicken breast halves.

◎ Combine ⅓ cup melted butter and ¼ cup chopped basil; stir well. Brush chicken lightly with melted butter mixture.

◎ Combine ½ cup softened butter, 2 tablespoons basil, Parmesan cheese, garlic powder, salt and pepper in a small bowl. Beat until mixture is well blended and smooth. Transfer to a small serving bowl; set aside.

◎ Grill chicken over medium coals 8 to 10 minutes on each side; basting frequently with remaining melted butter mixture.

◎ Serve grilled chicken with basil-butter mixture. Garnish with fresh basil sprigs, if desired.

Yield: 4 servings

TRY

Mediterranean Chicken

Very unusual, but very good! A great dish to serve to a crowd.

Preparation Time: 45 minutes
Chill Time: 4 hours
Cook Time: 30 minutes

12	chicken breast halves, boned and skinned	1	cup pitted prunes
	Vegetable cooking spray	½	cup green olives
½	cup red wine vinegar	½	cup capers, with a bit of liquid
½	cup olive oil	4	bay leaves
3	cloves garlic, crushed	1	cup brown sugar
4	tablespoons oregano	1	cup white wine
	Salt and pepper, to taste	¼	cup parsley, finely chopped

◎ Preheat oven to 350 degrees.

◎ Place chicken in single layer in large shallow baking dish coated with vegetable cooking spray.

◎ Combine red wine vinegar and olive oil; pour over chicken.

◎ Sprinkle with garlic, oregano, salt and pepper.

◎ Baste oil and red wine vinegar on chicken to wet spices, but not wash them off.

◎ Place prunes, green olives, capers and bay leaves around and between chicken breasts. Let marinate in refrigerator for 4 hours. Reserve a portion of the marinade.

◎ Before baking, sprinkle with brown sugar and pour white wine around the chicken.

◎ Bake for 30 minutes, basting frequently.

◎ Garnish with parsley and serve.

This recipe is still great without the capers or the prunes if you choose not to include these ingredients.

Yield: 8 to 12 servings

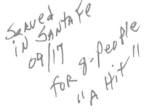
Served in Santa Fe 09/17 for 8-people "A Hit"

The Caper's the Culprit

Capers are the unopened bud of a shrub that grows wild all over the Mediterranean, North Africa and India. The green buds are picked by hand before sunrise, while they are still tightly closed, and then pickled.

✳ FYI

Chicken Cerveza

One of the best ways to cook chicken because the beer flavors and bastes the bird from the inside. Jaws will drop and eyes will pop!

Preparation Time: 35 minutes
Cook Time: 2 to 2½ hours

1 (12-ounce) can beer	1 large roaster chicken (4 to 5 pounds), washed, lumps of fat removed, and blotted dry
8 tablespoons Hot Pepper Rub; divided	3 tablespoons butter, melted
	½ teaspoon liquid smoke

◎ Preheat the oven to 350 degrees.

◎ Open the beer can and poke a few additional holes in the top. Pour out (or drink) half the beer and add 2 tablespoons of Hot Pepper Rub to the can.

◎ Sprinkle 2 tablespoons Hot Pepper Rub in the cavity of the chicken.

◎ Holding the chicken upright, insert the can into the cavity of the chicken. Place in a roasting pan, spreading out the legs to form a "tripod" so the chicken stands upright.

◎ Combine the butter and liquid smoke. Brush outside of bird with butter mixture.

◎ Sprinkle 4 tablespoons Hot Pepper Rub on the outside of the bird.

◎ Roast chicken until golden brown and fall-off-the-bone tender; 2 to 2½ hours.

◎ Present the bird upright on the beer can on a platter.

◎ Remove and discard the beer can, then carve chicken. (Caution: beer can will be very hot!)

Yield: 4 to 6 servings

HOT PEPPER RUB

¾ cup paprika	2 tablespoons chile powder
¼ cup ground pepper	2 tablespoons onion powder
¼ cup salt	2 teaspoons cayenne pepper
2 tablespoons garlic powder	

◎ Combine paprika, pepper, salt, garlic powder, chile powder, onion powder and cayenne pepper.

This recipe can be found in
Spanish in the **Otra Vez...En Español** section.

Soy Garlic Chicken

Perfect for outdoor grilling!

Preparation Time: 20 minutes
Chill Time: 4 hours
Cook Time: 24 minutes

¼ cup soy sauce	4 cloves garlic, minced
¼ cup vegetable oil	¼ teaspoon ground pepper
2 tablespoons ketchup	4 chicken breast halves, skinned and boned
1 tablespoon vinegar	

- ◎ Combine soy sauce, vegetable oil, ketchup, vinegar, garlic and pepper in a shallow dish or zip-top plastic bag; add chicken breasts. Cover or seal, and chill 4 hours, turning occasionally.
- ◎ Remove chicken from marinade, discarding marinade.
- ◎ Grill, covered with grill lid, over medium-high heat (350 to 400 degrees) for 12 minutes on each side.

Yield: 4 servings

Hot, Cool, and Clean All in One

That's the description of ginger in a nut shell. This versatile and compelling flavor is used in a variety of dishes; from soup to dessert and from breakfast to dinner. Covered with a tough, papery peel, the flesh inside is crispy, juicy and fibrous. Ginger is peeled and used sliced in stir-fries, minced and sautéed along with other aromatics like garlic and chiles, and grated or pressed to produce a pungent juice. To extract ginger juice, wrap grated ginger in cheesecloth and squeeze; use it in marinades and sauces. Ginger can also be found dried or crystallized.

Indirect or Direct Grilling

When you cook something over indirect heat, you are cooking the food at a lower heat and "next to" the fire, not over it. If a recipe calls for indirect cooking, preheat one side of your gas grill and put the food on the other side. Close the lid and the heat from the burner will warm the grill, much like an oven. Turkeys, roasts and other large cuts that require slow, even cooking are best cooked over indirect heat.

In direct grilling, the food is cooked directly over the hot fire. Fast cooking flat meats such as steaks, chops, kabobs and hamburgers are cooked directly over hot coals or lava rocks.

You can effectively turn your gas grill into a smoker by wrapping aromatic wood chips (such as hickory, alder, fruitwoods, maple, oak and pecan) that have been soaked in water for about 30 minutes in foil. Seal and poke holes in the top of the package and place under the grate directly over the burner. The same procedure can be done when grilling with charcoal; however the wood chips can simply be tossed into coals without wrapping them.

Minted Chicken Sauce

A versatile sauce for grilled or roasted
chicken that can be used for casual cookouts or formal dinners.

Preparation Time: 15 minutes
Chill Time: 1 hour

5 tablespoons mint leaves, finely chopped; divided	1 cup peanut oil
½ cup rice wine vinegar	½ teaspoon salt
2 tablespoons soy sauce	½ teaspoon ground pepper
4 egg yolks	1 teaspoon ground coriander

◎ Combine 4 tablespoons mint leaves, rice wine vinegar, soy sauce and egg yolks in a blender. While blending, slowly pour in peanut oil in a thin stream. Continue blending until smooth.

◎ Pour mixture into a bowl and add remaining 1 tablespoon mint leaves, salt, pepper and coriander. Refrigerate covered at least 1 hour.

◎ Use to complement grilled or roasted chicken.

Also good with chicken strips as an appetizer.

Yield: 2 cups sauce

Jalapeño-Glazed Cornish Hens

Delicious touch of the border to the classic Cornish hen!

Preparation Time: 15 minutes
Chill Time: 3 hours
Cook Time: 1 hour 20 minutes

3	(1½-pound) Cornish hens, split	2	teaspoons grated lime rind
½	teaspoon salt	⅓	cup lime juice
¼	teaspoon pepper	¼	cup vegetable oil
1	(10½-ounce) jar jalapeño jelly	1	tablespoon fresh cilantro, chopped

◎ Sprinkle Cornish hens with salt and pepper, and place cut side down in a large shallow dish. Set aside.

◎ Melt jalapeño jelly in a small saucepan over low heat. Add lime rind, lime juice, vegetable oil and cilantro.

◎ Pour marinade over hens, cover and refrigerate at least 3 hours; turn occasionally.

◎ For a charcoal grill, prepare fire, and let burn until coals are white. Rake coals to opposite sides of grill and place a drip pan between coals. For a gas grill, light one burner, placing drip pan on opposite side.

◎ Drain hens, reserving marinade. Place on food rack over drip pan. Cook, covered with grill lid, over medium-hot coals (350 to 400 degrees) 35 minutes.

◎ Brush with reserved jalapeño glaze.

◎ Cook an additional 40 minutes, or until done.

Yield: 6 servings

That's for the Birds

• Rock Cornish hens are 5 to 6 weeks old and weigh between 1 and 2 pounds. They are delicate, elegant miniatures that make an impressive and beautiful meal for a dinner party. They are wonderful roasted or split and grilled or broiled.

• Broiler-fryers, cut up into parts or whole, are the most common kind of chicken. They are about 45 days old and weigh between 3 and 4½ pounds. These tender birds are best broiled or fried, but can also be roasted, steamed or poached.

• Roasters are about 10 weeks old and weigh between 4½ pounds and 8 pounds. They have more meat than smaller birds and are perfect for roasting, with or without stuffing.

• Capons, 10-week-old cocks that were castrated when young, weigh between 8 and 10 pounds. They live a lazy life and grow big and fat! As a result, they are delicate and tender with an abundance of white meat. Their flavor is milder than that of chicken and their size makes them perfect for stuffing and roasting for a holiday dinner.

• Fowl or stewing hens are laying hens that have stopped laying. These tough old birds are 10 months or older and weigh between 3 and 7 pounds. Because they are older, their meat is stringy, but loaded with flavor. These chickens require slow, long, moist cooking or stewing to tenderize the meat and are best for making soup.

Fluted Mushrooms

Select firm, white mushrooms. Cut several slits at even intervals around each mushroom cap, cutting from the center of the cap to the edge and using a curving motion with a paring knife. Make another set of slits parallel to the first slits, allowing ¹⁄₁₆ inch between them. Remove and discard the tiny strips of mushroom between the slits.

Mahogany Marinated Duck Breasts

Impress your dinner guests with this dish which is as appealing to the eye as it is to the palate.

Preparation Time: 10 minutes
Chill Time: 12 hours
Cook Time: 30 minutes

1 cup soy sauce	½ teaspoon ginger, sliced
1 cup honey	1 duck breast per person
1 cup sugar	Vegetable oil
1 cup rice vinegar	Parmesan cheese, grated (optional)
¼ cup beef bouillon	Green onions, sliced (optional)
½ cup dry sherry	
4 teaspoons fresh garlic, minced	

◎ Combine soy sauce, honey, sugar, rice vinegar, beef bouillon, sherry, garlic and ginger to make marinade.

◎ Put duck breasts in shallow pan or heavy-duty zip-top plastic bag; pour marinade over duck and cover or seal. Marinate duck breasts overnight.

◎ Preheat oven to 400 degrees.

◎ Put a small amount of vegetable oil in a pan. When oil is hot, put in duck breasts, skin side down first. When skin starts to render fat, turn and brown on other side.

◎ Place duck breasts in a baking dish and put in oven. Cook for about 15 minutes or until duck reaches desired doneness (medium).

◎ Remove duck breast from pan, slice diagonally to get large pieces and serve. Garnish with a small amount of Parmesan cheese and green onions, if desired.

Yield: 8 to 10 servings

Grilled Marinated Turkey Steaks

You never tasted turkey this good!

Preparation Time: 15 minutes
Chill Time: 8 hours
Cook Time: 25 minutes

1 **(5-pound) bone-in turkey breast**	1 **tablespoon ground ginger**
½ **cup soy sauce**	1 **teaspoon dry mustard**
¼ **cup vegetable oil**	3 **cloves garlic, pressed**

◎ Purchase bone-in turkey breast from butcher. Ask him to cut in half lengthwise, and then cut each half crosswise into 1-inch thick steaks resembling large pork chops.

◎ Combine soy sauce, vegetable oil, ginger, dry mustard and garlic and pour over turkey. Cover and refrigerate 8 hours.

◎ Remove turkey from marinade, discarding marinade. Grill turkey, covered with lid, over medium-hot coals (350 to 450 degrees). Grill 8 to 10 minutes on each side.

A 5-pound boneless turkey breast may be substituted, cut in same manner.

Yield: 12 servings

Turkey Tips

• Buy a fresh turkey for Thanksgiving for a real treat.

• Wash anything that comes in contact with a raw bird thoroughly using hot, soapy water.

• Use a meat thermometer when cooking turkey. The internal temperature should be 170 degrees for the breast, 180 degrees for the thigh and 160 degrees for the stuffing.

• When storing leftovers, remove any stuffing from the carcass and refrigerate the turkey and stuffing separately.

• Reheat leftovers thoroughly. Boil leftover gravy for 1 minute before serving.

Quail

Quail is full of flavor with very rich and sweet meat. Because they are so small (between 6 to 8 ounces), they can easily be overcooked and become dry. Quail are best cooked by roasting, grilling, gently braising or sautéing over high heat. Sauté in butter or oil, turning to brown all sides and basting frequently. They will be done in just 15 to 20 minutes. Deglaze the pan quickly with port or Madeira for a wonderful sauce.

Figure on at least 2 quail per serving and encourage everyone to eat with their fingers!

Pierre's Quail Marinade

Move over, Colonel . . . this quail is "finger-lickin' good!"

Preparation Time: 10 minutes
Chill Time: 2 hours
Cook Time: 10 minutes

½	cup olive oil	1	juice and zest of lemon
¼	cup soy sauce	1	juice and zest of lime
1	clove garlic, chopped		White pepper, to taste
1	teaspoon fresh ginger, chopped	8	quail

- Combine olive oil, soy sauce, garlic, ginger, lemon juice and zest, lime juice and zest, and white pepper. Marinate quail a minimum of 2 hours.
- Grill quail 4 to 5 minutes on each side using low to medium heat.

Low-sodium soy sauce can be substituted for soy sauce.

Yield: 4 servings

Marinated Beef Tenderloin

Melts in your mouth!

Preparation Time: 15 minutes
Chill Time: 8 hours
Cook Time: 30 to 45 minutes

1	cup catsup	1	(4 to 6-pound) beef tenderloin, trimmed
2	teaspoons prepared mustard		Watercress (optional)
½	teaspoon Worcestershire sauce		Red grapes and green grapes (optional)
1½	cups water		
2	(.7-ounce) envelopes Italian salad dressing mix		

◎ Combine catsup, mustard, Worcestershire sauce, water and Italian salad dressing mix; blend well.

◎ Spear beef tenderloin in several places and place in a heavy-duty zip-top plastic bag. Pour marinade over meat and seal bag tightly. Place bag in a shallow pan and refrigerate 8 hours, turning occasionally.

◎ Drain off and reserve marinade.

◎ Place tenderloin on a rack in a baking pan; insert meat thermometer. Baste occasionally with reserved marinade while baking. Bake at 425 degrees for 30 to 45 minutes or until thermometer registers 140 degrees (rare), 150 degrees (medium rare), or 160 degrees (medium).

◎ Place on serving platter and garnish with watercress, red grapes and green grapes, if desired.

This marinade is also wonderful for venison backstrap.

Yield: 12 to 15 servings

This recipe can be found in Spanish in the **Otra Vez...En Español** section.

Not Just for Flavor

Marinades have a multitude of uses. They tenderize the tough, moisten the dry and enliven the bland. Although foods taste fine grilled just as they are, almost anything will benefit from the added flavor brought on by a marinade. For lean fish, beef and game, a marinade is essential.

Marinades are a combination of three ingredients: an acid (such as vinegar, tomatoes, buttermilk, yogurt, soy sauce, wine or citrus juice), oil and flavorings. The "acid" serves as the tenderizing agent. The best candidates for high-acid marinades are tough meats such as flank steaks, round steaks and shanks. "Oil" is a moisturizer. The most popular oil in marinades is olive oil, but sesame, nut and herb-flavored oils are also good to use. "Sugars," such as honey, molasses, and brown or granulated sugar, are the most common flavorings. Their sweetness takes the edge off the high-acid marinade and meats basted with sweetened liquids develop a rich, brown crust.

The length of time for a particular food to marinate depends on the strength of the marinade and the flavor and texture of the food. Fish should marinate no more than 30 minutes, and only in a delicately flavored marinade at that. Lean, strong-tasting game can and should marinate overnight. Keep foods well chilled while marinating, but bring the food to room temperature before grilling.

Grilling with Marinades

When grilling meats or poultry with marinades or sauces, know when to baste! Oil and vinegar or citrus-based marinades can be brushed on throughout the cooking process. However, when using sugar-based barbecue sauces, apply it toward the end of your cooking as it will burn.

Stuffed Mexican Pepper-Cheese Steaks

Now this is the way to spice up a steak!

Preparation Time: 10 minutes
Cook Time: 10 to 15 minutes

¾ cup onion, diced	½ cup (2 ounces) Monterey Jack cheese, shredded
1 (4½-ounce) can chopped green chiles, minced	½ cup Italian-seasoned bread crumbs
2 cloves garlic, minced	6 (4-ounce) beef tenderloin steaks, 1½-inches thick
1 tablespoon vegetable oil	

◎ Sauté onion, green chiles and garlic in hot vegetable oil in a large nonstick skillet until tender; remove from heat and stir in Monterey Jack cheese and Italian-seasoned bread crumbs.

◎ Cut a pocket into each beef tenderloin steak; spoon mixture into steak pockets. Secure with wooden picks.

◎ Grill, covered with lid, over medium-high heat (350 to 400 degrees) 10 to 15 minutes or until desired degree of doneness.

Yield: 6 servings

Grilled New York Strips with Blue Cheese Walnut Topping

You don't have to be a blue cheese lover to enjoy this!

Preparation Time: 10 minutes
Cook Time: 20 to 25 minutes

¼	cup walnut pieces, toasted	⅓	cup red wine
2	tablespoons butter	½	cup blue cheese, crumbled
3	green onions, finely chopped	4	tablespoons half-and-half
1	clove garlic, minced or pressed	4	New York strip steaks Seasoned salt, to taste

- ◎ Place walnut pieces on a cookie sheet and slightly toast under the broiler 2 to 4 minutes. Watch carefully so as not to burn. Set aside.
- ◎ Melt butter in a pan and add green onions; sauté until tender. Add garlic and sauté 1 minute longer.
- ◎ Add red wine and cook until reduced by ½, about 4 minutes.
- ◎ Add blue cheese, walnuts and half-and-half. Turn off heat to avoid scorching. Stir constantly while blue cheese melts.
- ◎ Season New York strip steaks with seasoned salt.
- ◎ Grill or broil until desired degree of doneness.
- ◎ Pour blue cheese sauce over cooked steaks and serve.

Yield: 4 servings

Prepared to Your Liking

There are several ways to tell when a steak is done. One way is to compare pressure points on your hand to the firmness of the cooked meat. Turn your palm up, spreading fingers as far apart as possible. Press the center of your palm—that's what a medium to well-done steak should feel like. Below your index finger feels like a medium steak; below your thumb is medium-rare and beneath your little finger is rare. If you are uncomfortable with the hand method, cut into the steak for a quick look at the interior:

- Medium-rare (cooked 5 to 6 minutes on each side) has a very pink center and is slightly brown toward the exterior.
- Medium (cooked 7 to 8 minutes on each side) has a light-pink center and the outer portion is brown.
- Well-done (cooked 9 to 10 minutes on each side) has a uniformly brown look throughout.

Hot Coals

When your recipe indicates grill temperature, don't just guess. Follow these simple guidelines:

• The grill is hot if you can hold your hand close to it for 2 to 3 seconds. The coals will be covered slightly with gray ash and may have low flames around them.

• The grill is medium temperature when you can hold your hand at grill level for 4 to 5 seconds. The coals should be well covered with ash and may glow red through the ash coating.

• The grill temperature is low when you can hold your hand at grill level for 6 to 7 seconds. The coals will be covered with a thick layer of ash.

Italian Rib-Eyes

Delicioso!

Preparation Time: 15 minutes
Cook Time: 16 minutes

1	green bell pepper, chopped
1	bunch green onions, cut into 1-inch pieces
3	cloves garlic, minced
2	cups fresh mushrooms, sliced
2	tablespoons dried Italian seasoning
¼	teaspoon salt

¼	teaspoon pepper
¼	cup olive oil
2	tablespoons butter or margarine
4	(1¼-inch thick) rib-eye steaks
	Seasoned salt, to taste
1	large tomato, chopped

◎ Sauté green bell pepper, green onions, garlic, mushrooms, Italian seasoning, salt and pepper in hot olive oil and butter in a large skillet until tender. Cover and keep warm.

◎ Season rib-eye steaks with seasoned salt, to taste.

◎ Grill rib-eye steaks, covered with grill lid, over high heat (400 to 500 degrees) about 16 minutes for medium or to desired degree of doneness, turning occasionally.

◎ Stir tomato into vegetable mixture; spoon over steaks.

Yield: 4 servings

Grilled Marinated Flank Steak

Delicious and perfect as a marinade for ribs also.

Preparation Time: 5 minutes
Chill Time: 3 hours
Cook Time: 15 minutes

¼ **cup vegetable oil**	¼ **cup whole peppercorns**
¼ **cup balsamic vinegar**	2 **cloves garlic**
2 **tablespoons barbecue sauce**	1 **tablespoon lemon juice**
1 **tablespoon Worcestershire sauce**	1 **(1½-pound) flank steak**

◎ Process vegetable oil, balsamic vinegar, barbecue sauce, Worcestershire sauce, peppercorns, garlic and lemon juice in a blender until smooth, stopping once to scrape down sides.

◎ Place flank steak in a shallow dish or heavy-duty zip-top plastic bag; pour mixture over steak. Cover or seal, and chill 3 hours.

◎ Remove flank steak from marinade, discarding marinade. Grill, covered with grill lid, over medium-high heat (350 to 400 degrees) 7 minutes on each side or to desired degree of doneness.

Yield: 6 servings

Safely Marinating

Marinate meats in the refrigerator, not at room temperature. Be careful with plates and utensils that have been touched by raw meat. Wash them before using them again with cooked food to keep bacteria from spreading. And finally, if you want to make a sauce for cooked food using the marinade, reserve a separate portion for dipping. Do not reuse any of the marinade used on the raw meat.

Making Meatloaf ✳

When preparing meatloaf, allow the meat to come to room temperature as it will combine more readily with the other ingredients; meat tends to become tough when it is overhandled. Rub meatloaf with cold water before putting it in the oven to prevent cracking.

Meatloaf with Sun-Dried Tomatoes and Herbs

This is guaranteed to please meatloaf lovers and haters alike.

Preparation Time: 15 minutes
Cook Time: 1 hour

1¼ cups sun-dried tomato halves; divided	2 cloves garlic, minced
1 medium onion, finely chopped	3 teaspoons dried basil; divided
1 medium green bell pepper, finely chopped	1 teaspoon dried oregano
1 tablespoon olive oil	1 teaspoon dried thyme
1 slice white bread	1¼ teaspoons salt; divided
2 tablespoons milk	1¼ teaspoons freshly ground pepper; divided
2 large eggs, lightly beaten	1 tablespoon flour
1 pound lean ground beef	1 cup half-and-half
1½ cups provolone cheese, shredded	1 tablespoon green onions, finely chopped
	Dried tomato halves (optional)

◎ Place tomato halves in a heavy saucepan; add water to cover. Bring to a boil over medium heat; reduce heat, and simmer 5 minutes. Drain and set aside.

◎ Cook onion and green bell pepper in olive oil in a skillet over medium heat, stirring constantly, until tender. Set aside.

◎ Tear bread into small pieces, and place in a large bowl; drizzle with milk. Add onion mixture, 1 cup reserved tomato halves, eggs, ground beef, provolone cheese, garlic, 2 teaspoons basil, oregano, thyme, 1 teaspoon salt and 1 teaspoon pepper; mix well.

◎ Press into a lightly greased 9 x 5 x 3-inch loaf pan. Bake at 350 degrees for 1 hour.

◎ Remove from oven, and invert onto a serving platter, reserving ¼ cup drippings for gravy mixture. Keep meatloaf warm.

◎ Heat drippings in a nonstick skillet over medium heat. Add flour and cook, stirring constantly, 1 minute. Gradually stir in half-and-half; cook, stirring often, until thickened and bubbly.

◎ Add remaining ¼ cup tomato halves, green onions, 1 teaspoon basil, ¼ teaspoon salt and ¼ teaspoon pepper; heat thoroughly. Serve over meatloaf. Garnish, if desired with dried tomato halves.

Double gravy recipe and serve over mashed potatoes.

Yield: 6 servings

Herb Crusted Pork Chops

✳ An easy and quick dinner full of flavor.

Preparation Time: 10 minutes
Cook Time: 40 minutes

6	(½ to 1-inch thick) pork chops
2	tablespoons Dijon mustard
¼	cup cornflakes cereal, crushed

2	tablespoons Parmesan cheese, grated
¼	teaspoon rosemary (crushed, fresh, or dried)
¼	teaspoon garlic salt

◎ Brush pork chops on both sides with Dijon mustard.

◎ Combine cornflakes cereal, Parmesan cheese, rosemary and garlic salt.

◎ Coat both sides of pork chops with cereal mixture.

◎ Place in shallow baking dish.

◎ Bake in preheated 350 degree oven for 40 minutes.

Yield: 4 to 6 servings

This recipe can be found in
Spanish in the **Otra Vez...En Español** section.

No-Sew Tablecloth

Create a tablecloth by overlapping sections of fabric yardage. Join the two pieces by tying them into swags with colorful ribbon. There is no sewing involved, and you can reuse the fabric for your next party.

Sauce is outstanding made often

Table Decorations and Simple Centerpieces

• Float candles and flowers in a glass bowl. Place the bowl on a mirror and surround with small votive candles.

• A centerpiece does not have to be one arrangement. Place miniature bud vases, small clay pots or vintage silver cups containing a beautiful flower at each place setting.

• Sheer organza ribbons accent candlesticks and flower arrangements and bring magic to your table.

• Fruits, vegetables and herbs make beautiful table arrangements. Miniature pumpkins, artichokes or apples can be hollowed out to make great votive candleholders. Cut a hole and hollow out a watermelon, cantaloupe, pineapple or honeydew and fill with flowers.

• Place candles of all different sizes on a heat resistant tray to make a dramatic centerpiece.

• Use flowers from your garden and place in coffee cans for a coffee or tea party.

• Fill a clear glass vase with fruit such as lemons, oranges, cranberries and kumquats. Then arrange large-stemmed flowers among the fruit.

• Load a basket with summer vegetables and fruit to create a fresh centerpiece for an outdoor barbecue.

Boneless Pork Chops with Ancho Cream Sauce

This creamy sauce is delightfully spicy and wonderful with the chops.

Preparation Time: 15 minutes
Cook Time: 20 to 25 minutes

4	(½-inch thick) boneless pork loin chops
¼	teaspoon salt
¼	teaspoon pepper
4	slices bacon
	Vegetable cooking spray
¼	cup Ancho Base
¾	cup whipping cream

◎ Sprinkle pork loin chops with salt and pepper. Wrap 1 slice bacon around each pork loin chop; secure with wooden picks, if desired.

◎ Coat food rack with vegetable cooking spray; place on grill over medium coals (300 to 350 degrees). Place pork loin chops on rack, and cook, covered with grill lid, 8 minutes on each side or until done.

◎ Combine Ancho Base and whipping cream in a saucepan, stirring with a wire whisk until smooth. Bring to a boil over medium heat, whisking constantly. Reduce heat, and simmer, whisking constantly, 5 minutes or until thickened.

◎ Spoon Ancho Cream Sauce onto plates; top each with a pork chop. Serve immediately.

Yield: 4 servings

ANCHO BASE

3	dried ancho chile peppers
4	ounces dried tomatoes
3	tablespoons garlic, minced
½	cup onion, chopped
4	beef-flavored bouillon cubes
1	tablespoon dried oregano
1	tablespoon brown sugar
2	tablespoons Worcestershire sauce
¼	cup tomato paste
1½	cups water

◎ Combine ancho chile peppers, dried tomatoes, garlic, onion, beef-flavored bouillon, oregano, brown sugar, Worcestershire sauce, tomato paste and water in a saucepan. Bring to a boil over medium heat; reduce heat, and simmer, stirring occasionally, 10 minutes. Cool about 15 minutes.

◎ Position knife blade in food processor bowl; add mixture. Process until smooth, stopping often to scrape down sides. Refrigerate up to 1 week or freeze up to 3 months.

Yield: 2¼ cups

Pork Medallions in Mustard Sauce

This dish will tantalize your taste buds!

Preparation Time: 15 minutes
Chill Time: 8 hours
Cook Time: 25 minutes

3 **tablespoons vegetable oil**	2 **(¾-pound) pork tenderloins**
1 **tablespoon coarse-grained mustard**	¼ **cup dry white wine**
½ **teaspoon salt**	**Mustard Sauce**
½ **teaspoon pepper**	**Fresh basil (optional)**

◎ Combine vegetable oil, coarse-grained mustard, salt and pepper, stirring well. Rub mixture over pork tenderloins; place in a heavy-duty zip-top plastic bag; refrigerate 8 hours.

◎ Place pork tenderloins on rack in a shallow roasting pan. Insert meat thermometer into thickest part of meat. Bake at 375 degrees for 25 minutes or until meat thermometer registers 160 degrees, basting every 10 minutes with white wine.

◎ Slice pork tenderloins into ¾-inch slices, and arrange 4 slices on each dinner plate. Spoon Mustard Sauce around pork on each plate. Garnish with fresh basil, if desired.

Yield: 4 servings

MUSTARD SAUCE

1¾ **cups whipping cream**	¼ **teaspoon salt**
¼ **cup coarse-grained mustard**	¼ **teaspoon white pepper**

◎ Heat whipping cream in a heavy saucepan until reduced to 1¼ cups (about 15 minutes). Do not boil. Stir in coarse-grained mustard, salt and white pepper and heat 1 minute.

Yield: 1¼ cups

Good Gravy ✳

Place flour in a small baking pan and bake at 350 degrees until medium brown, about 5 minutes. This eliminates a floury taste when preparing gravies or sauces. If gravy is too greasy, a bit of baking soda can be added without affecting the taste.

Apricot Grilled Lamb Kabobs

This savory marinade will have everyone "kabobbing" for more!

Prep Time: 5 minutes
Chill Time: 1 hour
Cook Time: 10 minutes

½ cup teriyaki baste-and-glaze sauce	2 teaspoons garlic, minced
3 tablespoons apricot jam	1 pound boneless lean lamb, cut into 1-inch pieces
1 tablespoon rice wine vinegar	1 large purple onion, quartered
1 teaspoon dried rosemary, crushed	Vegetable cooking spray

◎ Bring teriyaki baste-and-glaze sauce, apricot jam, rice wine vinegar, rosemary and garlic to a boil in small saucepan, stirring constantly. Cool completely. Reserve ⅓ cup mixture.

◎ Place lamb and purple onion in a shallow dish or large heavy-duty zip-top plastic bag; pour remaining teriyaki mixture over lamb. Cover or seal, and chill 1 hour, turning occasionally.

◎ Remove lamb and purple onion from marinade, discarding marinade.

◎ Alternate lamb and purple onion on 4 (8-inch) skewers.

◎ Coat food rack with vegetable cooking spray; place on grill over medium-high heat (350 to 400 degrees). Place kabobs on rack, and grill, covered with grill lid, 8 minutes or to desired degree of doneness, turning and basting occasionally with reserved teriyaki mixture.

Yield: 4 servings

Mint-Crusted Rack of Lamb

Utterly elegant!

Preparation Time: 10 minutes
Cook Time: 40 minutes

2	cups fresh mint leaves
8	cloves garlic, chopped
¼	cup olive oil
2	tablespoons coarse-grain salt

2	teaspoons freshly ground pepper
3	(8-rib) lamb rib roasts (2 to 2½ pounds each), trimmed

◎ Process mint leaves, garlic, olive oil, salt and pepper in a blender until smooth; spread evenly over lamb rib roasts. Place, fat side up, on a rack in a large roasting pan.

◎ Bake at 400 degrees for 10 minutes. Reduce heat to 375 degrees, and bake 30 minutes or until a meat thermometer inserted into thickest portion registers 145 degrees.

◎ Remove from oven; cover loosely with aluminum foil, and let stand 5 minutes or until thermometer reaches 150 degrees (medium-rare).

Yield: 8 servings

This recipe can be found in
Spanish in the **Otra Vez...En Español** section.

Tomato Rose

Using a sharp paring knife, cut a thin slice from bottom of tomato; discard. Beginning at top, peel a continuous paper-thin strip (about ¾ inch wide for regular tomatoes, and about ¼ inch wide for cherry tomatoes) from entire tomato. Beginning with first portion cut, shape the strip like a rose. With flesh side inward, coil the strip tightly at first to form the center of the rose, gradually letting it become looser to form the outer petals.

Beautiful Roses

Nothing is more spectacular than vases filled with every pastel rose—pink, ecru, pale yellow, cream and white. Buy roses at least two days ahead so that they will be in full bloom by the day of your party. When the roses start to fade, hang them upside down by their stems and let them dry. Dried roses keep their color and charm and make beautiful arrangements.

Grilled Veal Chops
with Mustard-Herb Butter

For an elegant night out. . . on the patio!

Preparation Time: 10 minutes
Cook Time: 10 to 12 minutes

4 tablespoons unsalted butter, softened	1 tablespoon chervil
1½ tablespoons Dijon mustard	1 tablespoon chives, chopped
1 shallot, minced	Freshly ground pepper, to taste
1 tablespoon parsley, chopped	2 veal chops

◎ In a mixing bowl or food processor, combine the butter, Dijon mustard, shallot, parsley, chervil, chives and pepper. Mix well and set aside (at room temperature).

◎ Cook veal chops on a grill over hot coals, turning them every 2 minutes and brushing with mustard herb butter.

◎ Check for doneness after 10 to 12 minutes (the veal should be light pink).

Yield: 2 servings

This recipe can be found in
Spanish in the **Otra Vez...En Español** section.

---

* Also good with thick cut boneless pork chops

Glazed Teriyaki Salmon

Grilled, broiled or baked - you can't go wrong with this recipe!

Preparation Time: 15 minutes
Chill Time: 30 minutes
Cook Time: 18 minutes

⅓	cup orange juice		1	teaspoon dry mustard
⅓	cup soy sauce		1	teaspoon lemon juice
¼	cup dry white wine			Pinch of sugar
2	tablespoons vegetable oil		1	clove garlic, minced
1	tablespoon fresh ginger, grated		½	teaspoon freshly ground pepper
			4	(4 to 6-ounce) salmon fillets

◎ Combine orange juice, soy sauce, white wine, vegetable oil, ginger, dry mustard, lemon juice, sugar, garlic and pepper in a shallow dish or large zip-top plastic bag. Add salmon fillets. Cover or seal and chill 30 minutes, turning once.

◎ Preheat oven to 450 degrees.

◎ Remove fillets from marinade, reserving marinade. Place fillets in a 13 x 9-inch pan.

◎ Bake for 10 minutes or until fish flakes easily with a fork. Remove from oven. Keep warm.

◎ Bring reserved marinade to a boil in a small heavy saucepan. Cook, stirring often for 6 to 8 minutes or until reduced by half. Pour over fillets.

Yield: 4 servings

Cannin' the Salmon

There are five different kinds of canned salmon on the market. Chinook, or king salmon, has a soft rich flesh that varies in color from deep red to white. It is often labeled as "Royal Chinook" and is a good choice for salads. Sockeye, or "red," salmon is firm-fleshed and deep orange in color; it works well in a variety of dishes. Coho, or silver salmon, is pink-fleshed and fine-textured; it is fine for cooking, but should not be used in salads. Pink salmon is very fine-textured and light pink in color; good for sandwiches. Chum salmon is very light-colored, sometimes almost gray and is inferior to other canned salmons.

Buying Fish

When figuring out how much fish to buy, keep in mind that the richer the choice, the smaller the quantity. It is also important to consider what else is being served with the fish and the richness of the sauce or garnish. Use the "Fish Portions" chart on the following page as your guide.

Sesame-Crusted Salmon with Ginger Vinaigrette

This versatile Ginger Vinaigrette makes a delicious salad dressing.

Preparation Time: 30 minutes
Cook Time: 12 minutes

1 large English cucumber, peeled and coarsely chopped	1 teaspoon hot sauce
½ cup plus 2 tablespoons rice wine vinegar; divided	½ teaspoon ground coriander
⅛ teaspoon salt	½ teaspoon dark sesame oil
2 tablespoons sugar	4 (4-ounce) salmon fillets
¼ cup water	1 tablespoon sesame seeds, toasted
¼ cup low-sodium soy sauce	1 large English cucumber, thinly sliced
1 tablespoon honey	Ginger Vinaigrette
	Fresh mint sprigs (optional)

◎ Preheat oven to 450 degrees.

◎ Position knife blade in food processor bowl; add cucumber. Process until smooth, stopping once to scrape down sides.

◎ Line a large wire-mesh strainer with cheesecloth or a coffee filter. Pour cucumber mixture through strainer, discarding pulp.

◎ Stir ½ cup rice wine vinegar and salt into cucumber liquid. Set aside.

◎ Combine sugar and water in a small saucepan. Cook over medium heat, stirring often, until mixture boils. Remove from heat, and stir into cucumber liquid mixture. Set aside.

◎ Combine soy sauce, 2 tablespoons rice wine vinegar, honey, hot sauce, coriander and dark sesame oil. Brush mixture over salmon fillets. Place salmon fillets in a lightly greased 13 x 9-inch baking pan. Sprinkle with sesame seeds.

◎ Bake for 10 to 12 minutes or until fish flakes when tested with a fork.

◎ Arrange salmon fillets and sliced cucumber evenly in 4 pasta bowls. Spoon cucumber liquid mixture evenly into each dish. Drizzle with a small amount of Ginger Vinaigrette. Garnish with fresh mint sprigs, if desired.

Yield: 4 servings

Sesame-Crusted Salmon continued

GINGER VINAIGRETTE

1	(1½-inch long) piece of fresh ginger, peeled	1	tablespoon honey
1	clove garlic	⅛	teaspoon dried crushed red pepper
2	tablespoons rice wine vinegar	¼	cup peanut oil
1	tablespoon low-sodium soy sauce	½	teaspoon dark sesame oil

◎ Position knife blade in food processor bowl. Add ginger and garlic. Process until smooth, stopping once to scrape down sides.

◎ Add rice wine vinegar, soy sauce, honey and crushed red pepper. Process for 10 seconds. Slowly pour peanut oil and dark sesame oil through food chute with processor's motor running, blending just until smooth.

Yield: 1 cup

Fish Portions

Fish:	Drawn
What's That?:	Whole fish, gutted and scaled; gills removed
Per Serving:	¾ to 1 pound
Fish:	Dressed
What's That?:	Whole fish, gutted and scaled; gills, fins and head removed
Per Serving:	¾ pound
Fish:	Split
What's That?:	Dressed round fish, split in half along the belly; bones and skin intact
Per Serving:	½ to ¾ pound
Fish:	Butterflied
What's That?:	Small round fish that have been dressed, then boned to lie flat
Per Serving:	⅓ to ½ pound
Fish:	Steaks with bone
What's That?:	Slices cut crosswise (¾ to 1¾ inches thick) and include a section of the backbone and skin
Per Serving:	½ pound
Fish:	Boned fillets and steaks
What's That?:	Sides of round or flat fish that are cut off the backbone; may or may not be skinned
Per Serving:	⅓ to ½ pound
Fish:	Medallions
What's That?:	Made from the fillet of a large fish that has been cut at an angle into regular slices of an even thickness
Per Serving:	⅓ to ½ pound
Fish:	Chunks
What's That?:	Trimming cut from large fish used to make a quick meal of chowder or kabobs
Per Serving:	⅓ to ½ pound

Under the Sea Pool Party

For invitations, cut fish shapes from clear transparency sheets; decorate with paint pens. Wrap in blue tissue paper and put in a Mylar bubble packing envelope and hand deliver. Decorations can include seashells, fish posters and fish netting. Hang iridescent Christmas ornaments from the ceiling or trees with fishing line to make ocean "bubbles." Use blue fabric for the tablecloths and tropical fabric for the napkins. Write names on snorkels and goggles as placecards. Put goldfish in big vases or fishbowls for centerpieces. Play a tape of ocean sounds. Draw fish on cards, making two of each kind. Shuffle and give each guest a card and ask them to find the person who has the mate to their card. Put the goldfish in plastic bags and give one to each guest as a party favor before they leave.

Lemon Orange Roughy

A simple and flavorful dish. Try other types of fresh fish fillets with this recipe.

Preparation Time: 5 minutes
Cook Time: 10 minutes

4	(4-ounce) orange roughy fillets
	Vegetable cooking spray
3	tablespoons lemon juice
1	tablespoon Dijon mustard

1	tablespoon margarine, melted
¼	teaspoon coarsely ground black pepper
	Pepper (optional)
	Lemon slices (optional)

◎ Place fillets on rack of broiler pan coated with vegetable cooking spray. Combine lemon juice, Dijon mustard, margarine and pepper. Stir well. Brush half of lemon juice mixture over fillets.

◎ Broil fillets 5½-inches from heat 8 to 10 minutes or until fish flakes easily when tested with a fork.

◎ Drizzle remaining lemon juice mixture over fillets. Transfer to a serving platter. If desired, sprinkle with pepper and garnish with lemon slices.

Yield: 4 servings

Grilled Tuna with Poblano Salsa

A great dish for spicing up your evening!

Preparation Time: 25 minutes
Chill Time: 30 minutes
Cook Time: 20 minutes

2 tablespoons lime juice	4 (4-ounce) tuna steaks
1 teaspoon olive oil	Vegetable cooking spray
	Poblano Salsa

◎ Combine lime juice and olive oil; brush on tuna steaks. Coat grill rack with vegetable cooking spray. Place on grill over medium-hot coals. Place tuna steaks on rack and cook, covered, 5 minutes on each side or until done. Serve with Poblano Salsa.

Yield: 4 servings

POBLANO SALSA

4 medium-size poblano chiles	¼ cup onion, diced
⅓ cup fresh or canned tomatillos, chopped	2 tablespoons fresh cilantro, chopped
1 small serrano or jalapeño chile, seeded and diced	2 tablespoons lime juice
½ cup tomato, chopped	½ teaspoon ground cumin
	½ teaspoon salt

◎ Place poblano chiles on a baking sheet. Broil 6 inches from heat, turning often with tongs until peppers are blistered on all sides. Immediately place in a plastic storage bag. Fasten securely, and let steam 10 to 15 minutes. Remove peel of each chile. Seed and dice chiles.

◎ Combine poblano chiles, tomatillos, serrano chile, tomato, onion, cilantro, lime juice, cumin and salt. Cover and chill for 30 minutes.

Pablano chiles can be substituted with 2 (4-ounce) cans chopped green chiles.

Yield: 2 cups

Flower Power

Edible flowers can be used to decorate a cake, dress up an entrée, or add color. Some of the more popular edible flowers include carnations, marigolds, Johnny-jump-ups, baby roses, nasturtiums, pansies, snapdragons, daisies, peonies, begonias, chrysanthemums, geraniums, lilies and violets. Edible flowers are generally not sold at a florist or nursery because they are sprayed with pesticides, but they can be located among the herbs at some grocery stores or in your very own backyard.

Pecan Catfish

Steamed green beans and tomato slices complete this southern dish.

Preparation Time: 16 minutes

4 catfish fillets (about 1½ pounds)	½ cup whipping cream
1 teaspoon salt; divided	2 tablespoons lemon juice
1 teaspoon pepper; divided	1-2 tablespoons parsley, chopped
1 cup pecans, finely chopped; divided	Lemon wedges (optional)
½ cup cornmeal	Fresh parsley, chopped (optional)
½ cup butter or margarine; divided	Pecans, chopped (optional)

◎ Sprinkle catfish fillets with ½ teaspoon salt and ½ teaspoon pepper.

◎ Stir together ½ cup pecans and cornmeal; dredge fish in mixture.

◎ Melt ¼ cup butter in nonstick 3-quart sauté pan over medium-high heat. Add catfish and cook 7 minutes on each side or until fish flakes easily with a fork. Remove from skillet.

◎ Melt remaining ¼ cup butter in pan over medium-high heat. Add remaining ½ cup pecans. Cook, stirring constantly, 1 minute. Add whipping cream, lemon juice, remaining ½ teaspoon salt and remaining ½ teaspoon pepper. Cook 1 minute. Remove from heat. Stir in parsley. Serve over catfish fillets. Garnish with lemon wedges, parsley and pecans if desired.

Yield: 4 servings

Grilled Swordfish
with Avocado-Lime Sauce

This combination of grilled fish and zesty sauce will make your tastebuds soar!

Preparation Time: 15 minutes
Cook Time: 10 minutes

1 lime	⅓ cup fresh cilantro, loosely packed
1 large avocado	½ jalapeño pepper, unseeded
¾ cup water	4 cloves garlic
½ teaspoon sea salt; divided	4 (1-inch thick) swordfish steaks (about 1½ pounds)
½ teaspoon freshly ground pepper; divided	2 teaspoons olive oil
½ teaspoon ground cumin	

◎ Peel lime with a vegetable peeler, reserving green rind only. Remove and discard pith. Cut lime into fourths, and place into blender; add rind. Cut avocado in half; scoop pulp into blender. Add water, ¼ teaspoon salt, ¼ teaspoon pepper, cumin, cilantro, jalapeño pepper and garlic. Process until sauce is smooth, stopping once to scrape down sides.

◎ Brush swordfish steaks with olive oil, and sprinkle with remaining ¼ teaspoon salt and ¼ teaspoon pepper.

◎ Grill, covered with grill lid, over high heat (400 to 500 degrees) for 5 minutes on each side or until fish flakes easily with a fork. Serve immediately with sauce.

Yield: 4 servings

This recipe can be found in Spanish in the **Otra Vez...En Español** section.

Avocados

Avocados are available in several varieties and should feel slightly soft, but not mushy. They freeze well when peeled and mashed. When ready to use, thaw in the refrigerator.

Peel Shrimp Quick

Use kitchen shears to peel and devein shrimp. Quickly snip down the back of the shrimp and expose the vein. Lift the dark vein from the slit and discard it; then remove the shell, leaving the tail intact, if desired.

Shrimp Scampi with Butter Sauce

This is an easy, decadent and delicious dish.

Preparation Time: 30 minutes
Cook Time: 50 minutes

Always Good

2 tablespoons butter	Salt and pepper, to taste
⅓ cup olive oil	3 pounds shrimp, peeled and deveined
1 tablespoon garlic, minced	Butter Sauce
½ teaspoon crushed red pepper	1½ pounds fettuccini or linguine, cooked according to directions
1 teaspoon parsley, chopped	
1 teaspoon basil, chopped	
¼ cup white wine	

◎ Melt butter in large skillet; add olive oil.

◎ Combine garlic, crushed red pepper, parsley, basil, white wine, salt and pepper. Stir into melted butter mixture. Add shrimp and cook until pink.

◎ Pour 1 cup Butter Sauce on scampi. Toss with fettuccini or linguine. Add extra Butter Sauce if needed.

Yield: 6 servings

BUTTER SAUCE

1 cup butter	⅓ cup white wine
1 tablespoon garlic, minced	½ lemon, juiced
1 (8-ounce) jar clam juice	1 teaspoon basil, chopped
¼ cup flour	Salt and pepper, to taste
1 tablespoon parsley, chopped	½ cup half-and-half

◎ Melt butter with garlic in skillet.

◎ Mix clam juice, flour and parsley. Pour into melted butter mixture. Stir until smooth.

◎ Stir in white wine, lemon juice, basil, salt and pepper.

◎ Gradually add half-and-half and stir until thickened. Simmer 30 to 40 minutes.

Spinach Tortellini Casserole

Served as an entrée or side dish, this flavorful pasta is a real winner!

Preparation Time: 15 minutes
Cook Time: 30 minutes

2   (10-ounce) packages cheese
    tortellini, cooked according
    to directions
¾   cup onion, chopped
2   tablespoons oil
1   (10-ounce) package frozen
    chopped spinach, thawed
    and drained *OR FResh SpiNAch*

Salt, pepper, garlic powder
    and onion powder, to taste
1   pint heavy whipping cream
2   cups Parmesan cheese;
    divided

◎ Place cooked cheese tortellini in a greased 3-quart casserole dish.

◎ Sauté onion in oil. Add spinach, salt, pepper, garlic powder, onion powder, whipping cream and 1 cup Parmesan cheese. Pour over tortellini.

◎ Sprinkle remaining cup of Parmesan cheese on top of tortellini mixture. Bake at 350 degrees for 30 minutes.

Yield: 6 to 8 servings

Reheating Pasta

One of the great things about microwaves is that pasta can be successfully reheated without drying it out! Microwave pasta (with or without the sauce) in a covered dish on high power for 1 minute. If the pasta is still cold, stir it and continue to microwave, checking it at 15-second intervals. Pasta can also be wrapped in aluminum foil and reheated in the oven at 350 degrees for 15 to 20 minutes.

It's in the Sauce

The shape of the pasta should dictate what type of sauce to be used. The rule is simple: the longer the pasta, the thinner the sauce; the shorter the pasta, the thicker the sauce. Pastina and orzo are the exceptions and are best served in a light broth.

Cajun Fettuccine Alfredo

This is a kicked up version of an old favorite.
Serve it with grilled chicken or fish for a heartier meal.

Preparation Time: 15 minutes
Cook Time: 20 minutes

½ cup chicken broth	¼ cup pimientos, chopped
2 teaspoons Cajun seasoning	1½ cups heavy cream
½ cup green onions (green part only), chopped	1 cup Parmesan cheese, grated; divided
1 teaspoon garlic, minced	1 pound dry fettuccine noodles
½ cup mushrooms, sliced	Crushed red pepper, to taste

◎ In a large skillet, combine chicken broth, Cajun seasoning, green onions, garlic, mushrooms and pimientos over high heat until boiling. Add heavy cream and ½ cup Parmesan cheese; continue cooking on high heat until mixture is reduced by ½. Lower heat.

◎ Cook fettuccine noodles; drain. Toss with cream mixture. Top with remaining ½ cup Parmesan cheese and crushed red pepper, to taste.

Yield: 4 servings

Chicken Tequila Fettuccine

A tasty pasta dish with Southwestern flair.

Preparation Time: 20 minutes
Cook Time: 40 minutes

1	pound dry spinach fettuccine (or 2 pounds fresh)		3	tablespoons jalapeño jelly, melted
1	cup fresh cilantro, chopped; divided		1¼	pounds chicken breast, diced in ¾-inch pieces
4	tablespoons garlic, minced		¼	medium red onion, thinly sliced
4	tablespoons jalapeño, minced		½	medium red bell pepper, thinly sliced
6	tablespoons unsalted butter; divided		½	medium yellow bell pepper, thinly sliced
1	cup chicken stock		½	medium green bell pepper, thinly sliced
4	tablespoons gold tequila		1½	cups heavy cream
4	tablespoons freshly squeezed lime juice			Salt and pepper, to taste
3	tablespoons soy sauce			

◎ Prepare rapidly boiling, salted water to cook spinach fettuccine; cook until al dente, 8 to 10 minutes for dry pasta, approximately 3 minutes for fresh. Pasta may be cooked slightly ahead of time, rinsed and oiled and then "flashed" (reheated) in boiling water or cooked to coincide with the finishing of the sauce.

◎ Cook ⅔ cup cilantro, garlic and jalapeño in 4 tablespoons butter over medium heat for 4 to 5 minutes. Add chicken stock, gold tequila and lime juice. Bring the mixture to a boil and cook until reduced to a paste like consistency; set aside.

◎ Mix together soy sauce and jalapeño jelly and pour over diced chicken; set aside for 5 minutes. Meanwhile cook red onion, red bell pepper, yellow bell pepper and green bell pepper, stirring occasionally, with remaining 2 tablespoons butter over medium heat. When the vegetables have wilted (become limp), add chicken and soy sauce mixture; toss and add reserved tequila paste and cream.

◎ Bring the sauce to a boil; boil gently until chicken is cooked through and sauce is thick (about 3 minutes). Add salt and pepper, to taste. When sauce is done, toss with well-drained spinach fettuccine and remaining 4 tablespoons cilantro.

◎ Serve family style or transfer to serving dishes, evenly distributing chicken and vegetables.

Yield: 4 to 6 servings

This recipe can be found in
Spanish in the **Otra Vez...En Español** section.

Counting Noodles

The usual pasta serving size is 4 ounces dried, but the cooked yield depends on the shape:

• 4 ounces uncooked spaghetti, vermicelli, capellini and linguine yield 2 cups cooked

• 4 ounces uncooked elbow macaroni, conchiglie (seashells), rotini, ruote (cartwheels), mostaccioli, ziti or penne yield 2½ cups cooked

• 4 ounces uncooked medium egg noodles or tagliatelle yields 3 cups cooked

Unusual Pastas

Conchigliette - little shells

Farfalle - butterflies or bow ties

Gemelli - twins; two short strands intertwined

Penne - straight tubes cut on the diagonal

Orecchiette - little ears or thumbprints

Radiatore - radiators or small ridged shapes

Rotelle - wheels

Semi de Melone - melon seeds

Tortellini - pasta stuffed with various fillings, folded over and shaped into a ring or hat

Ziti - long thin tubes

Creamy Rigatoni with Plum Tomatoes and Prosciutto

This pasta dish is rich and satisfying.
Add a fresh tossed salad and crunchy garlic bread to complete the meal.

Preparation Time: 10 minutes
Cook Time: 20 to 25 minutes

2 tablespoons butter	3 ounces sliced prosciutto, chopped
1 small onion, chopped	¾ cup whipping cream
2 cloves garlic, minced	1 cup Parmesan cheese, grated
1 tablespoon dried Italian seasonings, crumbled	8 ounces rigatoni, uncooked
1 (16-ounce) can Italian plum tomatoes with liquid, chopped	Salt and pepper, to taste

◎ Melt butter in heavy skillet. Add onion, garlic and Italian seasonings; sauté until onions are translucent.

◎ Add Italian plum tomatoes with liquid and prosciutto; simmer for about 10 minutes, stirring occasionally.

◎ Add whipping cream and ½ cup Parmesan cheese. Simmer until thickens slightly, about 4 minutes.

◎ Cook rigatoni in salted water. Drain and add to sauce. Stir to coat pasta. Season with salt and pepper, to taste.

◎ Serve, passing remaining ½ cup Parmesan separately.

Rigatoni can be substituted with penne or ziti.

Yield: 4 to 6 servings

TRY *Sounds good*

Shrimp and Feta Pasta

Want to create an easy and elegant dish for a dinner party? This is it!

Preparation Time: 30 minutes
Cook Time: 30 minutes

8	ounces vermicelli
1	pound medium shrimp, peeled and deveined
	Pinch of crushed red pepper flakes
¼	cup olive oil; divided
⅔	cup (4 ounces) feta cheese, crumbled
½	teaspoon garlic, crushed
1	(14½-ounce) can tomato wedges, with liquid
¼	cup dry white wine
¾	teaspoon dried basil
½	teaspoon dried oregano
¼	teaspoon salt
¼	teaspoon pepper
	Fresh basil (optional)

- ◎ Preheat oven to 400 degrees.
- ◎ Cook vermicelli according to the package directions. Drain, set aside, and keep warm.
- ◎ Sauté shrimp and red pepper flakes in 2 tablespoons olive oil in a large skillet 1 to 2 minutes or until shrimp are slightly pink.
- ◎ Arrange shrimp in a 10 x 6 x 2-inch baking dish; sprinkle with feta cheese, and set aside.
- ◎ Add remaining olive oil to skillet; sauté garlic over low heat. Add tomatoes with liquid; cook 1 minute. Stir in white wine, basil, oregano, salt and pepper; simmer, uncovered, 10 minutes. Spoon tomato mixture over shrimp.
- ◎ Bake, uncovered, for 10 minutes. Serve over vermicelli.
- ◎ Garnish with fresh basil, if desired.

Yield: 3 to 4 servings

Late Night Dinner for Two

When the children are small, it is sometimes very tough to have a nice evening out to celebrate a special event or just spend time together. Couple time is so special...plan a late night dinner in your own home after the kids are in bed. While one of you bathes the children, the other one puts the dinner together. Then you can enjoy some quiet time with some delicious food!

Sandy good

Chicken Lasagna Florentine

A delicious variation to a family classic.

Preparation Time: 30 minutes
Cook Time: 1 hour 15 minutes

9	lasagna noodles, uncooked
1	(10-ounce) package frozen chopped spinach, thawed and drained
2	cups cooked chicken, chopped
2	cups (8 ounces) cheddar cheese, shredded
⅓	cup onion, finely chopped
¼	teaspoon ground nutmeg
1	tablespoon cornstarch
½	teaspoon salt
¼	teaspoon pepper

1	tablespoon soy sauce
1	(10¾-ounce) can cream of mushroom soup, undiluted
1	(8-ounce) container sour cream
1	(4½-ounce) jar sliced mushrooms, drained
⅓	cup mayonnaise or salad dressing
1	cup (4 ounces) Parmesan cheese, freshly grated
	Butter-Pecan Topping

◎ Preheat oven to 350 degrees.

◎ Cook lasagna noodles according to package directions; drain and set aside.

◎ Drain spinach well, pressing between layers of paper towels.

◎ Combine in a large bowl spinach, chicken, cheddar cheese, onion, nutmeg, cornstarch, salt, pepper, soy sauce, cream of mushroom soup, sour cream, mushrooms and mayonnaise; stir well to blend.

◎ Arrange 3 lasagna noodles in a lightly greased 11 x 7 x 1½-inch baking dish. Spread ⅓ of chicken mixture over noodles. Repeat procedures with remaining noodles and chicken mixture. Sprinkle with Parmesan cheese and Butter-Pecan Topping.

◎ Bake, covered, for 55 to 60 minutes or until hot and bubbly. Let stand 15 minutes before cutting.

Yield: 8 servings

BUTTER-PECAN TOPPING

2	tablespoons butter or margarine	1	cup pecans, chopped

◎ Melt butter in a skillet over medium heat; add pecans, and cook for 3 minutes.

◎ Cool completely.

Yield: 1 cup

EASY

Spaghetti Bake

A great pasta dish your entire family will love.

Preparation Time: 15 minutes
Cook Time: 50 minutes

1	cup onion, chopped	2	teaspoons dried oregano
1	cup green *Red* bell pepper, chopped	1	pound ground beef, browned and drained
2	tablespoons butter or margarine	1	(12-ounce) package spaghetti, cooked and drained
1	(28-ounce) can chopped tomatoes, with liquid	2	cups (8 ounces) cheddar cheese, shredded
1	(4-ounce) can mushrooms, drained	1	(10¾-ounce) can condensed cream of mushroom soup, undiluted
1	(2¼-ounce) can sliced ripe olives, drained	¼	cup water
		¼	cup Parmesan cheese, grated

AND TOP W/ PARSLEY AS A ~~GAR~~ GARNISH

◎ Preheat oven to 350 degrees.

◎ In a large skillet, sauté onion and green bell pepper in butter until tender. Add tomatoes with liquid, mushrooms, olives, oregano and ground beef.

◎ Simmer, uncovered, for 10 minutes.

◎ Place half of the cooked spaghetti in a greased 13 x 9 x 2-inch baking dish.

◎ Top with half of the beef mixture. Sprinkle with 1 cup cheddar cheese. Repeat layers. Mix condensed cream of mushroom soup and water until smooth; pour over casserole.

◎ Sprinkle with Parmesan cheese. Bake, uncovered, for 30 to 35 minutes or until heated through. *garnish w/ parsley & serve*

Yield: 12 servings

Perfect Pasta

When cooking pasta, always start with at least one gallon of water for every pound of pasta. The water must be boiling rapidly during cooking; therefore, cook no more than two pounds of pasta at a time. If the water stops boiling, cover the pot until the boil returns. Stir as you add the pasta and continue to do so occasionally to keep it from sticking.

Pasta should be tasted to determine when it is done. Start testing fresh pasta after 30 seconds and dried pasta after 4 minutes. Fish a strand out and bite it: it should be firm yet tender with just a tiny chalky white center. The term "al dente" is used to describe perfectly cooked pasta which means that it should feel pleasurable to the touch of your teeth—not too soft, not too hard, just right!

Seafood Manicotti

This is a seafood lover's dream come true.

Preparation Time: 30 minutes
Cook Time: 1 hour 15 minutes

1	quart whipping cream
½	teaspoon salt
¼	teaspoon ground black pepper
¼	teaspoon ground red pepper
14	manicotti shells
2	pounds large fresh shrimp, unpeeled
3	tablespoons butter or margarine
1	cup onions, chopped

1	cup green bell pepper, chopped
¼	cup celery, chopped
1	clove garlic, minced
1	pound fresh crabmeat, drained and flaked
½	cup (2 ounces) cheddar cheese, shredded
½	cup (2 ounces) Monterey Jack cheese with peppers, shredded

◎ Preheat oven to 350 degrees.

◎ Combine whipping cream, salt, pepper and red pepper in a saucepan; cook over medium-high heat 30 minutes or until thickened and reduced to 2 cups. Set aside.

◎ Cook manicotti according to package directions. Drain and set aside.

◎ Peel shrimp, and devein, if desired. Chop and set aside.

◎ Heat butter in a large pot or Dutch oven over medium-heat; add onions, green bell pepper, celery and garlic. Cook, stirring constantly, 5 minutes or until tender.

◎ Add shrimp and crabmeat, and cook, stirring constantly, 5 minutes or until shrimp turns pink.

◎ Cool 10 minutes, and drain well.

◎ Combine seafood mixture and whipping cream mixture.

◎ Fill manicotti shells, and place in 2 lightly greased 11 x 7 x 1½-inch baking dishes. Sprinkle with cheddar cheese and Monterey Jack cheese with peppers, and cover with foil.

◎ Bake for 15 minutes.

◎ Uncover and bake 10 additional minutes. Serve immediately.

Yield: 6 to 8 servings

Shrimp Enchiladas in Tomatillo Sauce

You have to give this a try...indescribable!

Preparation Time: 20 minutes
Cook Time: 50 minutes

1	pound large fresh shrimp, unpeeled
1	large onion, finely chopped
2	teaspoons olive oil
1	tablespoon flour
1½	cups chicken broth
1	(12-ounce) can tomatillo sauce
1	teaspoon ground cumin
½	teaspoon dried oregano
8	corn tortillas
1½	cups (6 ounces) Monterey Jack cheese, shredded
½	cup sour cream

◎ Preheat oven to 350 degrees.

◎ Peel shrimp, and devein, if desired. Set shrimp aside.

◎ Cook onion in olive oil in a large nonstick skillet over medium-high heat, stirring constantly, until tender. Add flour, stirring until smooth; cook 1 minute.

◎ Stir in chicken broth, tomatillo sauce, cumin and oregano; cook 15 minutes or until thickened.

◎ Add shrimp; cook 5 minutes or until shrimp turn pink. Remove from heat, and cool slightly.

◎ Dip corn tortillas in shrimp mixture; place on a flat surface. Place 3 or 4 shrimp in center of each corn tortilla, using a slotted spoon; sprinkle each with about 1 tablespoon Monterey Jack cheese, and roll tightly.

◎ Place tortillas, seam side down, in a lightly greased 11 x 7 x 1½-inch baking dish. Pour remaining shrimp mixture over top, and sprinkle with remaining Monterey Jack cheese.

◎ Bake, covered, for 15 minutes. Uncover and bake 10 minutes or until cheese melts. Serve with sour cream.

Green chile sauce makes a spicy substitution for the tomatillo sauce used in this recipe.

Yield: 4 servings

This recipe can be found in Spanish in the **Otra Vez...En Español** section.

Time for Tomatoes

• Globe or slicing tomatoes are the familiar everyday tomatoes. They are good cooked, but best sliced and cut up for salads.

• Cherry tomatoes are bite-size tomatoes available year round. Buy cherry tomatoes in the winter when the globe tomatoes are tasteless. Cherry tomatoes come both red and yellow. The red have more flavor than the yellow.

• Plum, Italian or Roma tomatoes have thick, meaty walls, small seeds, little juice and rich flavor. They are the ideal cooking tomato. They are most often red, but can sometimes be found yellow.

• Yellow tomatoes always have a red counterpart, but are usually milder and less flavorful. Their brilliant color and uniqueness, however, make a wonderful presentation.

• Green tomatoes are immature tomatoes that have not ripened. They are firmer and more acidic than red tomatoes, but they are still good eating, particularly sliced and fried or cooked in relishes.

• Tomatillos are yellow or green tomatoes wrapped in papery husks. They are the essential tomato of Mexican and Southwestern cooking. Tomatillos are tart when eaten raw, but have a nice fresh, lemony, herbal flavor when cooked.

Garlic Smell...
Be Gone

To get the smell of garlic off your fingers after peeling or chopping it, simply rub your fingers on a stainless steel teaspoon. No one will ever know!

EASt

Tamale Pie

This is a crowd pleaser on a cold winter day.

Preparation Time: 25 minutes
Cook Time: 1 hour 30 minutes

1½ pounds ground beef	1 (8-ounce) can tomato sauce
3 cloves garlic, chopped	Salt and pepper, to taste
1 rib celery, chopped	1 cup cornmeal
1 large onion, chopped	1 teaspoon salt
1 green bell pepper, chopped	4 cups water
2 (10-ounce) cans tomatoes with chiles *Rotel*	½ pound Monterey Jack or cheddar cheese, shredded

◎ Preheat oven to 350 degrees.

◎ Brown ground beef; drain. Return meat to skillet and add garlic, celery, onion and green bell pepper. Cook vegetables and meat on medium heat until vegetables are soft, about 10 minutes.

◎ Add tomatoes with chiles and tomato sauce. Add salt and pepper, to taste.

◎ Cook until thick.

◎ Combine cornmeal, salt and water in a large pot. Cover and cook over medium heat until a thick mush forms, stirring often.

◎ Layer mush (reserving some for top layer), Monterey Jack cheese and meat mixture in a greased 2-quart casserole dish. Top with remaining mush.

◎ Bake, uncovered, for 1 hour.

Yield: 8 servings

Side Kicks

Side Kicks

Italian Artichoke Hearts

A great summer side dish!

Preparation Time: 10 minutes
Cook Time: 15 minutes

½	cup purple onion, minced	1	cup chicken broth
1	clove garlic, crushed	3	tablespoons lemon juice
1	tablespoon butter or margarine, melted	1	teaspoon dried whole oregano
2	(14-ounce) cans artichoke hearts, drained and halved	1	teaspoon salt

◎ Sauté onion and garlic in butter in a saucepan until onion is tender, but not browned.

◎ Add artichoke hearts, chicken broth, lemon juice, oregano and salt.

◎ Simmer 10 minutes or until heated, stirring gently.

Yield: 4 to 6 servings

Nothing to Choke On

Artichokes are a good source of vitamin A, vitamin C, calcium, iron and potassium. They are moderately high in protein, high in carbohydrates and low in fiber and fat. Not only are they very good for you, but they are rich in taste, as well. When flavoring artichokes, think of some of these enhancers: basil, black pepper, butter, chervil, cream, garlic, ginger, lemon, olive oil, oregano, Parmesan cheese, parsley, shallot and white wine.

Asparagus Tips

When buying asparagus, check the stalk color and tip for signs of freshness. Pick the greenest asparagus with straight, firm stalks; a duller khaki green indicates old age. The tips should be firm and tightly closed with a lavender tint.

Wrap asparagus, without cleaning first, in a plastic bag and store them in the crisper drawer of the refrigerator. Asparagus can also be stored upright by trimming the bottom ends and placing the asparagus in an inch of water in a deep, straight-sided container; cover the tops with a plastic bag.

One-half pound of asparagus per person will suffice. Next time you cook asparagus, make it special by flavoring it with some of the following: chives, lemon, nutmeg, orange, Parmesan cheese, parsley, poppy seeds, sage, sesame oil and seeds, tarragon and thyme.

Dilly Asparagus, Green Beans and Scallions

The secret to this vegetable medley is the hint of dill!

Preparation Time: 10 minutes
Cook Time: 20 to 25 minutes

1½ **pounds fresh asparagus, trimmed**	2 **tablespoons lemon juice**
2 **bunches scallions, trimmed**	2 **tablespoons dill, finely chopped**
1 **pound fresh green beans, trimmed**	**Salt and pepper to taste**
6 **tablespoons butter, melted**	8 **thin rings red or yellow bell pepper (optional)**

◎ Rinse asparagus and cut into 5 to 6-inch lengths. Lay flat in a skillet, layering if necessary, and cover with water. Cook uncovered about 7 minutes.

◎ Cook the scallions the same way as the asparagus, but for only 4 minutes.

◎ Drain the asparagus and the scallions well.

◎ Bring 1 quart salted water to a boil in a large saucepan. Add green beans slowly as to not lose the boil. Cook beans uncovered 10 to 15 minutes until crisp. Drain well.

◎ Combine vegetables in a baking dish, mounding in a criss-cross pattern.

◎ Combine butter, lemon juice, dill, salt and pepper in a small bowl. Pour over the vegetables.

◎ Keep vegetables warm in a low oven. Just before serving, overlap the bell pepper rings on top to garnish, if desired.

You can prepare this dish one day ahead and reheat in the microwave.

Yield: 12 servings

Lemon Pepper Broccoli

Simply seasoned with a zest of lemon,
this vegetable dish is a refreshing complement to any meal.

Preparation Time: 15 minutes
Cook Time: 10 minutes

1	**medium (1½ pounds) bunch broccoli, cut into 12 spears**
3	**tablespoons butter or margarine**
1	**(2-ounce) jar diced pimiento, drained**

2	**teaspoons lemon peel, grated**
	Pinch of salt
	Pinch of cayenne pepper

◎ Place broccoli spears in a 10-inch skillet and add enough water to cover. Bring to a full boil. Reduce heat to medium. Cook over medium heat 5 to 7 minutes until broccoli is crisp, but tender. Drain and return to skillet.

◎ Push broccoli to one side of skillet and add butter, pimiento, lemon peel, salt and cayenne pepper. Cook over medium heat 5 to 7 minutes, stirring all ingredients together until broccoli is heated through.

Yield: 4 servings

Bunch o' Broccoli

Always rinse broccoli before cooking it. If you are serving it raw, crisp it in cold water for 10 minutes, but not too long as some of the important vitamins in broccoli are water soluble. Never overcook broccoli regardless of how you prepare it, either by boiling, steaming, sautéing or pureeing. Broccoli tastes great, especially when enhanced by any of the following: basil, black pepper, caraway seeds, celery seeds, cheddar cheese, chile, curry powder, dill, garlic, lemon, marjoram, mustard, oregano, Parmesan cheese, sesame oil and seeds, tarragon and thyme.

Purple Broccoli?

When we think of broccoli, we think of a deep green vegetable. Sometimes broccoli can be found with purple heads. Green or purple, broccoli is rich in vitamins and nutrients.

Broccoli and Onion Au Gratin

Note the hint of rosemary in this broccoli and Swiss cheese dish.

Preparation Time: 20 minutes
Cook Time: 45 to 50 minutes

2 tablespoons plus ⅓ cup butter, melted; divided	1½ cups milk
2 tablespoons flour	1 cup Swiss cheese, shredded
½ teaspoon salt	2 cups broccoli flowerets
¼ teaspoon rosemary leaves, crushed	1 medium onion, cut into eight pieces
¼ teaspoon pepper	2 cups fresh bread crumbs
	¼ cup fresh parsley, chopped

◎ Preheat oven to 350 degrees.

◎ In a 1-quart saucepan, melt 2 tablespoons butter. Stir in flour, salt, rosemary and pepper. Cook over medium heat (30 seconds), stirring constantly, until smooth and bubbly.

◎ Stir in milk and continue cooking 4 to 5 minutes, stirring occasionally, until mixture thickens and comes to a full boil.

◎ Boil 1 more minute, then remove from heat.

◎ Stir in Swiss cheese until smooth; set aside.

◎ In a greased shallow 1-quart casserole or a 9-inch square baking pan, place broccoli and onion.

◎ Pour cheese sauce over vegetables.

◎ In a small bowl, combine bread crumbs, remaining ⅓ cup melted butter and parsley.

◎ Sprinkle on top of casserole.

◎ Bake for 35 to 40 minutes or until top is golden brown and broccoli is crisp, but tender.

Yield: 6 servings

This recipe can be found in
Spanish in the **Otra Vez...En Español** section.

Red Cabbage

You can make this tasty vegetable without even being at home!

Preparation Time: 10 minutes
Cook Time: 8 to 10 hours

1	small head red cabbage, washed and coarsely sliced
1	medium onion, chopped
3	tart apples, cored and quartered
2	teaspoons salt
1	cup hot water
1½	tablespoons sugar
½	cup vinegar
3	tablespoons butter, margarine or bacon grease

◎ Put red cabbage, onion, apples, salt, water, sugar, vinegar and butter in layers in exact order in a crock pot.

◎ Do not mix.

◎ Cook 8 to 10 hours.

◎ Stir before serving.

Yield: 6 to 8 servings

Cabbage for Kings

There are a variety of delicious cabbages available and one head can go a long way once you start slicing! (A 2-pound cabbage will yield 9 to 10 cups when thinly sliced.) Next time you go grocery shopping for cabbage, look for firm heads or leaves that are bright; avoid those that are discolored, limp or mushy. Flavor enhancers for cabbage are basil, bacon, black pepper, butter, caraway seeds, cayenne pepper, chile, dill, fennel seeds, ginger, marjoram, nutmeg, onion, sage, sesame oil, soy sauce, vinegar and wine. Try with one of these variations:

• Green cabbage: This is the most common variety. It has a mild flavor and can be eaten raw or cooked.

• Red cabbage: This cabbage looks just like green cabbage except for its deep reddish purple color. Red cabbage takes longer to cook than green. It is often finely chopped and mixed with green cabbage in cole slaws.

• Savoy cabbage: This is one of the prettiest cabbages. It is green with ruffled and veined leaves. Unlike the red and green cabbage, its leaves are loose. It is sometimes referred to as curly cabbage.

• Chinese, celery or Napa cabbage: These kinds of cabbage look more like a cross between lettuce and celery, with long pearly stalks and rumpled green leaves. Their flavor is more delicate than head cabbage with a very fresh, slightly peppery taste. They are excellent in stir-fries or raw in salads.

• Bok choy (pak choi): This cabbage resembles Swiss chard with its long, thick-stemmed, light green to pearly white stalks. The flavor is much like cabbage, just a bit fresher tasting. You can eat bok choy raw, but it takes just a quick stir-fry to mellow the flavor a bit while retaining its crisp texture.

Crunchy Carrots

Boil, steam, sauté, braise or bake carrots until they are just tender. They add sparkle and color to the dinner table and lend an intriguing flavor to salads, soups, stews, soufflés and purees. Buy them when they are smooth, firm and nicely shaped—the smaller, the more tender and sweet they will be. A pound of carrots will easily serve four people and two medium-sized carrots will yield one cup of shredded or sliced carrots.

Orange and Honey-Glazed Carrots

A tasty way to liven up those "good-for-you" carrots.

Preparation Time: 5 minutes
Cook Time: 20 minutes

1	pound baby carrots	⅛	teaspoon orange zest, grated
2	tablespoons butter	¼	teaspoon salt
1	clove garlic, halved	⅛	teaspoon pepper
2	tablespoons honey	1	tablespoon fresh chives, snipped

◎ In a large saucepan of boiling salted water, cook carrots 5 to 7 minutes, until tender. Drain.

◎ In a large skillet, melt butter over medium heat. Add garlic and cook, stirring for 2 minutes. Remove garlic and discard. Add honey, stirring to blend.

◎ Increase the heat to medium-high and add carrots, orange zest, salt and pepper. Cook, stirring occasionally, for 10 minutes, or until carrots begin to brown.

◎ Transfer to serving dish and garnish with fresh chives.

Yield: 4 servings

Good Summer dish

Corn and Okra Creole

Add this to your meal and you'll have a Southern-style feast fit for a king!

Preparation Time: 10 minutes
Cook Time: 25 to 30 minutes

1	cup green bell pepper, chopped
½	cup onion, chopped
2	tablespoons butter or margarine, melted
1½	cups (about 3 ears) white corn, cut from the cob
½	cup water

2	medium tomatoes, peeled, seeded and chopped
1½	tablespoons tomato paste
¼	teaspoon dried whole thyme
¼	teaspoon paprika
½	teaspoon salt
¼	teaspoon pepper
1½	cups okra, sliced

◎ Sauté green bell pepper and onion in butter in a large skillet until crispy-tender.

◎ Add corn and water; cover and cook 10 minutes over medium heat, stirring occasionally.

◎ Add tomatoes, tomato paste, thyme, paprika, salt and pepper. Cover and simmer 10 minutes, stirring occasionally.

◎ Add okra; cover and simmer 5 to 7 minutes or until okra is done.

Yield: 6 servings

Peeling Tomatoes

Fill a saucepan with water and bring to a boil. Cut a small "X" just through the skin on the bottom of the tomato. Place a tomato on the end of a long-handled fork and hold it in the water for 30 seconds. Remove the tomato, dip it in cold water to cool and peel off the skin, starting at the "X."

An Earful of Corn

Buy sweet corn in the summer, after the Fourth of July (in most parts) so you know it is local and fresh. Most off-season corn travels too far a distance to be fresh; in which case, canned, and frozen are a better bet. Fresh corn will have husks that are grass green, tightly wrapped and slightly damp. You can also check for freshness by seeing if the stem is moist or by pricking a kernel with your fingernail. If the juice looks like milk, the corn is new and sweet.

Shuck corn only moments before cooking it. Pull the husks off the ear and then remove the silks. Any stubborn silks can be brushed off with your hand or a soft vegetable brush. To cook corn in the husk, you still must remove the silk. Pull the husks down one by one until the corn is exposed; then pull off the silks. Carefully rewrap the corn in its husk and tie it at the top with kitchen string.

To cut the kernels off an ear of corn: shuck it and stand it on its stem on a cutting board or in a wide bowl. Using a sharp knife, cut off the kernels from top to the bottom, three or four rows at a time. Kernels from one medium-size ear of corn equal about ½ cup.

Corn can be boiled, roasted, steamed or sautéed. A note for all methods: do not salt it until you are ready to serve it...salt toughens the kernels!

Creamy Corn Bake

Oh boy, is this good! Serve it with barbecue or grilled meats and watch it disappear.

Preparation Time: 5 minutes
Cook Time: 45 minutes

½ cup butter or margarine, melted	1 (14½-ounce) can creamed corn
1 (14½-ounce) can kernel corn, half drained	1 (8-ounce) container sour cream
see below	1 small box cornbread mix

◎ Mix together butter, kernel corn, creamed corn, sour cream and cornbread mix. Put in greased 13 x 9 x 2-inch baking dish.

◎ Bake at 350 degrees for 45 minutes or until brown.

Spice up this recipe by adding hot pepper sauce, cayenne pepper or diced green chiles. *Add ½ to 1 cup*

Yield: 4 to 6 servings

This recipe can be found in
Spanish in the **Otra Vez...En Español** section.

EASY
VERY Good & moist

Eggplant and Tomato Casserole

Great as a vegetarian entrée or with pasta!

Preparation Time: 20 minutes
Cook Time: 1 hour 10 minutes

Vegetable cooking spray

1 cup (two 4-ounce containers) egg substitute

1 cup bread crumbs, unseasoned

1 medium (approximately 1¼ pounds) eggplant, cut into 10 to 12 slices

2 tablespoons vegetable oil

1 large clove garlic, finely chopped

½ cup onion, chopped

½ cup green bell pepper, cut into ½-inch wide strips

1 cup zucchini, cut into ¼-inch slices

2½ cups (approximately 3 medium) tomatoes, cut into ½-inch chunks

1½ teaspoons dried basil leaves

½ teaspoon dried oregano

¼ teaspoon salt

¼ teaspoon ground black pepper

1 cup mozzarella cheese, grated

◎ Preheat oven to 350 degrees and lightly coat 15 x 10½ x 1-inch jelly-roll pan with vegetable cooking spray. Set aside.

◎ Pour egg substitute and bread crumbs into 2 separate shallow dishes.

◎ Dip eggplant slices into egg substitute then into bread crumbs, coating both sides.

◎ Arrange eggplant on jelly-roll pan and bake for 30 to 35 minutes until fork-tender and lightly browned.

◎ In 12-inch skillet, over medium heat, pour vegetable oil. When sizzling, cook garlic for 1 minute, stirring constantly.

◎ Add onion, green bell pepper and zucchini. Cook 4 to 5 minutes, stirring occasionally, until onion is translucent.

◎ Stir in tomatoes, basil, oregano, salt and pepper. Cook 4 to 5 minutes, stirring often, until tomato cubes are soft, but still retain shape.

◎ Lightly coat 11½ x 8 x 2-inch glass baking dish with vegetable cooking spray.

◎ Spread half of eggplant slices in a single layer in baking dish.

◎ Spoon half of tomato mixture over eggplant.

◎ Sprinkle half of mozzarella cheese over tomato mixture.

◎ Keep layering until all ingredients have been added.

◎ Bake 20 to 25 minutes, until cheese is melted and sauce is bubbling.

Yield: 8 servings

Tomato Salads

• Cut tomatoes in thick slices and arrange them on a plate. Drizzle with olive oil and sprinkle with chopped shallots and freshly ground pepper. Chopped fresh parsley, basil, marjoram or oregano would be good too, as would a few drops of red wine vinegar. Let marinate one hour, then season lightly with salt before serving. If you buy winter tomatoes, add a bit of sugar with the pepper before marinating.

• A very popular Mediterranean salad: coarsely chopped tomatoes and minced red onion dressed in extra virgin olive oil, lemon or lime juice, a little chopped fresh herb and a grind of black pepper. The Portuguese add minced watercress and cilantro. The Greeks add a little basil and oregano, a lot of mint, a handful of black olives and crumbled feta cheese. The Italians add basil, minced garlic and fresh mozzarella.

• Arrange sliced tomatoes on a bed of spinach and top with crumbled crisp bacon and Roquefort cheese.

• Sprinkle sliced tomatoes with toasted sunflower or sesame seeds.

• Layer sliced tomatoes with thin slices of prosciutto and/or slices of fresh mozzarella, placing fresh basil leaves between each slice. Drizzle with extra virgin olive oil and balsamic vinegar.

Haricots Verts

A haricots verts is a slender, delicate French green bean. They cook in a flash, turn a deep, emerald green and taste delicious. They are not always readily available in the stores, so if you see them, be sure to buy some for your evening dinner!

Green Beans with Caramelized Onions

YUM!

Preparation Time: 30 minutes
Cook Time: 25 minutes

2	pounds fresh green beans
1	pound pearl onions
¼	cup butter or margarine

¼ cup brown sugar, firmly packed

◎ Arrange green beans in a steamer basket over boiling water. Cover and steam 15 minutes; set aside.

◎ Place onions in boiling water for 3 minutes; drain and rinse with cold water. Cut off root end of each onion and peel.

◎ Arrange peeled onions in steamer basket over boiling water. Cover and steam 5 minutes; set aside.

◎ Melt butter in a large skillet over medium heat; add brown sugar and cook, stirring constantly, until bubbly.

◎ Add onions and cook, stirring constantly for 3 minutes.

◎ Add green beans, cook, stirring constantly, until thoroughly heated.

Yield: 8 servings

Green Beans Provençal

The flavors of the French Riviera visit your own kitchen table!

Preparation Time: 5 minutes
Cook Time: 25 minutes

1	pound fresh green beans
½	cup water
1	onion, coarsely chopped
4	cloves garlic, minced
2	tablespoons olive oil
4	large tomatoes, peeled, seeded and coarsely chopped

½	cup dry white wine
1	(2¼-ounce) can sliced ripe olives, drained
1	tablespoon lemon juice
¼	teaspoon coarsely ground pepper

◎ Wash green beans; trim ends.

◎ Bring water to boil in a large saucepan; add beans. Cover and reduce heat to medium and cook 10 minutes or until beans are tender. Drain beans and set aside; keep warm.

◎ Sauté onion and garlic in olive oil in a skillet over high heat 5 minutes or until crisp, but tender.

◎ Stir in tomatoes and white wine; bring to a boil.

◎ Reduce heat; simmer, uncovered, 20 minutes, stirring occasionally. Stir in olives.

◎ Spoon sauce over green beans. Pour lemon juice over sauce; sprinkle with pepper and serve.

Yield: 6 servings

Snappy Green Beans

Green beans are often referred to as "string beans," but the string has been bred out and now occurs only when the bean is overripe. Green beans should be crisp when you buy them. Break one—if it does not snap, it is not fresh! Buy about ¼ pound per serving. Refrigerate them unwashed in open or perforated plastic bags for up to three days.

Cook green beans as simply as possible. First, trim the stem end (it is not necessary to trim the little tail). Drop them in boiling water to cover and gently cook, uncovered, until crisp-tender and still bright green. Check after five minutes; no more than ten minutes is necessary. Toss hot green beans in a little melted butter with other seasonings, or serve them at room temperature with a well-seasoned vinaigrette.

Romano Onion Bake

Onion rings at their best!

Preparation Time: 10 minutes
Cook Time: 25 minutes

4	cups onions, sliced	1	cup whipping cream
2	tablespoons butter or margarine, melted	¼	teaspoon salt
2	eggs, well beaten	¼	teaspoon pepper
		¼	cup Romano cheese, grated

- ◎ Preheat oven to 375 degrees.
- ◎ Sauté onion in butter until crispy-tender.
- ◎ Arrange in lightly greased 8-inch square baking dish.
- ◎ Combine eggs, whipping cream, salt and pepper; pour over onions.
- ◎ Bake for 20 minutes.
- ◎ Sprinkle with Romano cheese and bake an additional 5 minutes.

Yield: 6 servings

Good Side Dish
Tasty & Easy

Pecan Squash

*This wonderfully sweet side dish brings
festive holiday colors and flavors right to your plates!*

Preparation Time: 15 minutes
Cook Time: 20 to 25 minutes

2 **acorn squash (about 1 pound each)**	**⅓ cup butter or margarine, softened**
⅔ cup graham cracker crumbs or saltine cracker crumbs	**3 tablespoons brown sugar, firmly packed**
⅓ cup pecans, coarsely chopped	**⅛ teaspoon salt**
	¼ teaspoon ground nutmeg

◎ Pierce each whole squash in several places. Place 2 inches apart in the microwave and cook on high for 6 minutes.

◎ Cut squash crosswise in halves; remove seeds and arrange cut-side down on microwave-safe dish.

◎ Cover tightly with plastic wrap and microwave on high for another 7 to 9 minutes or until tender.

◎ Remove stems and arrange squash halves on dish with cut-side up.

◎ Mix graham cracker crumbs, pecans, butter, brown sugar, salt and nutmeg in a small bowl.

◎ Spoon ¼ of crumb mixture into each squash half.

◎ Microwave uncovered on high for 3 to 5 minutes, until filling is hot.

Add whole cranberry sauce and serve this delightful dish at Thanksgiving.

Yield: 4 servings

Pecans

Pecans are a southern favorite used in everything~from salads and vegetables to desserts. To shell pecans without breaking them into tiny pieces, soak the whole nut in salted water overnight. Store pecans in the refrigerator or freezer, never at room temperature.

Don't Squash Squash

Squash can be divided into two categories: summer and winter. Summer squash, which means they are harvested when they are immature and the skins and seeds are still edible, include pattypan, yellow squash and zucchini. Acorn, buttercup, butternut, chayote, golden nugget, hubbard, pumpkins, spaghetti and turban make up the winter squash family. Winter squash are picked fully mature; the skins are hard and the seeds are large and woody.

Squash Mexicali

This refreshing vegetable dish can be served year-round.

Preparation Time: 10 minutes
Cook Time: 20 to 25 minutes

← Sub 1-can of Rotel

1	teaspoon canola or olive oil	1	(14½-ounce) can stewed tomatoes
1	onion, diced	1	cup Monterey Jack cheese, grated
5	Mexican squash		

- ◎ Pour oil into large saucepan and heat; add onion and brown.
- ◎ Slice squash into ¼ to ½-inch slices and add to browned onions.
- ◎ Cover and let cook for 20 minutes or until squash is done.
- ◎ Add tomatoes as squash is cooking. Heat through.
- ◎ Place squash into a baking dish and top with Monterey Jack cheese.
- ◎ Place under broiler until cheese is melted.

Yield: 6 to 8 servings

God

Cheesy Chile Zucchini Bake

A delicious blend of Southwest ingredients!

Preparation Time: 15 minutes
Cook Time: 30 minutes

2	pounds zucchini, sliced
1	medium onion
1	tablespoon plus 2 teaspoons butter or margarine; divided
¾	cup Swiss cheese, grated
¾	cup cheddar cheese, grated

1	(4-ounce) can diced green chiles
1	(8-ounce) container sour cream
	Salt and pepper to taste
½	cup bread crumbs
¼	cup Parmesan cheese, grated

- Preheat oven to 350 degrees.
- In a large saucepan, add zucchini and onion; cover with water. Cook until tender.
- Grease a 2-quart baking dish with 1 tablespoon butter. Add zucchini and onion to baking dish.
- In a small bowl, mix Swiss cheese, cheddar cheese, green chiles, sour cream, salt and pepper together; sprinkle over zucchini and onion.
- Combine bread crumbs and Parmesan cheese; sprinkle on top of vegetables.
- Dot with remaining 2 teaspoons butter.
- Bake for 25 minutes.

Yield: 8 servings

This recipe can be found in
Spanish in the **Otra Vez...En Español** section.

Let's Talk Zucchini

By far, the most popular of the summer squash family is the zucchini because it is the most versatile. Its mild flavor and tenderness works well with so many other ingredients. Zucchini are available all year round, but the quality is best in late spring through summer. Buy zucchini that is firm and heavy for its size. The skin should be thin and tender (you can easily puncture it with your fingernail). Avoid those with bruises, soft spots, cuts and scrapes. Also, do not buy large zucchini. Anything over 7 to 8 inches is too big. The tiny zucchini are very tender, but the medium 5 to 7 inchers work best for most dishes. One medium zucchini, sliced, measures 2 cups or 1½ cups, shredded.

Spinach and Artichoke Parmesan

The addition of artichokes lends elegance to creamy spinach.

Preparation Time: 15 minutes
Cook Time: 30 to 35 minutes

2	(10-ounce) packages frozen chopped spinach
¼	cup butter or margarine
½	cup onion, finely chopped
1	(14½-ounce) can artichoke hearts, drained and quartered

1	(16-ounce) container sour cream
¼	teaspoon salt
¼	teaspoon pepper
½	cup Parmesan cheese, freshly grated; divided

- ◎ Preheat oven to 350 degrees.
- ◎ Cook spinach according to package directions; drain well, pressing between layers of paper towels; set aside.
- ◎ Melt butter in a large skillet over medium heat. Add onion and cook until tender.
- ◎ Gently stir in artichoke hearts, sour cream, salt and pepper.
- ◎ Stir in ¼ cup Parmesan cheese.
- ◎ Add spinach and toss.
- ◎ Spoon into a lightly greased 1½-quart casserole dish.
- ◎ Sprinkle with remaining Parmesan cheese.
- ◎ Bake for 25 to 30 minutes.

Serve this as a hot spinach appetizer with crackers, baguette slices or chips.

Yield: 6 servings

Skillet Spinach "Balsamico"

A mouth-watering way to prepare a healthy vegetable.

Preparation Time: 5 to 7 minutes
Cook Time: 10 minutes

4 slices bacon	2 tablespoons pecans, chopped
2½ tablespoons balsamic vinegar	¼ teaspoon salt
1 (10-ounce) package fresh spinach	¼ teaspoon pepper
	Pinch of sugar (optional)

◎ Cook bacon in a large skillet until crisp; remove bacon, reserving 1 tablespoon drippings in skillet.

◎ Crumble bacon and set aside.

◎ Add balsamic vinegar to skillet; bring to a boil over medium-high heat stirring to loosen bacon particles.

◎ Add spinach and cook, stirring constantly, for 1 to 2 minutes or until limp.

◎ Stir in bacon, pecans, salt and pepper. Sweeten with sugar, if desired.

◎ Serve immediately.

Substitute pine nuts for pecans and top with crumbled blue cheese.

Yield: 2 servings

Adding a Splash of Vinegar

It seems vinegar has been around forever, but is now being used for more than just canning, pickling and salad dressings. Vinegar can be also be used as a flavor accent for sauces, stews, meat, fish and vegetable dishes. It adds a zippy, clean taste that brings out the flavor of foods without adding fat or sodium. Next time a sauce tastes flat, add a dash of vinegar—you won't miss the salt at all! The wide range of flavored vinegars available allows for even more enhanced taste.

Vinegars will keep almost indefinitely if left unopened in a dark, cool place. Once opened, most vinegars will retain their flavors for a minimum of 2 to 3 months; cider vinegar will last up to 6 months. Keep vinegars tightly sealed after opening.

Full of Flavor

Fresh herbs lose their distinctive flavor when cooked a long time. Add some extra just before serving!

Herbed Tomato Tart

Don't let the word "tart" keep you from trying this scrumptious tomato dish!

Preparation Time: 40 minutes
Cook Time: 15 minutes

1	(17¼-ounce) package frozen puff pastry sheets, thawed
4	plum tomatoes, thinly sliced
1	teaspoon salt
½	tablespoon fresh oregano
½	tablespoon fresh basil
½	tablespoon fresh chives
½	tablespoon fresh sage
½	tablespoon fresh tarragon
½	tablespoon fresh rosemary

½	tablespoon fresh thyme
½	tablespoon fresh dill weed
1	(8-ounce) package shredded mozzarella cheese
1	(4-ounce) package crumbled feta cheese
¼	cup onion, chopped
1	clove garlic, minced
1	tablespoon olive oil

◎ Preheat oven to 400 degrees.

◎ Roll 1 pastry sheet into a 14-inch square on a lightly floured surface. Place on an ungreased baking sheet.

◎ Cut 4 (12 x 1-inch) strips from remaining pastry sheet and place along edges on top of pastry square, forming a border. Reserve remaining pastry for another use.

◎ Bake for 10 minutes or until golden brown. Transfer pastry shell to wire rack to cool.

◎ Place tomato slices in a single layer on paper towels; sprinkle evenly with salt. Let stand for 20 minutes.

◎ In a small bowl combine oregano, basil, chives, sage, tarragon, rosemary, thyme and dill weed; set aside.

◎ Place pastry shell on baking sheet.

◎ Sprinkle with mozzarella cheese, feta cheese, onion and garlic.

◎ Arrange tomato slices in a single layer on top. Sprinkle with mixed fresh herbs. Drizzle with olive oil.

◎ Bake 15 minutes or until cheese melts.

◎ Serve immediately.

You can substitute ½ tablespoon of fresh herbs for ½ teaspoon dried herbs.

Yield: 4 servings

TH

Garden Casserole

A deliciously pleasing medley of fresh vegetables; good anytime!

Preparation Time: 20 minutes
Cook Time: 1 hour 10 minutes

1	large onion, sliced	1	(10-ounce) package frozen cut green beans, thawed
2	medium red bell peppers, cut in strips OR chopped	2	cups Swiss cheese, shredded
2	cloves garlic, minced	1	cup half-and-half
3	tablespoons butter or margarine, melted	1 ~~2~~	teaspoon ~~dried whole~~ rosemary FResh
¼	cup flour	½	teaspoon salt
6	small baking potatoes, unpeeled and thinly sliced	¼	teaspoon pepper

◎ Sauté onion, red bell pepper and garlic in butter until crispy-tender. (Reserve 16 red bell pepper strips for garnish.)

◎ Add flour; cook for 1 minute, stirring constantly. Spoon half of the onion mixture into a lightly greased 13 x 9 x 2-inch baking dish.

◎ Layer half the potatoes, half the green beans and half the Swiss cheese over onion mixture. Repeat layering. Set aside.

◎ In a small bowl, combine half-and-half, rosemary, salt and pepper. Pour over vegetables.

◎ Cover and bake at 375 degrees for 1 hour or until the potatoes are tender.

◎ Uncover and sprinkle with remaining Swiss cheese. Garnish with red bell pepper strips and bake for another 5 minutes.   OR Chopped

Add a 4-ounce can of diced green chiles or 1 chopped chipotle chile for added flavor.

Yield: 8 to 10 servings

Vegetable Seasonings

Finely chopped combinations of vegetables, herbs and spices may be used to flavor other dishes. The most frequently used mixtures are:

• Finely chopped mushrooms and onions or shallots cooked in butter to a puree consistency. Known as duxelles, this combination is often used in stuffings, vegetable casseroles or gratins.

• Finely diced carrots combined with celery and seasoned with parsley, thyme and bay leaf is called a mirepoix.

The medley is cooked in butter and sautéed over low heat for 30 minutes until soft.

• Persillade is a mixture of parsley and garlic which may or may not be sautéed in butter when served with grilled meats.

• Sofrito is used in stuffings and gratins. It consists primarily of chopped tomatoes and onions and can include peppers and garlic along with meats, such as ham and sausage.

Tips for Grilling Vegetables

- Marinate or baste vegetables well during grilling to prevent them from drying out.

- Grill soft or juicy vegetables in a grill basket to facilitate turning.

- Foil-grilling is a convenient way to cook vegetables. Set the vegetables in an aluminum foil packet. Moisten with water, chicken stock or herbed butter and grill until done.

- Shorten the grilling time of larger vegetables (such as potatoes) by precooking them in the microwave for a few minutes.

Marinated Grilled Vegetables

There's nothing better than fresh vegetables cooked on the grill!

Preparation Time: 25 minutes
Chill Time: 1 hour
Cook Time: 15 minutes

½ cup balsamic vinegar	2 purple onions, cut into ¾-inch slices
¼ cup extra virgin olive oil	2 portobello mushrooms, quartered
2 tablespoons dry white wine	1 pound fresh asparagus, trimmed
1 tablespoon shallots, finely chopped	1 small eggplant, cut lengthwise into 1-inch slices
½ tablespoon garlic, minced	1 red bell pepper, quartered
½ tablespoon freshly ground black pepper	1 yellow bell pepper, quartered
1 teaspoon salt	1 tablespoon fresh chives, chopped
4 new potatoes, unpeeled	1 tablespoon fresh rosemary, chopped
4 Roma tomatoes, cut in half lengthwise	1 tablespoon fresh parsley, chopped
3 small zucchini, cut in half lengthwise	
2 ears yellow corn, cut into 3 inch pieces	

◎ Combine balsamic vinegar, olive oil, white wine, shallots, garlic, pepper and salt in a large bowl; set aside.

◎ Cook potatoes in boiling water 5 minutes; drain. Cut potatoes in half.

◎ Add potato halves, tomatoes, zucchini, corn, onions, mushrooms, asparagus, eggplant, red bell pepper and yellow bell pepper to vinegar mixture; toss gently to coat. Let stand for 1 hour, tossing occasionally.

◎ Remove vegetables from marinade; reserving marinade.

◎ Cook vegetables, covered with grill lid over medium heat (350 to 400 degrees) for 12 to 15 minutes, turning once. Remove vegetables to serving platter as they are done.

◎ Drizzle remaining marinade over cooked vegetables.

◎ Combine chives, rosemary and parsley; sprinkle over vegetables.

Yield: 8 servings

Sounds Good

Quick and Easy Blue Cheese Potatoes

Even if you don't like blue cheese,
you should try these potatoes anyway...they are delicious!

Preparation Time: 20 minutes
Cook Time: 30 to 45 minutes

3	tablespoons butter
6	cloves garlic, crushed
3	large baking potatoes (peeled, rinsed and patted dry)
½	cup mild blue cheese, crumbled

¼	cup Parmesan, Asiago and Romano cheeses, grated (available as a combination in a shaker can or you may use just Parmesan cheese)
1	pint whipping cream
1	teaspoon salt
1	teaspoon black pepper
½	teaspoon thyme
	Fresh parsley (optional)

◎ Preheat oven to 350 degrees.

◎ Vigorously rub cold butter in the bottom and sides of a 9 x 13 x 2-inch glass baking dish until the dish is thickly coated. Spread garlic over bottom of baking dish.

◎ Cut off the very ends of the dry, peeled potatoes. Slice in half lengthwise. Place the flat side down and using a very sharp knife, while holding the potato to keep its shape, cut very thin slices along the length of the potato half. Carefully pick up the sliced half and fan out the potatoes (like spreading a deck of cards) in a column in the baking dish. Continue with each potato half.

◎ Crumble blue cheese over potatoes; sprinkle mixed Parmesan, Asiago, and Romano cheeses over potatoes.

◎ Pour whipping cream over cheese and potatoes, making sure to coat potatoes well.

◎ Sprinkle salt, pepper and thyme over the top.

◎ Bake for 30 to 45 minutes. Check several times. Potatoes are done when cheese is very hot and bubbly and the potatoes and the cheese are slightly browned. Do not overcook. Thinly sliced potatoes cook quickly.

◎ Garnish with sprig of fresh parsley on individual plates, if desired.

The potatoes can also be cut into ½-inch cubes.
Yield: 6 servings

This recipe can be found in
Spanish in the **Otra Vez...En Español** section.

Types of Blue Cheese

Bleu d'Auvergne - This is the blue to use for a salad dressing. It is firm, not salty and has a sharp taste and aroma.

Bleu de Bresse - A creamy dessert cheese with a mild flavor and aroma that goes particularly well with dried apricots and dates.

Bleu de Gex - This marvelous blue cheese is a perfect melting cheese.

Bresse Blue - Creamy and mellow, this cheese complements a variety of cheeses and is great served with crisp apple wedges.

Gorgonzola - When young, Gorgonzola is sweet, creamy and smooth. As it ages, it becomes sharper and dry. Serve it for dessert with ripe pears and a glass of wine.

Maytag Blue - This pleasant-tasting blue is smooth and white with heavy mold throughout. It is considered one of the better domestic blues and is served with salads.

Roquefort - Made from sheep's milk under the strictest of regulations, this cheese looks white on the inside when it is first cut. After it is exposed to air, the characteristic blue-green veins appear. It is delicious with crusty bread, walnuts and raisins.

Good Pot Luck Dish

Try

Crunchy Potato Casserole

A quick and easy recipe that everyone will surely love!

Preparation Time: 15 minutes
Cook Time: 30 minutes

1	**(24-ounce) package frozen shredded hash brown potatoes, thawed and drained of excess water**
2	**cups sour cream**
¾	**cup butter, melted; divided**

1	**can cream of chicken soup**
½	**cup onion, chopped**
2	**cups cheddar cheese, shredded**
2	**cups cornflakes cereal, crushed** OR PANKO

◎ Combine hash browns, sour cream, ½ cup melted butter, cream of chicken soup, onion and cheddar cheese. Put in greased 9 x 13 x 2-inch casserole dish.

◎ Mix cornflakes cereal with remaining ¼ cup melted butter and sprinkle on top of potato mixture.

◎ Bake at 350 degrees for 30 minutes.

Yield: 10 to 12 servings

Garlic Roasted Potatoes

Crispy on the outside, soft on the inside, tasty all around!

Preparation Time: 15 minutes
Cook Time: 30 minutes

3 tablespoons butter, melted	¼ teaspoon salt
3 tablespoons olive oil	¼ teaspoon pepper
3-4 cloves garlic, minced	⅓ cup Parmesan cheese, grated
4 medium baking potatoes, cut into 1-inch pieces	

◎ Combine butter, olive oil, garlic, potatoes, salt and pepper in a 13 x 9 x 2-inch metal baking pan; toss gently to coat.

◎ Bake at 500 degrees for 25 minutes or until potatoes are tender, stirring every 10 minutes.

◎ Sprinkle with Parmesan cheese; bake an additional 5 minutes.

Add 1 large onion cut in strips and roast with potatoes.

Yield: 6 to 8 servings

Roasting Potatoes with Meat

There is nothing like the taste of potatoes cooked in the oven and basted with the drippings of a roast. Add the scrubbed quartered potatoes to the roasting pan 1 hour before the roast should be done. Baste them with the pan juices and turn several times to brown evenly.

Hot Mashed Potatoes

Mashed potatoes are best served at once, but in a pinch they can be kept warm in a pan over hot water. Or, put them in a buttered baking dish, film the top with cream, and keep them hot in a warm oven.

Stuffed Mashed Potatoes

A great variation to basic mashed potatoes.

Preparation Time: 25 minutes
Cook Time: 50 minutes

8 large (6 pounds) potatoes, peeled and chopped	¼ cup milk
½ cup butter; divided	1½ teaspoons salt
1 (3-ounce) package cream cheese, softened	½ teaspoon pepper
½ cup sour cream	1 medium onion, chopped
	12 large fresh mushrooms, sliced

◎ Put potatoes in a large covered pot with water to cover; boil 15 minutes or until tender. Drain.

◎ Mash potatoes with ¼ cup butter, cream cheese, sour cream, milk, salt and pepper until smooth.

◎ Melt remaining ¼ cup butter in a large skillet over medium heat; add onion and mushrooms and sauté until tender.

◎ Spoon ⅓ potato mixture into a lightly greased 2½-quart baking dish; top with ½ mushroom mixture. Repeat layers, ending with potato mixture.

◎ Bake at 350 degrees for 30 minutes or until lightly browned.

Yield: 10 to 12 servings

Gratin Potatoes with Boursin

Scalloped potatoes, move over!

Preparation Time: 20 minutes
Cook Time: 1 hour

2	cups whipping cream
5	ounces Boursin cheese
5	pounds red potatoes, unpeeled and thinly sliced

Salt and pepper, to taste
1½ tablespoons fresh parsley, chopped (optional)

◎ Preheat oven to 400 degrees.

◎ Grease a 9 x 13 x 2-inch baking pan, set aside.

◎ Stir together whipping cream and Boursin cheese in a saucepan over medium heat until cheese melts and mixture is smooth. Remove from heat.

◎ Layer half of the potatoes in the pan. Season with salt and pepper. Pour half of the cheese mixture over the potatoes. Layer remaining potatoes, salt, pepper and cheese mixture on top.

◎ Bake 1 hour.

◎ Garnish with parsley, if desired.

Yield: 8 to 10 servings

One Potato, Two Potato...

Buy potatoes that are firm, smooth, well shaped and heavy for their size. Do not buy potatoes with cracks, discoloration, withered skin or sprouts. Check carefully for any green tinge on the skin—they will taste bitter and could make you sick!

Keep your potatoes in a cool, well-ventilated place. Air circulation is important to the life of a potato because it keeps them dry. Take potatoes out of their plastic bags and put them in a net bag or basket. Potatoes can be kept in the refrigerator in paper bags, but only for a short while.

Starchy, dry potatoes (mature potatoes such as Russet and Idaho) are best for baking or frying; semi-starchy, moist potatoes (all-purpose potatoes) should be roasted or boiled; and new potatoes are great boiled or steamed.

Naturally Sweet

Sweet potatoes have a naturally sweet flavor and are low in fat. This versatile vegetable is a rich source of the antioxidant beta-carotene.

Sweet Potato Casserole

This recipe is not only great for holidays, but for any occasion.

Preparation Time: 20 minutes
Cook Time: 50 minutes

4 cups sweet potatoes, cooked and mashed	½ cup butter, melted
½ cup milk	½ teaspoon salt
½ cup sugar	2 eggs, slightly beaten
	Pecan Topping

◎ Combine sweet potatoes, milk, sugar, butter, salt and eggs until well blended.
◎ Place in greased 2-quart casserole dish.
◎ Sprinkle Pecan Topping over potatoes.
◎ Bake at 350 degrees for 30 to 40 minutes.

Yield: 6 to 8 servings

PECAN TOPPING

1 cup brown sugar	1 cup pecans, chopped
¼ cup butter, melted	⅓ cup flour

◎ Combine brown sugar, butter, pecans and flour.

Roasted Sweet Potatoes

The sweetness of the potatoes and the hint
of lime makes a great combination to complement any meal.

Preparation Time: 15 minutes
Cook Time: 15 minutes

Vegetable cooking spray	Salt and pepper, to taste
3 large (3 pounds) sweet potatoes, peeled and cut into 1-inch cubes	1 large clove garlic, minced
	2 tablespoons lime juice, freshly squeezed
4 tablespoons olive oil; divided	1½ tablespoons parsley, chopped

◎ Preheat oven to 400 degrees. Spray a baking sheet with vegetable cooking spray and set aside.

◎ In a medium bowl, toss the sweet potatoes with 2 tablespoons olive oil and season to taste with salt and pepper.

◎ Transfer to the prepared baking sheet and roast until potatoes can be pierced easily with a fork, about 15 minutes.

◎ Transfer the potatoes to a large serving bowl. Toss with the garlic, lime juice, parsley and remaining 2 tablespoons olive oil. Add more salt and pepper to taste, if necessary.

◎ Serve warm or at room temperature.

Yield: 4 to 6 servings

Sweet Potatoes

Buy small or medium sweet potatoes for they are the most tender. They should be firm, heavy and well shaped with no bruises or cuts. Many sweet potatoes have little hairs on them, which can be trimmed just before cooking (they do no harm). Do not buy sweet potatoes with twists or knobs as they make them too hard to peel. Peeling sweet potatoes is much easier done after they are cooked than before, plus more of the potato's vitamins and minerals will stay with the potato if the skin remains intact while cooking. Sweet potatoes can be baked, roasted or fried. They make great chips and wonderful hash browns as well!

Flavorful Rice

For full flavor enhancement to rice, substitute one of the following for all or part of the cooking water: apple, orange or pineapple juices; chicken, vegetable or beef stocks; wine; beer; sherry; cream; or milk.

Boost the flavor and appearance of reheated rice by adding: chopped dates and nuts; sliced mushrooms, green onions or shallots; chopped tomato, bell pepper, carrots, broccoli, onion, asparagus, green beans or celery; chopped ham, bacon, pork or seafood (nice for fried rice); chopped cilantro, parsley or other fresh herbs; minced fresh ginger or garlic; crushed pineapple, sliced mandarin oranges, chopped red or green apples, or raisins; sliced ripe or pimiento-stuffed olives; grated Romano or Parmesan cheeses, or crumbled feta cheese.

Three-Grain Rice

Three cheers for this dish!

Preparation Time: 15 minutes
Chill Time: 10 minutes
Cook Time: 55 minutes

⅔ cup orzo	1 tablespoon fresh thyme, chopped
2 tablespoons vegetable oil	1 tablespoon fresh sage, chopped
2 (14¼-ounce) cans chicken broth	1 teaspoon salt
½ cup water	¼ teaspoon ground white pepper
⅔ cup wild rice	
¾ cup long-grain rice	
1 bay leaf	

◎ Cook orzo in vegetable oil in a 3-quart saucepan over medium-high heat, stirring often, until lightly browned. Remove orzo from saucepan and set aside.

◎ Add chicken broth, water and wild rice to saucepan; bring to a boil over medium heat. Cover, reduce heat and simmer 10 minutes.

◎ Stir in orzo, long-grain rice, bay leaf, thyme, sage, salt and white pepper. Return to a boil; cover, reduce heat and simmer 40 minutes or until moisture is absorbed and rice is tender. Remove from heat and let stand 10 minutes. Remove and discard bay leaf.

May substitute 1 teaspoon dried herbs for fresh herbs.

Yield: 8 servings

Nutty Orange Rice

A delicious blend of flavors.

Preparation Time: 10 minutes
Chill Time: 2 hours
Cook Time: 20 minutes

1	(6-ounce) package wild and white rice mix
1	cup pecans, chopped
1	cup golden raisins
	Rind from one orange, grated
	Juice from one orange
¼	cup fresh mint, chopped
4	green onions, with tops, thinly sliced
¼	cup olive oil
	Salt and pepper, to taste

◎ Prepare wild and white rice mix according to package directions.

◎ Add pecans, golden raisins, orange rind, orange juice, mint, green onions, olive oil, salt and pepper; toss gently. Let mixture stand for two hours to allow flavors to develop.

◎ Serve at room temperature.

Yield: 4 to 6 servings

This recipe can be found in
Spanish in the **Otra Vez...En Español** section.

Nice Rice

Add a tablespoon of butter or oil to the water when cooking rice to keep grains separate.

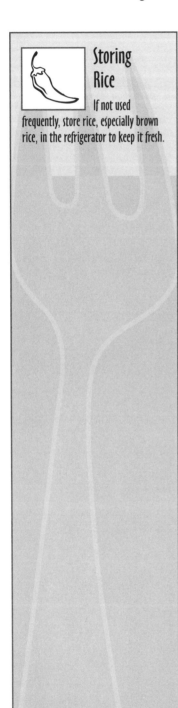

Storing Rice

If not used frequently, store rice, especially brown rice, in the refrigerator to keep it fresh.

Brown Rice Casserole

Two dishes in one ~ all you need is the meat to make a balanced meal.

Preparation Time: 20 minutes
Chill Time: Up to 24 hours
Cook Time: 1 hour 20 minutes

1 bunch green onions, chopped	¾ cup fresh parsley, chopped
3 medium carrots, scraped and chopped	¼ teaspoon freshly ground black pepper
½ cup butter or margarine; divided	1 cup Parmesan cheese, freshly grated
2 cups brown rice	2 eggs, beaten
4½ cups chicken broth	1 cup half-and-half
½ cup dry white wine	⅛ teaspoon ground nutmeg
2 cloves garlic, minced	Green onion slices (optional)
½ pound fresh mushrooms, sliced	

◎ Sauté green onions and carrots in ¼ cup butter in a large skillet 5 minutes. Add brown rice and cook 1 minute, stirring constantly. Add chicken broth and white wine. Bring to a boil; cover, reduce heat and simmer 45 minutes or until liquid is absorbed and rice is tender.

◎ Sauté garlic in remaining ¼ cup butter 1 minute; add mushrooms and cook 5 minutes. Drain. Stir in parsley and pepper.

◎ Layer half of rice mixture in a lightly greased 12 x 8 x 2-inch baking dish. Spoon mushroom mixture over rice; top with half of Parmesan cheese. Spread remaining rice mixture on top. Sprinkle with remaining Parmesan cheese.

◎ Combine eggs, half-and-half and nutmeg, mixing well. Pour over rice. Cover and refrigerate up to 24 hours.

◎ Remove rice from refrigerator and let stand 30 minutes. Bake at 350 degrees for 30 minutes or until thoroughly heated. Garnish with green onion slices, if desired.

Yield: 8 to 10 servings

Wild Rice with Cranberries and Onions

Cranberries add a speck of color to this
wonderful side that begs to go centerstage with game or lamb.

Preparation Time: 15 minutes
Cook Time: 1 hour 30 minutes

2	cups chicken broth	2	teaspoons brown sugar
1	cup brown and wild rice	1	cup dried cranberries
3	tablespoons butter	½	teaspoon orange zest, grated
3	medium onions, sliced		

◎ Combine chicken broth and brown and wild rice in medium sauce-pan. Bring to boil over medium-high heat, reduce to low; cover and simmer 45 minutes or until rice is tender and liquid is absorbed.

◎ Melt butter in a skillet over medium-high heat, add onions and brown sugar; cook 6 minutes or until liquid is absorbed and onions are tender and translucent. Reduce heat to low, cook stirring often for 25 minutes or until the onions are caramelized.

◎ Stir in cranberries, cover and cook over low heat for 10 minutes.

◎ Fold cranberry mixture and orange zest into rice.

Yield: 6 servings

Bright White Rice
Add a teaspoon of lemon juice to each quart of water used to cook rice. The grains will stay white and separated.

20 Ways to Eat Risotto

- Eggplant, fresh tomatoes, goat cheese and basil
- Goose or chicken livers
- Shrimp, garlic and parsley
- Gorgonzola and sage
- Zucchini, sun-dried tomatoes and fresh basil
- Shredded chicken, duck or goose
- Fresh herb pesto
- Truffles
- Porcini mushrooms, prosciutto and red wine
- Spinach and goat cheese
- Lobster, mussels, oysters and prawns
- Four cheeses including Gorgonzola, Parmesan, fontina and mozzarella
- Shrimp and peas
- Sausage and zucchini
- Chicken, beef, fish, duck or turkey stock
- Red wine or white wine
- Soaking liquid from dried wild mushrooms
- Vegetable juices or purees
- Juices and drippings from roasted meats and poultry
- Sun-dried tomato or black olive puree

Southwestern Risotto

A tasty side dish that goes well with grilled chicken or fish.

Preparation Time: 25 minutes
Cook Time: 35 to 40 minutes

½ cup onion, chopped	2 medium tomatoes, seeded and chopped
2 cloves garlic, crushed	1 jalapeño pepper, seeded and minced OR GRN Chile
2 tablespoons butter or margarine, melted	½ cup green onions, sliced
1 cup Arborio rice	½ cup Parmesan cheese, grated
½ cup dry white wine	2-3 tablespoons cilantro, minced
6 cups chicken broth; divided	Fresh cilantro sprigs and cubed tomatoes (optional)
½ cup whipping cream	

◎ Cook onion and garlic in butter in a large skillet or saucepan over medium heat, stirring constantly, until tender.

◎ Add Arborio rice; cook 2 to 3 minutes, stirring frequently. Add white wine and cook, uncovered, until liquid is absorbed.

◎ Add 1 cup chicken broth; cook, stirring constantly, over medium-high heat 5 minutes or until broth is absorbed. Continue adding broth, 1 cup at a time, cooking and stirring constantly until each cup is absorbed, about 25 to 30 minutes. (Rice will be tender and have a creamy consistency.)

◎ Stir in whipping cream, tomatoes, jalapeño pepper, green onions, Parmesan cheese and cilantro; cook 2 minutes.

◎ Garnish with cilantro sprigs and cubed tomatoes, if desired, and serve immediately.

Yield: 6 servings

Spinach and Onion Couscous

You'll go "couscous" over this!

Preparation Time: 5 minutes
Cook Time: 15 minutes

1	medium onion, chopped
1	clove garlic, pressed
2	tablespoons olive oil
1	(14½-ounce) can chicken broth
1	(10-ounce) package frozen chopped spinach
10	ounces (about 1¼ cups) couscous

¾	cup Parmesan cheese, freshly grated
2	tablespoons lemon juice
½	teaspoon salt
½	teaspoon freshly ground black pepper
½	cup pecans, chopped and toasted

◎ Sauté onion and garlic in hot olive oil in a large saucepan until tender.

◎ Add chicken broth and spinach; cook, stirring occasionally, until spinach thaws. Bring to a boil, stirring occasionally.

◎ Stir in couscous; cover, remove from heat and let stand 5 minutes or until liquid is absorbed.

◎ Stir in Parmesan cheese, lemon juice, salt, pepper and pecans. Serve immediately.

Yield: 6 to 8 servings

Risotto at Its Best

• Do not rinse the rice before cooking it. The starch that coats each grain is essential to making a creamy risotto.

• Keep the broth hot and the risotto at a lively simmer. If it cooks too quickly, the rice will be soft outside and chalky inside; if it cooks too slow, it will have a gluey texture.

• If adding seafood or vegetables that you want to remain crisp, sauté them before hand and add at the last minute. Some vegetables benefit from being sautéed with the rice.

• Start testing grains of rice for doneness after about 15 minutes of cooking. Risotto is done when you like it!

Coo Coo Over Couscous

A favorite in North Africa, couscous is steamed semolina or millet. Semolina is grain milled from durum wheat and is also used in making pasta. Millet was one of man's first cereals and still remains a popular diet in Asia, India and Africa.

Lemon Couscous

Fabulous is the only word needed to describe this dish!

Preparation Time: 10 minutes
Cook Time: 20 minutes

1	tablespoon lemon rind, grated
2	tablespoons fresh lemon juice
1	tablespoon butter or margarine
1/8	teaspoon salt
1	cup chicken broth
2/3	cup couscous

2	tablespoons pecan pieces, toasted
2	tablespoons fresh parsley, chopped
2	tablespoons red bell pepper, finely chopped
	Fresh mint sprigs and lemon slices (optional)

◎ Combine lemon rind, lemon juice, butter, salt and chicken broth in a saucepan; bring to a boil over medium-high heat.

◎ Add couscous, stirring well; cover, remove from heat and let stand 10 minutes.

◎ Stir in pecans, parsley and red bell pepper.

◎ Garnish with mint sprigs and lemon slices, if desired.

Yield: 2 servings

Green Chile Cheese Hominy

Spice up your breakfast with this tasty casserole.

Preparation Time: 10 minutes
Cook Time: 30 minutes

Add 1-cup Grn chile

3 (15-ounce) cans hominy, drained	1 (4-ounce) can chopped green chiles
1 (8-ounce) container sour cream	4-6 ounces sharp cheddar cheese, shredded
5 ounces Monterey Jack cheese, shredded	

◎ Mix hominy, sour cream, Monterey Jack cheese and green chiles together in a bowl. Pour into an 8 x 8-inch greased baking pan. Sprinkle with cheddar cheese.

◎ Bake uncovered at 350 degrees for 30 minutes.

Add some pico de gallo or salsa for extra spiciness.

Yield: 6 to 8 servings

Add Pico de gallo AS A GARNish
dRAiN well
Quick
EASy
Good

A Southern Favorite

Hominy is the kernels of dried corn with the hull and germ removed. Grits are the ground kernels. Look for the quick-cooking variety of grits in the cereal section of the grocery store. They take roughly 5 minutes to prepare as opposed to the 30 minutes for regular-cooking grits.

Letting Off Steam

Every time you open the oven door while baking, the temperature drops about 25 degrees. Try not to take a peek!

EASY

Swiss and Cheddar Baked Grits

No longer just a southern breakfast treat ...good anytime!

Preparation Time: 15 minutes
Chill Time: 15 minutes
Cook Time: 1 hour 15 minutes

4⅓ cups water	¼ teaspoon salt
½ teaspoon salt	¼ teaspoon pepper
1¼ cups quick-cooking grits	3 eggs, beaten
¼ cup butter or margarine	1¼ cups (5 ounces) Swiss cheese, shredded
1½ cups (6 ounces) cheddar cheese, shredded; divided	

◎ Bring water and salt to a boil in a heavy saucepan. Gradually stir in grits; return to a boil. Cover, reduce heat, and simmer, stirring occasionally, 5 minutes or until done.

◎ Remove from heat; stir in butter, 1¼ cups cheddar cheese, salt and pepper. Cool 15 minutes and stir in eggs.

◎ Pour ½ of grits into a lightly greased 12 x 8 x 2-inch baking dish; sprinkle Swiss cheese over top. Spoon remaining grits over cheese. Cover and bake at 350 degrees for 1 hour or until set.

◎ Uncover and sprinkle remaining ¼ cup cheddar cheese over top. Bake, uncovered, 5 minutes or until cheese melts.

Yield: 8 to 10 servings

Spicy Hot Beans

Add Chipotle Cornbread and call it a meal!

Preparation Time: 20 minutes
Chill Time: 8 hours
Cook Time: 2 to 3 hours

1	(16-ounce) package dried pinto beans
6	cups water
½	pound bacon, cut into ½-inch pieces
1	pound smoked link sausage, cut into ½-inch slices
2	medium onions, chopped
½	cup green bell pepper, chopped
4	cloves garlic, minced
¼	cup Worcestershire sauce
¼	cup brown sugar, firmly packed
2	tablespoons ground cumin
1	tablespoon chile powder
1	tablespoon pepper
1	tablespoon celery seeds
1-2	teaspoons hot sauce
1	teaspoon salt
1	bay leaf
1	(16-ounce) can tomatoes, with liquid, chopped

◎ Sort and wash beans; place in a large pot. Cover with water 2 inches above beans; let soak 8 hours. Drain beans and return to pot. Add 6 cups water.

◎ Combine bacon, smoked link sausage, onions, green bell pepper and garlic in a skillet; cook over medium heat until bacon is browned and vegetables are tender. Drain. Add to beans.

◎ Stir in Worcestershire sauce, brown sugar, cumin, chile powder, pepper, celery seeds, hot sauce, salt and bay leaf and bring mixture to a boil. Cover, reduce heat and simmer 2 to 3 hours or until beans are tender, stirring occasionally.

◎ Add tomatoes with liquid; cook 30 minutes longer.

◎ Remove bay leaf and serve.

Yield: 10 servings

This recipe can be found in
Spanish in the **Otra Vez...En Español** section.

Vodka Orange Slush

Frozen drinks are light and refreshing, particularly during the hot summer months. Whip up a batch of Vodka-Orange Slush to cool yourself down by combining 1 (6-ounce) can frozen orange juice concentrate, ¾ cup vodka, ¾ cup milk and 1 tablespoon sugar in a blender. Blend with ice until desired consistency.

Dressing Spoons

Dressings and stuffings have special spoons designed to serve them. Their 8-inch long handles give neat and easy access to this delicious side stuffed inside the turkey. Although ornate spoons are not a necessity, they do add history and beauty to the holiday table. If you have one, pull it out and use it~whether your dressing is inside or outside the bird. Browse for them in antique shops; an assortment of different patterns will make a lovely addition to your serving pieces.

Green Chile-Cornbread Dressing

Traditional cornbread dressing with a kick!

Preparation Time: 10 minutes
Cook Time: 40 minutes

¼ cup butter or margarine	3 tablespoons fresh parsley, chopped
2 cups onion, chopped	½ teaspoon poultry seasoning
1 cup celery, sliced	½ teaspoon salt
1 (14½-ounce) can chicken broth	¼ teaspoon dried oregano
1 (17-ounce) can whole kernel corn, drained	¼ teaspoon pepper
	6 cups cornbread crumbs
2 (4-ounce) cans chopped green chiles, drained	½ cup pecans, chopped and toasted

◎ Melt butter in a large pot; add onion and celery and cook over medium-high heat, stirring constantly, until tender.

◎ Stir in chicken broth, corn, green chiles, parsley, poultry seasoning, salt, oregano and pepper.

◎ Add cornbread crumbs and pecans, tossing until crumbs are moistened; spoon into a lightly greased 13 x 9 x 2-inch baking dish.

◎ Cover and bake at 350 degrees for 30 minutes or until thoroughly heated.

Yield: 8 to 10 servings

Sweet Sensations

Sweet Sensations

Warm Fudge-Filled Cheesecake

The warm chocolate center and the crunchy pistachio crust make this cheesecake decadent!

Preparation Time: 30 minutes
Cool Time: 1 hour
Cook Time: 1 hour 15 minutes

½	cup butter or margarine, softened
⅓	cup plus 1½ cups sugar; divided
1	cup flour
1	tablespoon vanilla extract; divided
⅔	cup pistachios, chopped
4	(8-ounce) packages cream cheese, softened
4	large eggs
1	(12-ounce) package semisweet chocolate miniature morsels
	Sweetened whipped cream (optional)
	Chocolate shavings (optional)

- ◎ Beat butter at medium speed with an electric mixer until creamy; add ⅓ cup sugar, beating well.
- ◎ Gradually add flour, beating at low speed until blended. Stir in 1 teaspoon vanilla extract and pistachios.
- ◎ Press into bottom and 1½ inches up sides of a 9-inch springform pan.
- ◎ Bake at 350 degrees for 12 to 15 minutes or until golden. Cool on a wire rack.
- ◎ Beat cream cheese at medium speed with an electric mixer until light and fluffy; gradually add 1½ cups sugar, beating well. Add eggs, 1 at a time, beating just until yellow disappears. Stir in remaining 2 teaspoons vanilla extract. Do not overmix.
- ◎ Pour ½ of batter into crust; sprinkle with chocolate morsels to within ¾ inch of edge and working toward center. Pour remaining batter over chocolate morsels.
- ◎ Place cheesecake on a baking sheet. Bake at 350 degrees for 1 hour or until set. Cool on a wire rack 1 hour.
- ◎ Serve slightly warm with sweetened whipped cream, if desired. Garnish with chocolate shavings, if desired.

Warm leftover slices in the microwave 30 seconds before serving.

Yield: 12 servings

This recipe can be found in Spanish in the **Otra Vez...En Español** section.

Melting Chocolate

Because it scorches easily, chocolate should be melted slowly over low heat. If using a double boiler, remove the pan from the heat when the chocolate is melted slightly more than halfway and stir until completely smooth. If using a microwave, heat at 50 percent power. Timing will vary based on the microwave and the type of chocolate being melted. If your chocolate begins to clump or harden when mixed with liquid, it can sometimes be corrected by immediately stirring in a small amount of vegetable oil, using a ratio of 1 tablespoon oil to 6 ounces of chocolate.

Chocolate-Wrapped Banana Cheesecake with Caramelized Bananas

There are no words to describe this incredible dessert!

Preparation Time: 30 minutes
Chill Time: 8 hours
Cook Time: 1 hour 15 minutes

Peanut-Graham Crust

3	medium ripe bananas
2	teaspoons lemon juice
2	(8-ounce) packages cream cheese, softened
1	cup sugar
1	cup mascarpone cheese
4	large eggs
1	tablespoon vanilla extract
1½	cups milk chocolate morsels
1½	tablespoons butter or margarine
	Caramelized Bananas

◎ Prepare Peanut-Graham Crust; set aside.

◎ Mash bananas with fork; stir in lemon juice until blended.

◎ Beat cream cheese and sugar at medium speed with an electric mixer until light and fluffy. Add mascarpone, beating until smooth. Add eggs, one at a time, beating well after each addition. Stir in bananas and vanilla extract. Pour into Peanut-Graham Crust.

◎ Bake at 325 degrees for 1 hour (center will be slightly soft). Remove from oven; run a knife around edge to loosen sides. Cool on a wire rack; cover and chill 8 hours.

◎ Microwave milk chocolate morsels and butter in a 1-quart microwave-safe bowl on high 60 seconds; stir until smooth. Let stand 30 minutes.

◎ Remove sides of springform pan. Spread ¾ of melted chocolate around sides of cheesecake.

◎ Arrange caramelized bananas on top; drizzle with remaining chocolate.

As a substitute for the mascarpone cheese, beat 1 (8-ounce) package cream cheese, 2½ tablespoons sour cream and 2 tablespoons whipping cream well at medium speed with an electric mixer. Use 1 cup mixture for cheesecake recipe, reserving remainder for other uses.

Yield: 12 servings

Chocolate-Wrapped Banana Cheesecake continued

PEANUT-GRAHAM CRUST

2	cups graham cracker crumbs	½	cup sugar
1	cup dry roasted peanuts, finely chopped	½	cup butter or margarine, melted

◎ Stir together graham cracker crumbs, peanuts, sugar and butter; press onto bottom and 1 inch up sides of a 9-inch springform pan.

◎ Bake at 375 degrees for 10 to 12 minutes. Cool on a wire rack.

Yield: crust for 1 (9-inch) cheesecake

CARAMELIZED BANANAS

4	medium bananas	¼	cup butter or margarine
½	cup light brown sugar, firmly packed		

◎ Cut bananas diagonally into ⅓-inch thick slices.

◎ Cook brown sugar and butter over high heat in a small skillet, stirring constantly, 5 minutes or until thickened. Remove from heat; stir in bananas. Cool.

Yield: 1¼ cups

Peanut Butter Fun Dough

Little hands can create works of art with Peanut Butter Fun Dough:

2 cups nonfat dry milk powder

2 cups powdered sugar

1¾ cups creamy peanut butter

1¾ cups honey

Beat all ingredients with an electric mixer until smooth. Mold or shape dough into imaginative shapes or pat and cut out the dough using a cookie cutter.

Yield: 5 cups

Cap it with Coffee

- **Café au lait:** Brew strong black coffee. Simultaneously pour coffee and an equal amount of scalded milk into cup. Add sugar if desired.

- **Café Brûlot:** In a chafing dish, combine 6 teaspoons sugar, 6-8 whole cloves, 2 cinnamon sticks, 4 lemon twists and 4 orange twists. Pour 8 ounces of either cognac or Cointreau over mixture. Flame. Add 4 cups very strong hot coffee. Stir and heat 1 minute.

- **Café Viennese:** To a cup of strong hot coffee, add 1 ounce cognac. Top with sweetened whipped cream and a sprinkle of nutmeg.

- **Café con Canela:** To a cup of strong hot coffee, add 1 ounce coffee-flavored liqueur and 1 teaspoon vanilla. Top with sweetened whipped cream and a sprinkle of grated semi-sweet chocolate or cinnamon. Garnish with a cinnamon stick.

- **Irish Coffee:** Add 1 ounce Irish whiskey and 1 to 2 teaspoons sugar to a cup of strong hot coffee. Top with sweetened whipped cream.

- **Tropical Coffee:** To a cup of strong hot coffee, add 1 tablespoon coconut cream and 1 ounce dark rum. Top with sweetened whipped cream. Garnish with grated toasted coconut.

Pumpkin Cheesecake with Caramel Swirl

This delicious cheesecake is a new twist for a traditional holiday dessert and can be prepared one day ahead of time.

Preparation Time: 40 minutes
Chill Time: 8 hours
Cook Time: 1 hour 15 minutes

Gingersnap Crust	9 tablespoons whipping cream; divided
4 (8-ounce) packages cream cheese, room temperature	1 teaspoon cinnamon
1⅔ cups sugar	1 teaspoon allspice
1½ cups canned solid pack pumpkin	4 large eggs
	1 tablespoon caramel sauce
	1 cup sour cream

- Prepare Gingersnap Crust; set aside.
- Preheat oven to 350 degrees.
- Beat cream cheese and sugar in large bowl with electric mixer until light. Transfer ¾ cup mixture to small bowl; cover tightly and refrigerate to use for topping.
- Add pumpkin, 4 tablespoons whipping cream, cinnamon and allspice to mixture in large bowl and beat until well combined.
- Add eggs, one at a time, beating until just combined.
- Pour filling into Gingersnap Crust (filling will almost fill pan). Bake until cheesecake puffs, top browns and center moves only slightly when pan is shaken, about 1 hour 15 minutes.
- Transfer cheesecake to rack and cool 10 minutes. Run small sharp knife around cake pan sides to loosen cheesecake. Cool. Cover tightly and refrigerate overnight.
- Bring remaining ¾ cup cream cheese mixture to room temperature. Add remaining 5 tablespoons whipping cream to cream cheese mixture and stir to combine.
- Press down firmly on edges of cheesecake to even thickness. Pour cream cheese mixture over cheesecake, spreading evenly.
- Spoon caramel sauce in lines over cream cheese mixture. Using tip of knife, swirl caramel sauce into cream cheese mixture.
- Release pan sides from cheesecake. Spoon sour cream into pastry bag fitted with small star tip (do not stir before using). Pipe decorative border around cheesecake and serve.

Pumpkin Cheesecake continued

GINGERSNAP CRUST

1½ cups gingersnap cookie crumbs

1½ cups (about 6 ounces) pecans, toasted

¼ cup brown sugar, firmly packed

¼ cup unsalted butter, melted

- Finely grind cookies, pecans and brown sugar in food processor.
- Add butter and blend until combined.
- Press crust mixture onto bottom and up sides of 9-inch springform pan with 2¾-inch high sides.

Yield: 12 servings

Don't Crack the Cheesecake!

The reason cheesecakes crack is because they have been overcooked. Overcooking causes proteins to shrink and the cake to dry out, leading to cracks.

The simplest way to avoid cracks is to shorten the cooking time, but you can also play with other variables. Sugar slows cooking by blocking the coagulation of proteins, so adding more provides an extra barrier against overcooking. Another option is to cut an egg out of the recipe. Fewer eggs mean fewer proteins, a slower rate of coagulation and slower cooking.

Cooking on a High

Baking does not have to be tricky at high altitudes. Follow these basic guidelines:

For cakes: Baking at higher elevations causes cakes to expand. Therefore, increase the oven temperature by 20 degrees and decrease the baking time slightly. Up to elevations of 3000 feet, you should not need to adjust the ingredients in the recipe, although you should take care not to overbeat the eggs when baking at any higher elevation. At elevations of 3000 feet or more, use the following chart for adjustments:

Ingredient:	Liquid: add for each cup
3000 feet:	1-2 tablespoons
5000 feet:	2-4 tablespoons
7000 feet:	3-4 tablespoons

Ingredient:	Baking powder or soda: decrease for each teaspoon
3000 feet:	$\frac{1}{8}$ teaspoon
5000 feet:	$\frac{1}{8}$-$\frac{1}{4}$ tablespoon
7000 feet:	$\frac{1}{4}$ tablespoon

Ingredient:	Sugar: decrease for each cup
3000 feet:	0-1 tablespoon
5000 feet:	0-2 tablespoons
7000 feet:	1-3 tablespoons

Refer to the suggestions on the following page for additional tips when cooking at high altitudes.

Caramel Cake

The Caramel Frosting is well worth the effort.
It transforms this cake into an elegant dessert for special occasions.

Preparation Time: 1 hour
Chill Time: 1 hour
Cook Time: 55 minutes

1	(8-ounce) container sour cream	2	teaspoons baking powder
¼	cup milk	½	teaspoon salt
1	cup butter, softened	1	teaspoon vanilla extract
2	cups sugar	1	teaspoon rum extract (optional)
4	eggs		Caramel Frosting
2¾	cups flour		

◎ Combine sour cream and milk.

◎ Cream butter with an electric mixer; gradually add sugar, beating well at medium speed. Add eggs, 1 at a time, beating well after each addition.

◎ Combine flour, baking powder and salt; add to creamed mixture alternately with sour cream mixture, beginning and ending with flour mixture. Mix after each addition. Add vanilla extract and rum extract, if desired.

◎ Pour batter into 2 greased and floured 9-inch round cake pans. Bake at 350 degrees for 30 to 35 minutes or until a wooden pick, inserted in center, comes out clean.

◎ Cool in pans 10 minutes; remove and cool completely on wire racks.

◎ Spread Caramel Frosting between layers and on top and sides of cake.

Yield: 14 to 16 servings

CARAMEL FROSTING

3	cups sugar; divided	¾	cup butter or margarine
1	tablespoon flour	1	teaspoon vanilla extract
1	cup milk		

◎ Sprinkle ½ cup sugar in a shallow, heavy 3½-quart pot; cook over medium heat, stirring constantly, until sugar melts (sugar will clump first) and syrup is a light golden brown. Remove from heat.

◎ Combine remaining 2½ cups sugar and flour in a large saucepan, stirring well; add milk and bring to a boil, stirring constantly.

Caramel Cake continued

◎ Gradually pour about ¼ of hot mixture into caramelized sugar, stirring constantly; add remaining hot mixture (mixture will lump, but continue stirring until smooth).

◎ Cover and cook over low heat 2 minutes. Uncover and cook, without stirring, over medium heat until a candy thermometer reaches 238 degrees. Add butter, stirring to blend.

◎ Remove from heat and cool without stirring until temperature drops to 110 degrees (about 1 hour).

◎ Add vanilla extract and beat with a wooden spoon or at medium speed of an electric mixer until spreading consistency (about 7 or 8 minutes).

Cooking on a High
(continued)

For cookies, biscuits and muffins: A recipe should need little adjustment when baking cookies, biscuits or muffins at higher altitudes. Try reducing the sugar and baking powder slightly and increasing the liquid. Also, to keep the cookies from drying out, increase oven temperature by 20 degrees and decrease the baking time.

For yeast doughs: Yeast doughs rise more rapidly at higher altitudes. It is necessary to punch the dough down after it has risen once and allow it to rise again. Add more liquid to the dough if it seems dry, and remember to decrease the amount of flour you use the next time!

For pies: Higher altitudes mean greater evaporation. Add a little more liquid to your pastry.

For candy: Candy temperatures need to be lowered 8 degrees to prevent excessive water evaporation.

For deep-frying: Deep-fat frying requires a lower temperature. Lower fat temperature 2 degrees for each 1000 feet of elevation.

Note: The altitude in El Paso is 3900 feet.

Cake Cutting 101

For a clean well-defined cut, heat the blade of a thin sharp knife (either serrated or straight-edged) by running it under hot water and drying it before cutting. A serrated edge with small compact teeth produces cleaner cuts. Serrated edges work well with angel food cakes and dental floss works well with cheesecakes.

Maple Nut Cake

Maple syrup is not just for breakfast - this nutty cake
and rich creamy maple frosting will be devoured any time of day!

Preparation Time: 30 minutes
Cook Time: 30 to 35 minutes

1	cup shortening	½	teaspoon salt
½	cup brown sugar, firmly packed	2	teaspoons nutmeg
1	cup maple syrup	½	cup hot water
2	large eggs	½	cup sherry
2½	cups flour	1	cup pecans, chopped and toasted
2	teaspoons baking powder		Maple Frosting
½	teaspoon baking soda	12-15	pecan halves

◎ Beat shortening at medium speed of an electric mixer until fluffy; gradually add brown sugar, beating well. Add maple syrup and eggs, beating until blended.

◎ Combine flour, baking powder, baking soda, salt and nutmeg; add to shortening mixture alternately with hot water and sherry, beginning and ending with flour mixture. Beat at low speed until blended after each addition.

◎ Stir in chopped pecans.

◎ Pour batter into a greased and floured 13 x 9 x 2-inch pan.

◎ Bake at 350 degrees for 30 to 35 minutes until a wooden pick, inserted in center, comes out clean. Cool cake completely in pan on wire rack.

◎ Spread Maple Frosting on top of cake; place a pecan half on each serving.

Yield: 12 to 15 servings

MAPLE FROSTING

¼	cup butter, softened	2-3	tablespoons milk
2¼	cups powdered sugar; divided	½	teaspoon maple extract

◎ Beat butter at medium speed of an electric mixer until creamy; gradually add 1 cup powdered sugar, beating well. Add remaining powdered sugar and milk, beating until spreading consistency. Beat in maple extract until blended.

Yield: 1 cup

Flan Cake

This Mexican-style cake is easy to prepare and gives the impression that you worked for hours!

Preparation Time: 20 minutes
Cook Time: 45 to 50 minutes

1 **(12-ounce) can evaporated milk**	**Vegetable cooking spray**
1 **(14-ounce) can sweetened condensed milk**	½ **cup Cajeta (Mexican caramel) or caramel ice cream topping**
3 **eggs**	1 **box butter cake mix**
1 **tablespoon vanilla extract**	

◎ In large bowl, mix evaporated milk, sweetened condensed milk, eggs and vanilla extract with a spoon. Set aside.

◎ Spray 12-cup Bundt pan very liberally with vegetable cooking spray. Spread Cajeta into bottom of Bundt pan. (Microwave the caramel for 30 seconds on high to make it easier to spread).

◎ Prepare cake mix as directed on back of box. Pour cake batter on top of Cajeta in Bundt pan. Slowly, pour flan mixture over cake batter (flan mixture will sink to the bottom of the pan).

◎ Bake at 325 degrees for 45 to 50 minutes. Cool in pan 15 minutes; invert onto serving platter and cool completely.

Substitute spice cake mix or another cake mix of your choice instead of butter cake mix.

Yield: 12 to 14 servings

This recipe can be found in
Spanish in the **Otra Vez...En Español** section.

Splatter-proof

Avoid splatters while using your electric mixer by punching holes in a paper plate; insert beaters through the holes and into the mixer. Keeping the surface of the plate even with the top of the bowl, begin beating mixture.

Chocolate Truffle Cake

This recipe may seem elaborate, but the finished cake is a work of art!

Preparation Time: 2 hours
Chill Time: 2 hours
Cook Time: 25 to 30 minutes

Chocolate Truffles	**Satiny Chocolate Frosting**
2-3 tablespoons milk	2 (2-ounce) bottles chocolate
Rich Chocolate Cake	sprinkles

◎ Prepare Chocolate Truffles.

◎ Combine milk and reserved ¾ truffle mixture; beat at high speed of an electric mixer until mixture is spreading consistency.

◎ Spread between layers of Rich Chocolate Cake.

◎ Spoon about 1 cup Satiny Chocolate Frosting into a decorating bag fitted with large tip Number 2110. Spread remaining frosting on top and sides of cake, spreading it smoothly with a long metal spatula. Pat chocolate sprinkles on sides of cake. Pipe 12 (1-inch) rosettes of frosting around top edge of cake. Place a truffle on each rosette. Chill until serving time.

Yield: 12 to 14 servings

CHOCOLATE TRUFFLES

1 (12-ounce) package semisweet chocolate morsels	¼ cup plus 2 tablespoons powdered sugar, sifted
4 egg yolks	2 tablespoons chocolate sprinkles
¼ cup plus 2 tablespoons butter or margarine, cut into cubes	

◎ Place chocolate morsels in top of a double boiler; bring water to a boil. Reduce heat to low; cook until chocolate melts. Remove container of chocolate from boiling water.

◎ Beat egg yolks until thick and lemon colored.

◎ Gradually stir about ¼ hot chocolate into yolks; add back to remaining hot mixture, stirring constantly.

◎ Add butter and powdered sugar; beat at medium speed of an electric mixer until butter melts and mixture is smooth.

◎ Place about ¼ mixture in a bowl; cover with a paper towel, and let stand in a cool dry place 1 hour (do not refrigerate). Set aside remaining ¾ truffle mixture to spread between layers of cake.

Chocolate Truffle Cake continued

◎ After ¼ of truffle mixture has set for 1 hour, shape into 12 equal balls; roll balls lightly in chocolate sprinkles. Let stand 1 hour, uncovered.

Yield: 1 dozen truffles and filling for a 3-layer cake

RICH CHOCOLATE CAKE

1	cup cocoa	1½	teaspoons vanilla extract
2	cups boiling water	2¾	cups flour
1	cup butter or margarine, softened	2	teaspoons baking soda
2½	cups sugar	½	teaspoon baking powder
4	eggs	½	teaspoon salt

◎ Combine cocoa and boiling water, stirring until smooth. Set aside to cool.

◎ Cream butter, sugar, eggs and vanilla extract at high speed of an electric mixer until light and fluffy, about 5 minutes.

◎ Combine flour, baking soda, baking powder and salt. Add to creamed mixture alternately with cocoa mixture; beat at low speed of an electric mixer, beginning and ending with flour mixture.

◎ Pour batter into 3 greased and floured 9-inch cake pans. Bake at 350 degrees for 25 to 30 minutes. Cool in pans 10 minutes; remove from pans and let cool completely on wire racks.

Yield: 12 to 14 servings

SATINY CHOCOLATE FROSTING

1	(6-ounce) package semisweet chocolate morsels	1	cup butter or margarine
½	cup milk	2½	cups powdered sugar, sifted

◎ Combine chocolate morsels, milk and butter in a saucepan; cook over medium heat, stirring constantly until melted and smooth.

◎ Remove from heat; blend in powdered sugar.

◎ Set saucepan in a bowl of ice water; beat at medium speed of an electric mixer until frosting holds its shape.

Yield: about 3 cups

The Refreshing Flavor of Mint

Mint-flavored chocolate morsels are wonderful in recipes, but sometimes difficult to find in the store. When not available, make them on your own by pouring a bag of semisweet chocolate morsels into a heavy-duty zip-top plastic bag and adding ½ teaspoon mint extract. Close the bag and toss to coat the chocolate morsels. Remove as much air from the bag as possible and seal. Let the bag sit overnight and the chocolate morsels will absorb the mint flavor and be ready for use in any recipe.

The Sweet Smell of Lemon

• Lemons will keep at least three to four days at room temperature or up to four weeks in the refrigerator.

• If a recipe calls for both lemon juice and zest, pour the lemon juice over the zest to keep it moist and flavorful.

• Lemon juice and lemon zest freeze well.

• To extract the most juice, make sure the lemons are at room temperature. Roll them under your palm on a countertop before squeezing. For best results, use a lemon juicer; however, if you do not have one, squeeze a lemon half around the tines of a fork. Thick-skinned lemons are the juiciest.

• Grate or remove the zest first, then squeeze for juice.

• To remove the zest in strips, use a very sharp paring knife, a vegetable peeler or a special tool called a lemon zester. Remove only the colored part of the peel, leaving the bitter white pith on the lemon. If necessary, turn the strips over and scrape any white with a sharp knife.

• Do not cut lemons with a carbon steel knife or cook in aluminum pots.

Lemon Meringue Cake

The creamy lemon filling and light meringue topping make this an elegant dessert.

Preparation Time: 1 hour
Cook Time: 45 minutes

¼ cup plus 1 tablespoon butter or margarine; divided	⅓ cup milk
1¾ cups sugar; divided	½ teaspoon vanilla extract
4 eggs, separated; divided	1 cup water
1 egg, whole	½ teaspoon lemon rind, grated
1⅓ cups flour; divided	¼ cup lemon juice
1 teaspoon baking powder	½ teaspoon cream of tartar

◎ Cream ¼ cup butter with an electric mixer; gradually add ½ cup sugar, beating at medium speed. Add 2 egg yolks and 1 whole egg to creamed mixture; mix well.

◎ Combine 1 cup flour and baking powder; add to creamed mixture alternately with milk, beginning and ending with flour mixture. Mix after each addition. Stir in vanilla extract.

◎ Pour batter into a greased and floured 9-inch round cake pan. Bake at 350 degrees for 28 to 30 minutes or until a wooden pick, inserted in center, comes out clean.

◎ Cool in pan 10 minutes. Remove from pan and cool completely.

◎ Combine remaining 2 egg yolks and water; set aside. Combine ¾ cup sugar and remaining ⅓ cup flour in a heavy saucepan; add egg yolk mixture and lemon rind. Cook over medium heat, stirring constantly, until mixture thickens and comes to a boil. Boil 2 minutes. Remove from heat. Stir in lemon juice and remaining 1 tablespoon butter. Cover with wax paper and cool.

◎ Place cake layer on baking sheet. Spoon filling onto cake.

◎ Beat 4 egg whites (at room temperature) and cream of tartar at high speed of an electric mixer 1 minute. Gradually add remaining ½ cup sugar, 1 tablespoon at a time, beating until stiff peaks form and sugar dissolves (2 to 4 minutes). Spread over lemon filling.

◎ Bake at 350 degrees for 12 to 15 minutes or until meringue peaks are lightly browned.

Yield: 12 servings

Pumpkin Praline Cake

The moist cake and crunchy praline center will have everyone asking for the recipe.

Preparation Time: 40 minutes
Cook Time: 1 hour

1 **package yellow cake mix (without pudding)**	1 **teaspoon allspice**
½ **cup oil**	1 **(15-ounce) can pumpkin**
¾ **cup brown sugar, firmly packed**	¼ **cup water**
1 **teaspoon cinnamon**	3 **eggs**
½ **teaspoon nutmeg**	**Praline Mix**
	Cream Cheese Icing
	Pecans, chopped (optional)

◎ Combine yellow cake mix, oil, brown sugar, cinnamon, nutmeg, allspice, pumpkin and water. Beat with an electric mixer until blended. Add eggs, 1 at a time, beating well after each addition.

◎ Pour ½ of the mixture into a greased and floured Bundt pan. Sprinkle the Praline Mix over the batter; pour remaining batter over Praline Mix.

◎ Bake at 350 degrees for 1 hour or until wooden toothpick inserted in center comes out clean.

◎ Cool in pan 15 minutes; invert onto serving platter and cool completely.

◎ Top with Cream Cheese Icing and sprinkle with chopped pecans, if desired.

Yield: 12 to 14 servings

PRALINE MIX

½ **cup pecans, chopped**	½ **cup butter, softened**
⅓ **cup brown sugar, firmly packed**	

◎ Blend pecans, brown sugar and butter with a fork until mixture is crumbly.

CREAM CHEESE ICING

1 **(8-ounce) package cream cheese, softened**	4 **cups powdered sugar**
4 **tablespoons butter or margarine, softened**	1 **teaspoon vanilla extract**

◎ Blend cream cheese and butter with an electric mixer; add powdered sugar and vanilla extract. Mix until creamy.

Pumpkin Patch

The spotting of pumpkins is the first sign that summer is over and the fall harvest is here. Big pumpkins, or "face" pumpkins, are not only good for making jack-o-lanterns, but they serve as vases for huge bouquets of harvest foliage on buffet tables. Tiny baby pumpkins are scooped out and baked or steamed to hold individual portions of soup. The pumpkins grown for jack-o-lanterns are very different from those grown to make canned pumpkin. Those pumpkins are known as "cheese" pumpkins. So next time you feel like getting "domestic" and want to try to puree your own pumpkin meat...don't. This is one of the few times when canned is actually better than homemade.

Preparing the Pan

To avoid having a cake stick to the pan, grease or oil the bottom and sides of the pan and dust with flour. For chocolate cakes, use cocoa as the dusting agent.

Sinful Bundt Cake

This easy-to-make cake filled with creamy candy bars is sure to be a favorite!

Preparation Time: 30 minutes
Cook Time: 1 hour 15 minutes

6 chocolate-covered caramel nougat candy bars, coarsely chopped	2½ cups flour
	¼ teaspoon baking soda
1 cup butter or margarine, softened; divided	1¼ cups buttermilk
2 cups sugar	2 teaspoons vanilla extract
4 large eggs	1 cup pecans, chopped
	Creamy Chocolate Glaze

◎ Melt chocolate-covered caramel nougat candy bars and ½ cup butter in a heavy saucepan over low heat, stirring until smooth. Set aside.

◎ Beat remaining ½ cup butter and sugar at medium speed with an electric mixer until fluffy. Add eggs, 1 at a time, beating until blended after each addition.

◎ Combine flour and baking soda; add to sugar mixture alternately with buttermilk, beginning and ending with flour mixture. Beat at low speed after each addition.

◎ Stir in candy mixture, vanilla extract and pecans.

◎ Pour into a greased and floured 12-cup Bundt pan or 10-inch tube pan.

◎ Bake at 350 degrees for 1 hour 15 minutes or until a wooden pick, inserted in center, comes out clean.

◎ Cool in pan on wire rack 10 minutes; remove from pan and cool completely on wire rack.

◎ Drizzle Creamy Chocolate Glaze over cake.

Yield: 12 to 14 servings

CREAMY CHOCOLATE GLAZE

2¼ cups powdered sugar, sifted	¼ cup butter or margarine, softened
3 tablespoons cocoa	6 tablespoons milk

◎ Stir together sugar and cocoa in a large mixing bowl.

◎ Add butter and milk and beat at medium speed with an electric mixer until smooth.

American Apple Pie

A new twist on an old favorite - crunchy oatmeal crust and topping make this pie a special treat for 4th of July, Thanksgiving, or any time of year!

Preparation Time: 20 minutes
Cook Time: 45 minutes

2 **cups flour**	4 **cups (about 3 large) apples, peeled and thinly sliced**
1 **cup brown sugar, firmly packed**	¾ **cup sugar**
½ **cup regular oats**	1 **tablespoon cornstarch**
¾ **teaspoon salt; divided**	½ **teaspoon vanilla extract**
⅓ **cup pecans, chopped**	½ **cup water**
¾ **cup butter, melted**	

◎ Combine flour, brown sugar, oats, ½ teaspoon salt and pecans in a large bowl; add butter and stir until blended. Measure 1 cup firmly packed mixture and set aside for pie topping. Press remaining mixture in bottom and up sides of a well greased 9-inch deep-dish pie plate.

◎ Arrange apples on top of crust in pie plate. Set aside.

◎ Combine sugar, cornstarch, ¼ teaspoon salt and vanilla extract in a small saucepan. Stir in water. Cook over medium heat until mixture boils.

◎ Pour hot mixture evenly over apples; crumble reserved topping mixture evenly over pie.

◎ Bake at 375 degrees for 40 minutes, covering with foil the last 15 minutes, if necessary, to prevent excess browning.

Granny Smith apples work well for this pie. It's delicious with ice cream!

Yield: 8 servings

Pleasant Pie Crusts

To prevent pie crust edges from overbrowning, fold a 12-inch square of aluminum foil into quarters. Cut out the center, leaving an 8-inch hole. Unfold and place foil over the partially baked pie crust to shield the edges.

Bumbleberry Pie

Lots of fresh fruit and a packaged pie crust make this a fresh and easy summertime pie. Serve warm with vanilla ice cream for rave reviews.

Preparation Time: 15 minutes
Cook Time: 50 to 55 minutes

2 large cooking apples, peeled and chopped	1 cup sugar
1 cup fresh rhubarb, chopped	½ cup flour
1 cup fresh raspberries	1 tablespoon fresh lemon juice
1 cup fresh blueberries	1 (15-ounce) package refrigerated pie crusts
1 cup fresh strawberries, halved	Vanilla ice cream

◎ Combine apples, rhubarb, raspberries, blueberries, strawberries, sugar, flour and lemon juice in a large bowl, stirring gently.

◎ Fit 1 pie crust into a 9-inch pie plate according to package directions; spoon fruit mixture into crust.

◎ Roll remaining pie crust with a rolling pin to press out fold lines; cut into ½-inch strips, and arrange in a lattice design over filling. Fold edges under and crimp.

◎ Place pie on a baking sheet. Bake at 400 degrees for 25 minutes; reduce heat to 350 degrees and bake 25 to 30 more minutes, shielding edges of pie with strips of aluminum foil to prevent excess browning if necessary.

◎ Serve with vanilla ice cream.

Frozen rhubarb and berries, thawed and drained, may be substituted for fresh fruit.

Yield: 6 to 8 servings

Chocolate Banana Pecan Cream Pie

An easy and delicious pie that is good to the last bite!

Preparation Time: 40 minutes

¼ cup butter or margarine, softened

1 (3-ounce) package cream cheese, softened

1½ cups plus 3 tablespoons powdered sugar, sifted; divided

1¼ cups whipping cream; divided

½ teaspoon vanilla extract

3 bananas, sliced

1 (6-ounce) can pineapple juice

1 9-inch pastry shell, baked

½ cup pecans, chopped and toasted

2 (1-ounce) squares semisweet chocolate

◎ Beat butter and cream cheese at medium speed with an electric mixer until creamy; gradually add 1½ cups powdered sugar alternately with ¼ cup whipping cream, beginning and ending with powdered sugar.

◎ Stir in vanilla extract. Set filling aside.

◎ Toss banana slices in pineapple juice; drain. Pat slices dry with paper towels.

◎ Spoon half of filling into baked pastry shell. Arrange banana slices over top of filling. Top with remaining filling and sprinkle with pecans. Set pie aside.

◎ Melt semisweet chocolate in a heavy saucepan over low heat. Spoon into a small heavy-duty zip-top plastic bag. Snip a tiny hole at corner of bag; drizzle over pecans and filling. Set aside.

◎ Beat remaining 1 cup whipping cream at low speed with an electric mixer until foamy; gradually add remaining 3 tablespoons powdered sugar, beating until soft peaks form.

◎ Spoon whipped cream into a large heavy-duty zip-top plastic bag. Snip ½ inch from corner of bag. Pipe dollops of whipped cream around outside edge.

Yield: 8 servings

Cutting-Edge Pie Crusts

With ready-made pie dough available, you can now spare more time to "spiff" up the edges. Here's how:

• A string of stars: Place one of the two prepackaged crusts in the pie plate. Unfold the second and make stars using a tiny cookie cutter. Lay them down on the edge of the crust one by one, overlapping until the circle is completed.

• Scallop: Turn the bowl of a spoon upside down and cut dough with the tip of the spoon; discard the dough removed.

• Herringbone: Indent the pastry with tines of a fork at a 45-degree angle, alternating direction each time. If the fork sticks to the dough, dip it in flour.

On a Pie High

• Pie dough will keep in the refrigerator for up to three days or in the freezer for six months. Thaw frozen dough in the refrigerator, then let stand at room temperature for 30 minutes before rolling it out.

• Use a pizza wheel to trim rolled pastry or cut lattice strips for the top of a pie.

• Moist pies should be stored at room temperature, covered loosely with aluminum foil or plastic wrap to keep them crisp. Store custard and cream pies in the refrigerator, but let them warm to room temperature before serving.

Raspberry Cream Pie

The raspberries add a sensational surprise to this creamy pie.

Preparation Time: 20 minutes
Cook Time: 50 to 55 minutes

1 cup sugar	1 9-inch pastry shell
⅔ cup flour; divided	⅓ cup brown sugar, firmly packed
2 large eggs, lightly beaten	⅓ cup pecans, chopped
1⅓ cups sour cream	3 tablespoons butter, softened
1 teaspoon vanilla extract	Whipped cream and fresh raspberries (optional)
3 cups fresh or frozen raspberries, thawed	

◎ Combine sugar, ⅓ cup flour, eggs, sour cream and vanilla extract in a large bowl, stirring until smooth.

◎ Gradually fold in raspberries.

◎ Spoon into pastry shell.

◎ Bake at 400 degrees for 40 to 45 minutes or until center is set.

◎ Combine remaining ⅓ cup flour, brown sugar, pecans and butter; sprinkle over hot pie.

◎ Bake at 400 degrees for 10 minutes or until golden, shielding edges with foil, if necessary, to prevent excessive browning.

◎ Garnish with whipped cream and fresh raspberries, if desired.

Yield: 8 servings

Mango Colada Pie

A taste of the tropics comes right to you with this creamy pie and delicious crunchy crust!

Preparation Time: 20 minutes
Chill Time: 8 hours
Cook Time: 10 minutes

Coconut Crust

2	(8-ounce) packages cream cheese, softened
1	cup sugar; divided

2	ripe mangoes, chopped in small pieces
2	(8-ounce) containers heavy cream
¾	cup coconut

- ◎ Prepare Coconut Crust; set aside.
- ◎ Beat cream cheese and ⅔ cup sugar with an electric mixer until creamy.
- ◎ Fold in mangoes.
- ◎ In a separate mixing bowl, beat heavy cream and remaining ⅓ cup sugar until stiff peaks form. Fold in the mango mixture.
- ◎ Pour into cooled Coconut Crust. Garnish with coconut.
- ◎ Chill for at least 8 hours or overnight before serving.

Decorate each plate with some raspberry puree and fresh raspberries.

Yield: 8 to 10 servings

COCONUT CRUST

½	cup almonds, finely chopped
¼	cup sugar
¼	cup walnuts, finely chopped

1	cup graham cracker crumbs
1	cup coconut
½	cup unsalted butter, melted

- ◎ Combine almonds, sugar, walnuts, graham cracker crumbs and coconut.
- ◎ Add butter and stir until blended.
- ◎ Press into bottom and up sides of a deep-dish pie plate.
- ◎ Bake at 300 degrees for 10 minutes. Cool.

This recipe can be found in
Spanish in the **Otra Vez...En Español** section.

Toasting Coconut

To toast coconut in the oven: Preheat the oven to 325 degrees. Spread the coconut in a thin layer on a baking sheet and place on a center rack in the oven. Toast until golden brown, 7 to 10 minutes. Shake the pan a couple of times while toasting and start checking coconut after 5 minutes to make sure it does not burn.

To toast coconut in the broiler: Preheat the broiler. Spread the coconut in a thin layer on a baking sheet. Broil 4 to 5 inches from the heat until golden brown, about 2 to 4 minutes. Be sure to watch the coconut very carefully as it can burn quickly.

"Unseparating" Separated Eggs

Egg yolk which gets into the white when the egg is separated can be removed by touching it with a corner of a cloth that has been moistened with cold water. The yolk adheres to the cloth, the white does not. (An easy way to separate several egg yolks from their whites is to use a kitchen funnel.)

Ice Cream Pie with Meringue Pecan Crust and Caramel Raisin Sauce

A refreshing ice cream dessert with a delicious sauce.

Preparation Time: 30 minutes
Chill Time: 1 hour
Cook Time: 12 minutes

1	egg white	1	quart vanilla ice cream, softened
¼	cup sugar		Pecan halves (optional)
1½	cups pecans, chopped		Caramel Raisin Sauce

- Beat egg white (at room temperature) at high speed of an electric mixer; gradually add sugar, 1 tablespoon at a time, beating until stiff peaks form and sugar dissolves.
- Fold in pecans.
- Spread mixture on bottom and up sides of a greased 9-inch pie plate.
- Bake at 400 degrees for 12 minutes or until lightly browned. Cool completely.
- Spread ice cream evenly over crust; cover and freeze until ice cream is firm.
- Garnish with pecan halves, if desired.
- Spoon Caramel Raisin Sauce over each serving of pie.

Use vanilla frozen yogurt for a reduced fat version.

Yield: 8 servings

CARAMEL RAISIN SAUCE

3	tablespoons butter or margarine	½	cup whipping cream
1	cup light brown sugar, firmly packed	½	cup golden raisins
		1	teaspoon vanilla extract

- Melt butter in a small saucepan.
- Add brown sugar and whipping cream; stir over low heat until sugar dissolves.
- Add raisins and vanilla extract; stir well.

Yield: 1½ cups

Caramel Turtle Truffle Tart

An elegant, rich tart with very few ingredients.

Preparation Time: 30 minutes
Chill Time: 1 hour 30 minutes
Cook Time: 15 minutes

Sugar Cookie Crust	¾ **cup whipping cream; divided**
1½ **cups semisweet chocolate**	1 **(14-ounce) package caramels**
morsels	2 **cups pecans, chopped**

◎ Prepare Sugar Cookie Crust; set aside.

◎ Combine semisweet chocolate morsels and ¼ cup whipping cream in a small microwave-safe bowl; microwave on high 1 to 1½ minutes until chocolate melts, stirring once. Spread 1 cup mixture evenly in bottom of baked pastry, reserving remaining mixture. Chill pastry 30 minutes.

◎ Combine caramels and remaining ½ cup whipping cream in a heavy saucepan; cook over low heat, stirring constantly, until the caramels melt and mixture is smooth. Stir in pecans and spread evenly over chocolate layer.

◎ Spoon reserved chocolate mixture into a small heavy-duty zip-top plastic bag. (If chocolate is firm, microwave on high 30 seconds or until soft.) Cut a small hole in corner of plastic bag; drizzle chocolate over tart.

◎ Chill at least 1 hour. Let stand 30 minutes before serving.

Commercial caramel ice cream topping can be substituted for packaged caramel candies; just omit ½ cup whipping cream.

Yield: 12 servings

SUGAR COOKIE CRUST

1⅓ **cups flour**	1 **large egg**
⅓ **cup sugar**	1 **teaspoon vanilla extract**
½ **cup butter, cut into slices**	

◎ Position knife blade in food processor bowl; add flour, sugar and butter. Process 1 minute or until mixture is crumbly. Remove food pusher. Add egg and vanilla extract through chute with processor running; process until dough forms a smooth dough.

◎ Press dough into bottom and up sides of an 11-inch tart pan; prick bottom generously with a fork.

◎ Bake at 400 degrees for 10 minutes or until golden brown; cool.

Tips for Tarts

• Partially bake the crust for a custard or fruit tart before filling so that the crust remains a separate layer.

• Bake unfilled shells in the middle of your oven; bake the shell with filling in the lower third so that the bottom browns.

• Once baked, the shell will shrink from the side of the pan. When the tart is completely cooled, the outside ring can be removed.

• Glaze fresh fruit on a tart by brushing it with melted red currant or apple jelly. If you melt a jelly with seeds for glazing, be sure to press it through a sieve.

• Sprinkle sugar over the top of fresh fruit tarts before baking for a nice glazed finish.

Fine Grind

To finely grind nuts, cookies or crackers, put them in your coffee grinder and churn away.

Key Lime Tart in Coconut Crust

A refreshing no-bake dessert that's ready in no time!

Preparation Time: 10 minutes
Chill Time: 1 hour
Cook Time: 5 minutes

Coconut Crust	⅓ **cup Key lime juice**
4 **egg yolks**	**Whipped cream**
1 **(14-ounce) can sweetened condensed milk**	**Fresh mint sprigs and lime twists (optional)**
1 **teaspoon lime rind, grated**	

◎ Prepare Coconut Crust; set aside.

◎ Beat egg yolks with a wire whisk until lemon colored; add sweetened condensed milk, lime rind and Key lime juice, stirring well.

◎ Spoon filling into Coconut Crust. Chill until firm.

◎ Pipe or dollop whipped cream on pie. Garnish with mint sprigs and lime twists, if desired.

Yield: 10 servings

COCONUT CRUST

1 **cup flaked coconut**	½ **cup graham cracker crumbs**
½ **cup gingersnap cookie crumbs**	¼ **cup butter or margarine, melted**

◎ Combine coconut, gingersnap cookie crumbs, graham cracker crumbs and butter, mixing well. Firmly press mixture evenly over bottom and ¾ inch up sides of a 9-inch springform pan.

◎ Bake at 350 degrees for 5 minutes. Chill.

This recipe can be found in
Spanish in the **Otra Vez...En Español** section.

Banana Bars

A very moist, light dessert that's wonderful for a crowd.

Preparation Time: 30 minutes
Cook Time: 20 minutes

1 cup butter or margarine, room temperature	1 cup sour cream
1½ cups sugar	1 teaspoon vanilla extract
3-4 ripe bananas, mashed with a fork	2 cups flour
2 eggs	½ teaspoon salt
	1 teaspoon baking soda
	Cream Cheese Frosting

◎ In a large bowl, cream butter, sugar, bananas, eggs, sour cream and vanilla extract with an electric mixer until well blended.

◎ Add flour, salt and baking soda until well mixed.

◎ Pour batter into a greased and floured 15 x 10 x 1-inch jelly-roll pan.

◎ Bake at 350 degrees for 20 minutes or until light brown.

◎ When cake is cooled completely, ice with Cream Cheese Frosting.

Yield: 24 bars

CREAM CHEESE FROSTING

½ cup butter or margarine, softened	2 cups powdered sugar
1 (8-ounce) package cream cheese, softened	¼ teaspoon vanilla extract

◎ In a medium bowl, cream butter, cream cheese, powdered sugar and vanilla extract until it reaches frosting consistency.

Banana-rama

• Purchase yellow bananas with green tips and ripen at room temperature for 2 to 3 days. When bananas achieve a golden color and a moist, slightly sticky flesh, use them immediately to make breads and cakes.

• To speed ripening, place bananas in a brown paper bag with an apple. To slow the ripening process, place in the crisper bin of the refrigerator. The thick skin will turn brown, but the inside will remain firm until ready to use.

• Sprinkle banana flesh with lemon juice to prevent darkening.

Grating Chocolate

For grated chocolate, refrigerate a large piece of chocolate until hard. Hold it with a paper towel so your hand does not warm it. Grate it into a large bowl or over a piece of waxed paper. A rotary grater works well because your hands do not warm the chocolate.

If you need a lot of grated chocolate, cut it into small chunks, put it in the food processor and process with on/off pulses. The food processor works best with semisweet or bittersweet chocolate. Grating or chopping unsweetened chocolate is best done by hand.

Candy Bar Brownies

With the addition of candy bars to already rich brownies, this dessert will satisfy even the sweetest sweet tooth!

Preparation Time: 15 minutes
Cook Time: 30 to 35 minutes

4	large eggs, lightly beaten
2	cups sugar
¾	cup butter or margarine, melted
2	teaspoons vanilla extract
1½	cups flour
½	teaspoon baking powder

¼	teaspoon salt
⅓	cup cocoa
4	(2.07-ounce) chocolate-coated caramel-peanut nougat bars, coarsely chopped
3	(1.55-ounce) milk chocolate bars, finely chopped

◎ Combine eggs, sugar, butter and vanilla extract in a large bowl.

◎ Combine flour, baking powder, salt and cocoa; stir into sugar mixture.

◎ Fold in chocolate-coated caramel-peanut nougat bars.

◎ Spoon into a greased and floured 13 x 9 x 2-inch pan; sprinkle with chopped milk chocolate bars.

◎ Bake at 350 degrees for 30 to 35 minutes. Cool and cut into squares.

Yield: 30 brownies

Cranberry Caramel Bars

A luscious treat to serve to drop-in guests during the holidays or anytime.

Preparation Time: 20 minutes
Cook Time: 35 minutes

1 cup fresh cranberries	1 cup butter or margarine, melted
2 tablespoons plus ½ cup sugar; divided	1 (10-ounce) package dates, chopped
2⅓ cups flour; divided	¾ cup pecans, chopped
½ teaspoon baking soda	1 (12-ounce) jar caramel sauce
2 cups regular oats	
½ cup light brown sugar, firmly packed	

- ◎ Preheat oven to 350 degrees.
- ◎ Stir together cranberries and 2 tablespoons sugar in a small bowl; set aside.
- ◎ Combine 2 cups flour, baking soda, oats, remaining ½ cup sugar and brown sugar; stir in butter until crumbly. Reserve 1 cup flour mixture.
- ◎ Press remaining mixture into bottom of a lightly greased 13 x 9-inch baking dish.
- ◎ Bake for 15 minutes. Sprinkle with dates, pecans and cranberry mixture.
- ◎ Stir together caramel sauce and remaining ⅓ cup flour; spoon over cranberries.
- ◎ Sprinkle with reserved 1 cup flour mixture.
- ◎ Bake 20 minutes more or until lightly browned. Cool on a wire rack. Cut into bars.

Yield: 24 bars

Frosted Grapes

Place grapes on a wire rack. Using a soft pastry brush, paint grapes lightly with egg substitute. While grapes are still wet, sprinkle them with granulated sugar to create a frosted look; allow them to dry in a cool place (about 1 hour). Do not refrigerate frosted grapes because the moisture will melt the sugar. The same procedure can be followed for fresh cranberries.

Second Base for No-Base Cakes

To free the bottom of a springform pan for another cake, cover a cardboard round that fits in the bottom with plastic wrap or foil and set it on the metal base in the pan. After removing the pan sides, slide the cake along with the cardboard round onto a serving plate.

Jam-It Bars

You'll be "jam-in" these in your mouth, they're so good!

Preparation Time: 25 minutes
Cook Time: 35 to 40 minutes

2 cups flour	⅛ teaspoon nutmeg
½ cup sugar	¾ cup butter or margarine
½ teaspoon vanilla extract	1 cup pecans, chopped; divided
¼ teaspoon salt	1 (10-ounce) jar peach jam or preserves
⅛ teaspoon cinnamon	

◎ Combine flour, sugar, vanilla extract, salt, cinnamon and nutmeg; cut in butter with a pastry blender until mixture resembles coarse meal.

◎ Stir in ½ cup pecans.

◎ Remove ¾ cup mixture and set aside.

◎ Press remaining mixture evenly into a lightly greased 9-inch square pan. Spread peach jam over crumb mixture; sprinkle with remaining ½ cup pecans.

◎ Sprinkle reserved crumb mixture over pecans.

◎ Bake at 350 degrees for 35 to 40 minutes. Cool and cut into bars.

Yield: about 24 bars

Coconut-Macadamia Cookies

The tropical flavor of these cookies makes them the perfect treat for a luau or beach party.

Preparation Time: 20 minutes
Cook Time: 7 to 10 minutes

½ cup sugar	1¼ cups flour
½ cup light brown sugar, firmly packed	1 cup quick-cooking oats
½ cup butter or margarine, softened	½ cup flaked coconut
1 large egg	½ teaspoon baking soda
1 teaspoon vanilla extract	¼ teaspoon salt
	1 cup macadamia nuts, coarsely chopped

- ◎ Beat sugar, brown sugar, butter, egg and vanilla extract at medium speed with an electric mixer until fluffy.
- ◎ Combine flour, oats, coconut, baking soda, salt and macadamia nuts. Add ½ of mixture at a time to sugar mixture, beating at low speed until blended.
- ◎ Drop dough by heaping teaspoonfuls 2 inches apart onto lightly greased baking sheets.
- ◎ Bake at 350 degrees for 7 to 10 minutes or until edges are golden brown. Cool on baking sheets 1 minute. Remove to wire racks to cool.

Yield: 36 cookies

A Cookie Tea (For Ladies of All Ages)

Mothers and daughters can get together for a fancy holiday cookie-swap party. The hostess can provide a cookie recipe for a dozen cookies to each Mother/Daughter "team" for them to bake, package and swap with the other guests. The hostess should also bake extras for sampling. The sample cookies can be placed on nice silver trays and the packaged versions (possibly wrapped in colorful cellophane and tied with a holiday ribbon) can be put on a separate table. Each guest receives a holiday bag to take their cookie "loot" home.

Good Report Card

When someone receives good news from school, it is definitely worth celebrating! Prepare a fun meal that everyone will enjoy and create some simple decorations to tie in to the school spirit. Get some brightly colored balloons to put around the room and make a big star construction paper placemat for the honoree.

Lunitas de Fresa

No one would guess that it only takes a few
ingredients to create these pretty cookies with the beautiful name.

Preparation Time: 45 minutes
Cook Time: 15 to 20 minutes

1 (8-ounce) package cream cheese, softened	1 small jar strawberry preserves
1 cup butter, softened	Powdered sugar
3 cups flour	

- Let cream cheese and butter soften at room temperature. Combine cream cheese, butter and flour with hands to form dough.
- Shape dough into 1-inch balls and flatten with a small flat-bottomed glass dipped in flour.
- Put a small dollop of strawberry preserves in the middle of each round and fold dough over preserves pressing edges with tip of a fork.
- Place cookies on a cookie sheet and bake at 350 degrees for 15 to 20 minutes or until lightly browned.
- Sprinkle with powdered sugar and let cool.

Yield: 50 small cookies

This recipe can be found in
Spanish in the **Otra Vez...En Español** section.

Crispy Oatmeal-Toffee Lizzies

A great spin on the old-fashioned oatmeal cookie.

Preparation Time: 15 minutes
Chill Time: 1 hour
Cook Time: 12 minutes

1 **cup butter-flavored shortening**	2 **cups flour**
1 **cup sugar**	1 **teaspoon baking soda**
1 **cup brown sugar, firmly packed**	1 **teaspoon salt**
2 **large eggs**	2 **cups quick-cooking oats**
1 **tablespoon milk**	2 **cups semisweet chocolate morsels**
1 **teaspoon vanilla extract**	¾ **cup almond brickle chips**
	½ **cup pecans, chopped**

◎ Beat butter-flavored shortening at medium speed with an electric mixer until fluffy; gradually add sugar and brown sugar, beating well. Add eggs, one at a time, beating until blended after each addition.

◎ Add milk and vanilla extract, beating until mixture is blended.

◎ Combine flour, baking soda and salt; gradually add to shortening mixture, beating at low speed until blended.

◎ Stir in oats, semisweet chocolate morsels, almond brickle chips and pecans; cover and refrigerate 1 hour.

◎ Shape dough into 1¼-inch balls; place 2 inches apart on lightly greased baking sheets. Flatten cookies to ¼-inch thickness with a flat-bottomed glass dipped in flour.

◎ Bake at 350 degrees for 12 minutes or until cookies begin to brown around edges. Remove to wire racks to cool.

Yield: 72 cookies

Movie Theatre Party

Create decorative invitations on paper and cover plastic video boxes with them. Go to the local video store and ask for old displays and posters; place them all around your home. Get popcorn bags from a local movie theater and fill with popcorn for the kids to snack on while watching a favorite video. Turn your kitchen into a concession stand by hanging up bags of chips, cookies and candy on a string with clothes pins. Give each child a popcorn bag full of goodies to take home.

Cookie Tips

- For consistent results, form drop cookies with either a teaspoon or tablespoon.

- When making bar cookies, use the size of pan called for in the recipe. Altering the pan size will affect the consistency of the cookies.

- If the dough for rolled cookies is sticky and hard to work with, chill it for a few minutes in the freezer before continuing with the instructions.

- Grease cookie sheets only if specified in the recipe.

- For chewy cookies, choose the low range of a recipe's baking time. For crisp cookies, bake for the longer time allotted.

- To prevent overbaking, let cookies cool on cookie sheets 1 minute; then remove to wire racks in order for them to cool completely (unless recipe specifies otherwise).

- Cool bar cookies completely before cutting.

- To soften cookies that have become hard, place an apple wedge or a slice of bread in the airtight container with them. Remove the next day.

- For best results, bake only one sheet of cookies at a time, placing the sheet in the center of the oven.

Praline Cookies

Made with ingredients you probably have on hand, these cookies are great for a picnic or barbecue or that bake sale your kids forgot to tell you about!

Preparation Time: 20 minutes
Cook Time: 10 minutes

1 egg, beaten	1 teaspoon vanilla extract
¼ cup plus 2 tablespoons butter or margarine, melted	1 cup plus 2 tablespoons flour
1¼ cups brown sugar, firmly packed	¼ teaspoon salt
	1¼ cups pecan halves

◎ Preheat oven to 350 degrees.
◎ Combine egg, butter, brown sugar and vanilla extract, stirring well.
◎ Add flour and salt, stirring well.
◎ Stir in pecans.
◎ Drop by tablespoonfuls onto ungreased cookie sheets.
◎ Bake for 10 minutes. Do not overbake.

Yield: 36 cookies

White Chocolate Orange Cookies

A surprisingly different and sinfully delicious blend of flavors.

Preparation Time: 20 minutes
Cook Time: 10 minutes

2¼ **cups flour**	½ **cup light brown sugar, firmly packed**
¾ **teaspoon baking powder**	1 **egg, room temperature**
½ **teaspoon salt**	3 **teaspoons orange peel, grated**
1 **cup butter, softened**	2 **cups white chocolate morsels**
½ **cup sugar**	

- ◎ Preheat oven to 350 degrees.
- ◎ Combine flour, baking powder and salt in a bowl; set aside.
- ◎ In a large mixing bowl, beat butter, sugar and brown sugar until creamy on medium speed of an electric mixer.
- ◎ Add egg and orange peel until blended.
- ◎ Slowly add in the flour mixture.
- ◎ Fold in the white chocolate morsels.
- ◎ Drop heaping tablespoons of dough onto an ungreased cookie sheet.
- ◎ Bake for 10 minutes, just until light gold in color. Do not overcook. They will look unfinished, but are meant to be moist, not crunchy.
- ◎ Remove from oven and let stand for 2 minutes. Remove to a plate and let cool 10 more minutes.

Yield: 36 cookies

Chocolate Dipped Fruit

One of the simplest sweets with after-dinner coffee is a perfectly ripe strawberry, raspberry, banana slice or tangerine section dipped in chocolate. The best chocolate for dipping is bittersweet chocolate~ Caillebaut, Tobler, Suchard or Ghirardelli.

Melt the chocolate in the top of a double boiler over hot water. Pick the fruit up on a toothpick, dip it into the chocolate and swirl it gently to cover. Let the excess chocolate drip off; stick the toothpick with the fruit atop into a piece of Styrofoam or a piece of firm fruit (such as canteloupe) that will hold the fruit while it dries. Put the fruit in the refrigerator to harden and set the chocolate.

Teddy Bear Tea Party

Invitations can be on construction paper cut out in the shape of teddy bears, and say "Bring your special teddy bear, come play dress up with me; we'll have lots of fun while we drink tea!" Let the young hostess set her own tea party table with teapots, cups and china. Have a lot of dress up clothes available for spontaneous play.

Fudge in a Bag

A great no-cook recipe for kids to make - it's all done in a plastic bag!

Preparation Time: 10 minutes

1 (3-ounce) package cream cheese, softened	½ cup cocoa
½ cup butter, softened	1 teaspoon vanilla extract
4 cups powdered sugar	Pecans or walnuts (optional)

◎ Put cream cheese, butter, powdered sugar, cocoa and vanilla extract in a one gallon heavy-duty zip-top plastic bag. Squeeze all air out of bag, then seal.

◎ Knead the bag until the fudge pulls away from the bag.

◎ Remove from bag and spread on platter or pie plate.

◎ Garnish with nuts, if desired. Cut into squares.

Yield: 24 1-inch squares

Lemon Blackberry Crisp

A nice, refreshing dish for the hot summer months.

Preparation Time: 20 minutes
Cook Time: 30 minutes

4 cups fresh blackberries	¼ cup flour
¼ cup sugar	½ teaspoon cinnamon
2 tablespoons cornstarch	½ cup butter or margarine, melted
3 tablespoons fresh lemon juice	Ice cream or sweetened whipped cream (optional)
25 vanilla wafer cookies, crushed	
½ cup regular oats	
½ cup light brown sugar, firmly packed	

◎ Place blackberries in a lightly greased 11 x 7-inch baking dish. Sprinkle with sugar.

◎ Stir together cornstarch and lemon juice; stir into berries.

◎ Combine vanilla wafer cookie crumbs, oats, brown sugar, flour and cinnamon. Stir in butter until crumbly. Sprinkle over berries.

◎ Bake at 400 degrees for 30 minutes or until lightly browned. Serve with ice cream or sweetened whipped cream, if desired.

Yield: 6 to 8 servings

Substitute blackberries with any fresh fruit of your choice.

Got the Winter Blues?

When winter time has you feeling a little blue, plan an indoor picnic! A winter picnic can be done indoors with cold weather versions of all the summer foods you love. Spread out a blanket in the middle of the family room and give everyone brightly colored paper plates and napkins. The winter blues will quickly disappear when supper is barbecue, beans, cornbread and fruit crisp with ice cream!

Chocolate Éclair Dessert

An easy, tasty dessert with the authentic flavors of a chocolate éclair; everyone will want the recipe!

Preparation Time: 20 minutes
Chill Time: 1 to 2 hours
Cook Time: 2 to 3 minutes

3 cups milk	2 (3.4-ounce) boxes instant vanilla pudding
1 (8-ounce) container frozen whipped topping, thawed	8 large graham cracker squares
	Chocolate Glaze

- Mix milk, whipped topping and vanilla pudding in large bowl. Set aside.
- Arrange graham crackers to cover the bottom of a greased 13 x 9-inch pan.
- Pour ½ of pudding mixture over graham crackers; top with another layer of graham crackers and pour remaining pudding mixture on top; put last layer of graham crackers on top of pudding.
- Pour Chocolate Glaze on top. Chill and serve.

Yield: 14 to 16 servings

CHOCOLATE GLAZE

1 cup sugar	¼ cup butter
½ cup cocoa	1 teaspoon vanilla extract
¼ cup milk	

- Mix sugar, cocoa and milk in a saucepan; bring to a boil. Allow to boil for 1 minute.
- Remove from heat and add butter and vanilla extract.
- Let cool for 3 minutes.

Chocolate Trifle

A beautiful dessert that will satisfy every "chocoholics" cravings.

Preparation Time: 45 minutes
Chill Time: 8 hours
Cook Time: 25 to 30 minutes

1   **(19.8-ounce) package fudge brownie mix**

½   **cup Kahlúa or coffee-flavored liqueur**

3   **(3.9-ounce) packages instant chocolate pudding mix**

1   **(12-ounce) container frozen whipped topping, thawed**

6   **(1.4-ounce) English toffee-flavored candy bars, crushed**

◎ Prepare fudge brownie mix and bake according to package directions in a 13 x 9 x 2-inch pan.

◎ Remove from oven and prick top of warm brownies at 1-inch intervals using a fork; drizzle with Kahlúa. Let cool, and crumble.

◎ Prepare pudding mix according to package directions, omitting chilling.

◎ Place ⅓ of crumbled brownies in bottom of a 3-quart trifle dish. Top with ⅓ of pudding, ⅓ of whipped topping and ⅓ of crushed English toffee-flavored candy bars. Repeat layers twice with remaining ingredients, ending with crushed candy bars. Chill 8 hours.

4 tablespoons strong brewed coffee and 1 teaspoon sugar may be substituted for coffee-flavored liqueur.

Yield: 16 to 18 servings

Do the "Cordial" Thing!

Crème de Menthe: Both green and white, this familiar liqueur evokes the flavor of peppermint. The white is especially nice mixed with brandy for stingers and the green is simply poured over ice to dilute the intense flavor and color.

Drambuie: This velvety spirit is perfect in front of a roaring fire on a cold winter night.

Frangelico: This lightly sweet and rich liqueur exudes the very essence of toasted hazelnuts. Put a splash in some Irish Crème and relish.

Grand Marnier: This sweet liqueur is an infusion of the finest Cognac with the peels of luscious Curaçao oranges. A delightful complement to a demitasse of strong coffee.

Kahlúa: This thick coffee-flavored liqueur is a unique blend that can be mixed with cream or hot chocolate for a wonderful mocha drink.

Chocolate Curls

Melt squares or morsels of semisweet chocolate over hot water in a double boiler; cool slightly. Pour chocolate out onto a waxed paper-lined baking sheet. Spread chocolate with a spatula into a 3-inch-wide strip. Smooth the top of the strip with a spatula. Let stand at room temperature until chocolate cools and feels slightly tacky, but not firm. (If chocolate is too hard, curls will break; if it is too soft, chocolate will not curl.) Gently pull a vegetable peeler across length of chocolate until curl forms, letting chocolate curl up on top of peeler. Insert wooden pick inside curl to transfer. Chill until ready to use.

Chocolate Mousse au Grand Marnier

Very nice dessert for an elegant dinner party.

Preparation Time: 20 minutes
Chill Time: 1 hour
Cook Time: 5 minutes

1 (4-ounce) package sweet baking chocolate	2 cups whipping cream
4 (1-ounce) squares semisweet chocolate	½ cup powdered sugar, sifted
¼ cup Grand Marnier or other orange-flavored liqueur	Chocolate curls, optional

◎ Combine sweet baking chocolate, semisweet chocolate and Grand Marnier in a heavy saucepan; cook over low heat until chocolate melts, stirring constantly. Remove from heat and cool to lukewarm.

◎ Beat whipping cream until foamy; gradually add powdered sugar, beating until soft peaks form.

◎ Gently fold about ¼ of whipped cream into chocolate; fold in remaining whipped cream.

◎ Spoon into individual serving dishes. Chill until ready to serve. Garnish with chocolate curls, if desired.

Yield: 6 servings

Black and White Crème Brûlée

This custard dish is not only very rich, but beautiful too! The custard should be made one day ahead and the topping broiled at the last minute.

Preparation Time: 30 minutes
Chill Time: 8 hours
Cook Time: 50 to 55 minutes

2½ **cups whipping cream; divided**	½ **cup sugar**
5 **(1-ounce) semisweet chocolate squares**	1 **teaspoon vanilla extract**
6 **egg yolks**	6 **tablespoons light brown sugar; divided**

◎ Cook ½ cup whipping cream and semisweet chocolate in a heavy saucepan over low heat, stirring constantly, until chocolate melts and mixture is smooth. Pour into a large bowl.

◎ Whisk together remaining 2 cups whipping cream, egg yolks, sugar and vanilla extract until sugar dissolves and mixture is smooth.

◎ Whisk 1 cup egg mixture into chocolate mixture until smooth. Cover and chill remaining egg mixture.

◎ Pour chocolate mixture evenly into 6 (8-ounce) custard cups; place cups in a 13 x 9-inch pan. Add hot water to pan to a depth of ½ inch.

◎ Bake at 325 degrees for 30 minutes or until almost set. (Center will be soft.)

◎ Slowly pour remaining egg mixture evenly over custards, and bake 20 to 25 more minutes or until set. Cool custards in water in pan on a wire rack. Remove from pan; cover and chill at least 8 hours.

◎ Sprinkle each custard with 1 tablespoon brown sugar; place custards in a pan. Broil 5½ inches from heat (with electric oven door partially open) until sugar melts (about 2 minutes). Let stand 5 minutes to allow sugar to harden.

Try arranging one strawberry sliced in a fan shape on top of each custard as a garnish.

Yield: 6 servings

Brûlée Basics

• Don't panic when you see the term "water bath." A water bath is simply a roasting pan filled with water. The water creates a cushion from the heat of the oven, allowing the custards to bake slowly without curdling.

• Don't burn yourself! Before you take the water bath out of the oven, remove some of the water with a basting bulb or a long-handled ladle.

• When you broil the brown sugar, get the crème brûlées as close to the heating element as possible. To do this, place an inverted roasting pan on the top shelf of the oven; then place the crème brûlées on a baking sheet on top of the roasting pan. An adventurous alternative to the broiler is a welding torch.

• Crème brûlée is even more extraordinary if the custard is cold and firm when you crack into the caramelized topping. Place the custards in a roasting pan filled with ice and then broil them. The ice keeps the custards cold while the sugar melts.

• You can bake the crème brûlées ahead of time, but do not caramelize the sugar until serving time.

Turn a Sunday afternoon into a Sundae Party

Create a "sundae bar" by setting out the following: containers of ice cream; several sauces and syrups; and bowls of candies, chopped nuts, crumbled cookies, toasted coconut, colored sprinkles and mounds of whipped cream. Guests concoct their own monster treats!

Frozen Lemon Soufflé with Raspberry-Amaretto Sauce

A light, delicious combination of tart lemon and sweetened raspberry flavors.

Preparation Time: 45 minutes
Chill Time: At least 2 hours
Cook Time: 15 minutes

1 envelope unflavored gelatin	⅛ teaspoon salt
½ cup lemon juice	1 cup whipping cream, whipped
3 eggs, separated	3 coconut macaroon cookies, crumbled
¾ cup sugar; divided	Raspberry-Amaretto Sauce
2 teaspoons lemon rind, grated	

◎ Sprinkle gelatin over lemon juice in a small saucepan; let stand 1 minute. Cook over low heat, stirring until gelatin dissolves; set aside.

◎ Beat egg yolks and ¼ cup sugar in a large bowl at medium speed of an electric mixer until thick and lemon colored. Add gelatin mixture, remaining ½ cup sugar and lemon rind, stirring well.

◎ Beat egg whites (at room temperature) and salt until stiff peaks form. Gently fold egg whites and whipped cream into lemon mixture.

◎ Spoon ¾ of mixture into a 1-quart soufflé dish. Sprinkle with macaroon crumbs, and spoon remaining lemon mixture over crumbs. Cover and freeze.

◎ To serve, spoon into individual serving dishes and top with Raspberry-Amaretto Sauce.

Yield: 6 servings

Frozen Lemon Soufflé continued

RASPBERRY-AMARETTO SAUCE

1 pint fresh raspberries	½ cup sugar
¼ cup water	2 tablespoons amaretto
1 tablespoon lemon juice	

- Combine raspberries, water and lemon juice in processor or blender. Process until pureed. Strain and discard the seeds.
- Pour raspberry puree into a saucepan; add sugar. Bring to a boil over medium heat; reduce heat and simmer 10 minutes.
- Stir in amaretto.
- Refrigerate until ready to serve.

1 (10-ounce) package frozen raspberries can be substituted for the fresh berries. Thaw raspberries and reserve ¼ cup juice for use in place of ¼ cup water. Try this sauce over vanilla ice cream too.

Yield: 1 cup

Frozen Sweets

With so many frozen sweets to choose from in the grocery, let these reminders help you grab the kind you need:

- Ice cream is a rich mixture of cream, milk, milk fat, and sugar or sweeteners.

- Ice milk contains less milk fat than ice cream does, making it lighter and lower in calories.

- Frozen yogurt can be made from whole milk or low-fat and nonfat milk sweetened with sugar or artificial sweeteners. These products can be lower in fat but not necessarily lower in calories.

- Sherbert is usually made from sweetened fruit juice, milk and water.

- Sorbet contains no milk, a good choice for those who need to stay away from dairy.

- Granita is water and sugar combined with fruit juice, wine or coffee. This one is a firm slush of icy crystals.

Chocolate Leaves

Select leaves such as mint leaves, that are nonpoisonous. Wash leaves and dry thoroughly. Melt 1 or 2 ounces semisweet chocolate over water in a double boiler; cool slightly. Using a tiny brush, paint chocolate on the back of each leaf, spreading to the edges. Place leaves, chocolate side up, on waxed paper-lined baking sheets. Chill until firm, at least 10 minutes. Then grasp the leaf at stem end, and carefully and quickly peel leaf from chocolate. Chill chocolate leaves until ready to use.

Tiramisu

An easy recipe for a traditional Italian favorite.

Preparation Time: 30 minutes
Chill Time: 8 hours

4	large eggs, separated	1	large package (or 2 small packages) ladyfinger cookies
½	cup Kahlúa or coffee-flavored liqueur	½	cup espresso
1	pound mascarpone cheese	2	(1-ounce) squares semisweet chocolate, grated
½	cup sugar		

◎ Put egg yolks in a large bowl and egg whites in a separate large bowl.

◎ Add Kahlúa to egg yolks and stir until blended.

◎ Add mascarpone cheese and beat with an electric mixer until blended.

◎ Beat egg whites with an electric mixer on high speed until soft peaks form. Continue to beat while gradually adding sugar, a little at a time, until stiff peaks form.

◎ Add half of the egg whites to the cheese and egg yolk mixture and blend well. Fold in the rest of the egg whites. Set aside.

◎ Dip ladyfingers quickly in espresso (do not saturate). Arrange ladyfingers flat side down in a 9 x 12-inch pan.

◎ Layer half the cheese mixture on top of the ladyfingers and smooth. Sprinkle half of the grated chocolate over the cheese layer. Place another layer of espresso-dipped ladyfingers on top of chocolate. Then spread the rest of the cheese mixture over the cookies; cover with remaining grated chocolate.

◎ Cover and refrigerate overnight.

Yield: 14 to 16 servings

ACKNOWLEDGMENTS (continued)

Stephanie Ketcher

Julie Kirk

Hulda Kitchen

Maria Klein

Robin Langford

Gloria Lavis

Margaret Leachman

Laura Leslie

Nancy Licon

Monica Lohf

Karen Loper

Lynn Lopez

Patricia Lopez

Rose Lucero

Gloria Macias-Viramontes

Dominique Mailloux

Terry Mailloux

Donna Mangan

Amy Marcus

Shelly Martin

Katherine Masel

Marina Mata-de la Garza

Susan Mayfield

Michelle McCown

Sandy Mead

Laura Montalvo

Marcia Montez-Smith

Monica Morton

Melanie Mullings

Emily Neeld

Carolyn Niland

Nancy Nordell

Laura Norwich

Susan Nowak

Leslie Olson

Henrietta R. Owen

Patty Palafox

Lourdes Pearson

Vrony Pernter

Jeannie Pitluck

Debbie Price

Teeni Provencio

Patti Psencik

Sue Ramsey

Julie Reiser

Stacy Retzloff

Angie Ricono

Michelle Roetzer

Christine Rook

Steve Rubin

Shelly Ruddock

Lark Saad

Sandra Sancehz-Almanzan

Margie Santascoy-Tippin

Trina Schafer

Genevieve Schatzman

Lisa Ann Schoenbrun

Linda Schuster

Shari Schwartz

Tania Schwartz

Suzie Schwitters

Candace Scudday

Lori Shapiro

Virginia Shapiro

Joan Shepack

Nancy Skokan

Linda Smith

Ana Stevens

Armida Stevens

Linda Stevens

Tish Szurek

Laura Tate-Goldman

Jane Thomas

Shawna Thomson

Jana Tippin

Kathy Vandenburg

Cindy Villalba-Holguin

Kathryn Viola

Lynda Vitoulis

Sharon Voelz

Lori Waite

Kelley Walker

Carmen Blanchi Weinstein

Ann Renee Wilsey

Teresa Windham

Janice Woods Windle

Maria Woody

Jamie Young

Wendy Zimmerman

Index

Seasoned with Fun

Seasoned with Fun

Seasoned with Fun

Seasoned with Fun

Seasoned with Fun

Seasoned with Fun